Helmut Krausnick was born in Wenden near Braunschweig in 1905, and studied History at Breslau, Heidelberg and Berlin. Since 1951 he has been at the Institute of Contemporary History, becoming its General Secretary in 1959. He is on the editorial committee of the Institute's Quarterly.

Martin Broszat was born in Leipzig in 1926. He studied History at Leipzig and Cologne, taking his doctorate in 1952. Since 1955 he has been at the Institute of Contemporary History in Munich and is on the editorial committee of the Institute's Quarterly.

G000049002

HELMUT KRAUSNICK
MARTIN BROSZAT

Anatomy of the SS State

Translated by
Dorothy Long and Marian Jackson

A PALADIN BOOK

GRANADA
London Toronto Sydney New York

Published by Granada Publishing Limited in 1970
Reprinted 1973, 1982

ISBN 0 586 08028 7

Originally published under the title *Anatomie des SS-Staates*
Copyright © Walter-Verlag A.G. 1965
First published in Great Britain by
William Collins Sons and Company Limited 1968
English translation copyright © William Collins Sons and
Company Limited 1968
Glossary copyright © Brian Melland
Preface copyright © Max Hastings
This edition comprises two of the five essays from the
original book of the same name.

Granada Publishing Limited
Frogmore, St Albans, Herts AL2 2NF
and
36 Golden Square, London W1R 4AH
515 Madison Avenue, New York, NY 10022, USA
117 York Street, Sydney, NSW 2000, Australia
100 Skyway Avenue, Rexdale, Ontario, M9W 3A6, Canada
61 Beach Road, Auckland, New Zealand

Printed and bound in Great Britain by
Cox & Wyman Ltd, Reading
Set in Monotype Ehrhardt

Granada ®
Granada Publishing ®

Contents

Preface
by Max Hastings

If Heinrich Himmler or Alfred Rosenburg had been charged in the civilian courtroom of a western democracy with the killing of a single Jew, and had they advanced in their own defence the arguments by which they sought to justify the murder of six million people, it would have been fascinating to speculate whether they would merely have been imprisoned for life, or found criminally insane. For those of us born out of the time and place of nazism's crimes against humanity, it remains extraordinarily difficult to understand first, how such a contemptible group of men were able to rule a great European state; and second, how they found so many willing tools to execute their homicidal will.

In recent years, the SS have been the subjects of many books that can only be classified among the pornography of death, dwelling mindlessly on their uniforms, customs, military achievements, leaders' lives and atrocious cruelties. These works debase both their writers and their readers.

But Krausnick and Broszat's dispassionate analysis of the force that made Hitler's tyranny possible is in another class altogether. The authors are scholars. Their purpose is to set aside the emotional horror of what the SS did, and to present before the bar of history the evidence as to how and why it was done. Although they carried out their research more than 20 years ago, their study remains as valid today as when it was first offered to the courts in 1963.

Hitler himself, as the authors show, wished to remove the Jews from the map of Europe merely because he disliked them. It was left to Himmler, Rosenburg, Heydrich and their colleagues to create the fantastic edifice of scientific racial theory which they employed to justify the Final Solution. 'Gentlemen,' said Hans Frank to the assembled leaders of the SS, 'I must ask you to arm yourselves against all considerations of pity.' Himmler told them: 'I have to expect of you superhuman acts of inhumanity. But it is the Führer's will.'

Among the most fascinating passages of the book are those which trace the progressive destruction of justice in Germany in

9

the 1930s. Hitler achieved a brilliant perversion of politics with his Night of The Long Knives in June 1934, which silenced the fears of conservative German politicians about the rising tyranny of the SA, only to make way for the far more deadly government of the SS. The authors chronicle the protests of the handful of officials and lawyers who dared to question the creation of the labour camps, the arrests and finally the executions without trial. The SS, armoured with Hitler's absolute support, were able to sweep aside even the objections of the German army to their excesses.

Himmler began to create his industrial empire around the SS and the labour camps. By 1937, the inmates of Dachau were making Yuletide candleholders on a profit-making basis. By 1942, in the words of the authors, the concentration camps had become 'an SS-owned arsenal of compulsory labour'. Industry's willing exploitation of the slave labour hired to the factories by Himmler remains among the damning evidence of the German nation's support for nazism.

At one of the decisive conferences about the death-camp programme, held on 20 January 1941 – by a macabre irony at Interpol headquarters – Heydrich sketched a programme for the ultimate extinction of 11 million Jews as far afield as Britain, Ireland and Turkey. By an exercise of insane logic, it was decreed that it was essential to kill those Jews who survived the forced labour programme, since they were clearly the strongest racial stock, and thus those whom it would be most intolerable to allow to reproduce. Throughout their career, the creators of the concentration camps displayed some grotesque confusions of purpose. Herding millions of human beings to slave labour or death created immense logistical problems. At one moment the SS were preoccupied with the difficulties of organizing industrialized mass-murder. Yet at the next, they were troubled by the high death rate from sickness or starvation among those inmates who survived. The book shows the diabolical ingenuity of the SS in compelling their victims to pay the costs of their own transportation and extinction.

It is a fragment of history that makes terrible reading. Yet if anyone should ask why it is vital to record it, and to ensure that posterity reads of it, it is only necessary to compare the story of the SS and The Holocaust with that of Stalin's death camps.

Most of us would like to believe that the Russian policy of absolute suppression of evidence does not succeed. Yet however often we are reminded that Stalin's acolytes murdered more people than those of Hitler, most of us find it difficult to see the Russian crimes anything like so vividly. We have never been allowed to see either photographs, film, or authentic official documents about them.

The Holocaust, on the other hand, has a direct and awful meaning for almost all of us because of the great mass of evidence of it that has been presented to us. Today, almost 40 years after the event, there is a danger that even this is not enough to preserve the truth for future generations. It might have seemed impossible to debase the memory of the Six Million. But the extravagant vulgarities of a succession of Hollywood films; the terrible error of some modern Israeli politicians in attempting to use The Holocaust as a mere trump card on the negotiating table of Middle Eastern politics; and the persistent propagandizing of some Germans who claim that the crimes of nazism have been grossly exaggerated – all these things make it essential to maintain unsullied a calm, scholarly, factual record of the unspeakable nature of the SS state. To this purpose, Krausnick and Broszat make a contribution which has not been surpassed.

Foreword to the Original Edition

Concentration camp crimes and mass murder of Jews were essential features of National Socialist tyranny. Many people for various reasons forget this fact. For some the whole Third Reich business can be summed up in the word Auschwitz; they are incapable of seeing further than the stark fact that this hell on earth actually happened. As a result they lose sight of the historical truth as a whole. Their answer to the question how this horrifying phenomenon could occur and why it was tolerated consists solely of generalized moral and cultural philosophizing, leaving the intellectual and political background out of account. Another section of opinion holds the view that these crimes were the work of a misguided body of men who had no place in the main stream of German history of the period; apart from the more notorious crimes they have little to say about the policy of the Hitler period. However different the views of these two categories may be, they have one thing in common: both lack any insight into the realities of the Hitler régime; in particular, both fail to see the connexion between the form of political tyranny adopted and the mass crime called for by its ideology.

In the numerous trials of National Socialist criminals now being conducted in Germany, the question of the connexion between political tyranny and ideological crime is inevitably a relevant issue. The importance of these trials lies more in the fact that they pose the necessity of finding an answer to this question, than in their ostensible task of meting out justice for wrong committed. The case of an accused who took part in these crimes can only be judged rightly if the whole moral, political and organizational background leading to his action is surveyed. The task of the historical expert is to assist the Court by painting as clearly as possible a picture of this background. He is not there to concern himself with the case of any particular accused. Investigation into the circumstances of each individual case and pronouncement of guilt or innocence is exclusively the prerogative of the Court. It is for the expert to provide a picture of the historical and political landscape in which each individual occurrence took place. For this reason during these trials of National

Socialist criminals, it has been thought advisable, contrary to normal Court procedure, to hear the experts *before* the witnesses, since thereby a better factual background is available to the Court against which it can measure the witnesses' statements.

The close connexion between the actions of the accused and the political background against which their crimes were committed presents the Court with a particular problem in the formation of its judgement. Many Germans, for instance, wrestling with their own conscience are apt to allow their sense of communal political and moral guilt to overshadow the specific crimes of specific individuals; this is a widespread tendency to which the Court must not give way. A man may reproach himself for having been politically mistaken or having shown himself a coward, but between him and the man who actively and wholeheartedly participated in the régime's dirty business there is a difference not of degree but of kind. Actual violations of the law must not be allowed to become lost in general philosophizing about being caught in the toils of fate and carried into crime. No right-thinking person whose sense of right and wrong has not been warped can declare a man innocent if he has murdered thousands of defenceless human beings, no matter whether or not he can cite an order bidding him to do so.

A central feature of these submissions is the anatomy of the SS state. In other words we are concerned not so much with the details of what the SS *did* but with the question of how an instrument of power such as that formed by the combination of the SS and the police could arise, and how it functioned – in fact we are concerned with the day-to-day practice of totalitarian tyranny. The instrument was extraordinarily complex and differed in many important aspects from a normal state executive. This also is a relevant point in these trials. Ever since the Nuremberg War Crimes Trials, the accused have been using a highly developed technique to evade judicial establishment of the facts by taking refuge in the jungle of organizational channels and overlapping authorities. In order adequately to answer the question how this system functioned we must not confine ourselves to the organizational and institutional aspects but must deal also with certain intellectual angles of the problem, such as the SS mentality and the special features of the National Socialist form of anti-Semitism.

When presenting the history of the National Socialist period to a Court of Justice, a special effort must be made to do so rationally and dispassionately, for the facts presented are not merely the subject of an historical analysis which commits no one, but may have a decisive influence on the fate of the accused. Those taking part in public discussion before a Court are in duty bound to weigh their words, and this is to the good in that it constitutes an effective counterweight to the widespread habit of painting a highly emotional picture of the past in order to highlight certain major truths, but at the price of historical exactitude regarding facts and circumstances. Since Hitler's dictatorship is so obviously to be condemned from all points of view, people are tempted to think too little about it. This is why, although we possess an immense mass of literature about the Third Reich, so little intelligent use has been made of it. The superficiality of many words on the subject is no more than a reflection of the popular tendency; people prefer vivid writing (and it is difficult not to write vividly about Auschwitz); people try to evade the rationalism of the historican and prefer moralistic emotional theorizing. The current phrase is 'conscience awakening'. But a sleepy conscience is like a sleepy man: if a man is shaken hard enough he will wake up – and then after one or two half-waking moments will quickly go to sleep again. That which man's intellect once grasps however will remain and will not disappear. So in order to come to terms intellectually with National Socialism and its era, the Germans have need not of emotionalism or some moral evangelistic movement but of sober work combined with intelligence and common sense. Otherwise we run the risk of drawing the wrong lessons from the past. The strict rules of the judicial proceeding point the way to a standard of rationalism of which we are in dire need. This was the standard which the authors of these submissions strove to maintain.

I The Persecution of the Jews

Translated by Dorothy Long

Helmut Krausnick

Introduction

History has seen many instances of persecution of the Jews – but never a State-inspired persecution planned with such diabolical consistency and carried through so cold-bloodedly and systematically, and on such a scale and with such terrible consequences, as that persecution set in motion by the National Socialist regime, with all the administrative and technical resources at its command, in the territories under its control.

In any study of the subject the German historian has a duty, now more than ever, to keep firmly in mind that this was no chance development and that even Hitler was no mere 'accident' of German history. For this reason, while analysing the fact of anti-Semitism as the core of National Socialist 'ideology', it would seem proper, as far as space allows, to examine the philosophy behind the National Socialist persecution of the Jews – and the temptations to which not only the instigators of the movement and their catspaws, but also sections of modern 'educated' society, principally in Germany, had been exposed for a considerable time, and to which they had finally succumbed. Only thus is it possible to recognize and understand the true nature of the persecution.

Modern Anti-Semitism
It is generally accepted that the first thing to be taken into account in regard to modern anti-Semitism is the disastrous change in the status of the Jewish people that took place during the second half of the nineteenth century under the influence of a highly questionable 'science of race'. No expert would, of course, assert that the influence of theories of this kind was decisive. The deepest roots of hatred of the Jews has always lain in the latent tendency of many people to look askance at those of their fellows who do not 'conform', and both before and after the turn of the century an attitude of vulgar, unthinking hostility towards the Jews was the distinguishing mark of the anti-Semite. The less such a sentiment could be justified either morally or intellectually, the more it always seemed to prevail. Arguments for discrediting the Jews and discriminating against them – whether based on religious grounds, on grounds of social or economic necessity,

or on some sort of ideological principle (as could be sensed in German romanticism and in the early manifestations of nationalism) – gradually gained widespread and uninformed acceptance, and survived in modern anti-Semitism. Such ideas were nourished by the 'sociological minority problem' which had been thrown up in the course of history and had never been completely solved, although it had dwindled to very small proportions by 1900: after this date, in fact, there can no longer be said to have been any serious 'group tensions'.

Nevertheless the change that I have mentioned remains of the highest significance, especially when looked at in conjunction with the upsurge of nationalism and the triumphal progress of the natural sciences of the mid-nineteenth century as it affected the Jews. That race was the decisive factor in historical development was the theme of the French Count Gobineau's *Essay on the Inequalities of the Human Race* [Paris, 1853–5] – a work which, although not the first in the field and lacking in scholarship, nevertheless had a decisive influence. Count Gobineau, whose aim it was to gain admission for 'the science of history' into the 'family of natural sciences', drew a distinction between the 'higher' and the 'lower' races and postulated that different natural characteristics had different values. He tried to prove that only the white races were possessed of true creative power; of these the most valuable was the Aryan group, among whom the Germanic or 'Nordic' peoples held pride of place. Gobineau, and even more so his compatriot, Ernest Renan, and their disciples instituted a comparison between these races and the Semites who, they alleged, were fundamentally uncreative. And although Gobineau never dreamed that his romantically aristocratic theories would be put to an inhuman use, they did in fact lead to the establishment of an arbitrary racial order which his successors made more crudely inflexible and to which they gave outward expression as anti-Semitism. The validity of the racial factor, operating presumably as a law of nature, gained acceptance; the 'Jewish question' became a 'racial question'.

What was new about this development was not that it rejected the Jews as a 'worthless' minority group, but that it condemned them to such a status for all time. According to this new school of thought it was no longer possible for a Jew to throw off the shackles of his racial origins by Christian baptism. Hitherto

Christian dogma had recognized the right of individual Jews to escape the curse of Judaism by entry into the Christian Church. And even when enlightenment weakened Christian dogma (or when the saving grace of Christianity was withheld), the humanist creed of the perfectibility of man through upbringing and education still held out to the Ghetto Jew the hope of raising himself in the social hierarchy. 'The doctrine of anti-Semitism', according to a more modern scholar, Alexander Bein, who made a penetrating study of its consequences,

broke completely with this faith. To hold that race is the decisive, the conclusive and the only determining factor in the destiny of peoples and of mankind is to undermine the very foundation of the optimist's belief in the ability of the individual to improve himself by his own efforts. Good and evil, worth and futility, cultural fecundity and cultural nihilism – all are dependent on racial origin. Race – that is the iron law, unshakable, unalterable as the word of God, and to be changed only by the mercy of Divine Providence. There was no room for compromise or pity in this false or only half-understood, and thus easily perverted, doctrine; nature remained eternally responsible for man's salvation or damnation.

In the final count, so the more extreme anti-Semites averred, this applied so particularly to 'the Jewish element' that their most determined efforts at assimilation were 'doomed to failure'. In short, because of his race, every Jew was a 'natural' second-class citizen and condemned so to remain. He must therefore be treated as a 'parasite', and must be eliminated as such.

These new doctrines of anti-Semitism found some acceptance in France and elsewhere, but it was in Germany that they enjoyed the greatest acclaim. To many people who disliked the Jews and had hitherto had to excuse themselves on religious, economic or on any other grounds, these racial theories served as the so-called 'secondary rationalization' which provided them with a legitimate reason for their feelings of aversion just when the sanction of religious conviction was beginning to lose its potency, due to the growth of secular influences.

By and large the Jews in Germany at that time enjoyed a high degree of legal parity with the rest of the population and their cultural assimilation, within the compass of a general economic prosperity, was far advanced. At the same time a Jew could only become an officer in the reserve in exceptional cases. And how much it counted, status-wise, in German society of those days, to be 'an officer in the reserve'! Under the surface, moreover, antipathy towards the Jews as a recognizable minority group must have been prevalent among the broad middle-classes – the 'separateness' of the Jews, like that of the Jesuits and the Free-masons, serving to nourish the suppressed fantasies of so 'rational' a period. Two extraneous factors, one of an incidental and temporary nature and the other basic and permanent, were particularly instrumental in activating the Germans' latent hostility towards the Jews after 1870. The first was the protracted *economic crisis of 1873* – the collapse of the unhealthy economic boom that followed the ending of the Franco–Prussian war. This experience, which had its parallel in France and in Austria with the same results, reawakened the anti-capitalist sentiments to which the lower-middle and peasant classes, vulnerable as they were to economic change, were prone from time to time in their attitude towards the Jews. And even if, as Hans Günter Zmarzlik has recently stressed, the theme of the apparently decisive in-fluence of the Jews on modern capitalism is illustrative of a prejudice characteristic of the next century, spokesmen of the current anti-Semitic movement found no difficulty in exploiting the *historically* limited role played by the Jews in certain branches of the modern economy for the purpose of arousing ill-feeling among that broad stratum of society always anxious for some simple 'explanation' in time of crisis. The second factor, which is of greater significance in the present context, was the powerful drive, initiated by the authorities, to complete the national unity achieved by Germany by the creation of a *single German nation*. It is well known how this tendency has also asserted itself in relation to national minorities, in particular the Poles, in the guise of a definitive and militant nationalist policy. This policy did not *of necessity* entail any very pronounced or consistent 'racial evaluations', and was therefore all the more easily able to win acceptance among the forward-looking and educated sections of our people, including the liberal upper-middle classes. That minorities – or groups which seemed to belong to that category – should be assimilated, appeared to 'modern' public opinion as an obvious no less than an essential minimum requirement. It was a short step, however, from the impatience with which a people awakened to prejudice watched the process of integration to the doubts such people felt about the readiness of those concerned for assimilation or indeed their ability to become assimilated. So much is clear from the pronouncements of Treitschke, who declared that there must be no 'racial anti-Semitism' although he had already launched the senseless and sinister slogan 'the Jews are our misfortune'. 'Anti-capitalist' and 'nationalist' themes not only had an equally pervasive influence on public opinion; potentially both could also be linked with racially anti-Semitic arguments to form a spectrum or shades of opinion and stress. Whether such opinions were more or less extreme depended largely on temperament – that is to say, on self-control and conscience; for nationalism was already developing a tendency to reject ideas of equality and tolerance. The more general anti-liberal attitudes of the second half of the nineteenth century, which we have yet to examine, favoured and encouraged a fusion of the various anti-Semitic themes, and it needed only the right external stimulus for them to find expression in public utterance.

This was provided by the serious economic crisis of 1873, which was followed by a series of publications in the German-speaking countries, stigmatizing the Jews as parasites and demanding that they should, at least, be made subject to special laws. The authors of these works had apparently not been influenced by Gobineau's ideas – these were not disseminated in Germany until later. In the prevailing climate of opinion, if they had been available, they would have been thought so much the more worthy of consideration.

Wilhelm Marr, in a pamphlet which reached twelve editions, called for a fight between 'Germanism' and the 'threatening world domination' of 'Judaism', and declared categorically that the Jewish people were 'racially inflexible'; they could not change themselves, nor could they be changed; it was impossible to live with them in peace and on equal terms because of their deliberately fostered characteristics; there was only one alternative: Us or Them! Claiming a philosophical, biological and historical foundation for anti-Semitism, the Berlin philosopher and economist, Eugen Dührung, cast aside (in 1881) the last vestiges of tolerance – even, and perhaps especially, towards baptized Jews. To be sure he reserved 'solutions' like 'exile' and 'deportation' to a more 'robust future', but he considered, more or less seriously, the possibility of 'interning' Jews under 'international law'. He wished to see them 'held off from the sphere of the community in general', that is to say, made subject to special legal restrictions – as a first and preliminary step, of course. For in Dühring's opinion the tenacity of Judaism could be destroyed only by the destruction of the Jews themselves. He denied 'conclusively' that 'Christianity was still essentially interwoven with Judaism' and declared that it was the first duty of every Christian to turn against Judaism with all the force at his command. Finally, in 1887, the oriental scholar, Adolf Wahrmund, expressed satisfaction at 'the large number of books published in Austria-Hungary, Germany and France' which inveighed against 'the domination' of the Jews – a race of 'nomads', so he arrogantly claimed, who lived by exploiting the foreign economies into which they had forced their way by dishonest means, and whose religious practices made them the very 'embodiment of the anti-Christian principle'. In his own book – *The Laws of the Nomads and the Contemporary Domination of the Jews* – Wahrmund argued that the 'deep-seated laws of evolution' were all-powerful. If this fact were recognized, history would reveal itself in a new light; an ideal central Europe, in which there would be no place for the 'Asiatic' or 'nomadic' way of life represented by the Jews, could be rebuilt on this basis.

In ways like these 'nationalist' and 'economic' arguments combined to produce the anti-Semitic polemic of the seventies and eighties. As a means of furthering the growing interest in German pre-history and encouraging dedication to the cult of all things 'Germanic', the new racial doctrines were worth a great deal. The fact that already during this period these widely circulated literary outpourings led to political demonstrations and organizations of an anti-Semitic character is well known. 'Take care not to arouse the beast in man', warned the left-wing, liberal member of Parliament, Eugen Richter, in 1880, 'for it will stop at nothing'. The protagonists of an extreme anti-Semitism were not fighting a lone battle. There were also the men of comparatively 'moderate' views, who spoke and wrote against the Jews; it was perhaps they who were mainly responsible, just because of their so-called 'moderation', for making anti-Semitism socially acceptable among well-to-do bourgeois circles. As we have already seen, this applied particularly to Heinrich von Treitschke, who managed to preserve his innate liberalism in face of considerable odds so that when he attacked the Jews, in his role as champion of the new Reich, his outbursts made all the more powerful an impression; his moral influence on his more radical followers – in particular, Heinrich Class, President of the All-German Association – and on future generations was very strong. There were also men like the famous oriental scholar and critic, Paul de Lagarde (1827–91) who were not racially anti-Semitic in the narrow sense and did not condemn assimilation unconditionally. Lagarde demanded that the spiritual and economic power of the Jews – which was held to be so dangerous a threat – should be broken. He asserted that the Jews were the exponents of all those features which he and many others most disliked in the economic and pluralistic development of the day – that is to say, materialism and the commercialization of life and thought, spiritual indifference, the 'debasement of morals', and the 'un-German' western ideas of a free-thinking middle-class. He talked, in short, about 'the purveyors of decadence', which the Jews (as foreign bodies in the State) must always be: 'We simply cannot tolerate a nation within a nation.' In Lagarde the anti-capitalist and nationalist themes directed against the Jews were allied to a protest against the general lowering of cultural standards and led to the rejection of tolerance and humanity. It is true that he went so far as to say, almost as an aside: 'We shall not succeed in subduing Judaism by any form of persecution.' At the same time he allowed himself to make out a case which could only encourage ideas about the Jews, which, if accepted and implemented, were bound to promote and justify the institution of inhuman measures against them. He preached hatred and contempt for those who pleaded 'humanitarian principles' in defence of speaking in favour of the Jews, and for those who were too weak-kneed to trample these 'profiteering vermin' underfoot. 'One does not have dealings with pests and parasites; one does not rear them and cherish them; one destroys them as speedily and thoroughly as possible.' It must not be forgotten, in this context, that Lagarde's precepts came back into fashion in an exaggerated form, particularly among members of the German youth movement, as part of the widespread revolt against the rationalism of modern technical civilization that occurred after the First World War, nor that his 'admonitions' were exploited as propaganda in a most obvious way by the National Socialists after 1933 and during the Second World War.

The promotion of genuinely racial theories in Germany was due, as much as anything else, to Richard Wagner the Younger's *Bayreuther Kreis* (The Bayreuth Set) and its mouthpiece, the *Bayreuther Blätter,* in which the 'Germanic cult' played so important a rôle. It was here that Gobineau's philosophy was precisely defined – his book was translated into German by a member of the set, L. Schemann. Richard Wagner's own expressed attitude to hostility towards the Jews, which was predominantly emotional in origin [his world of ideas made a profound impression upon Hitler, as the latter acknowledged], was most likely to have been influenced in a racially anti-Semitic sense by Gobineau, and was certainly so influenced by Houston Stewart Chamberlain. Chamberlain, born an Englishman, a naturalized German and well known as Wagner's son-in-law, was a spiritual disciple of Gobineau's. It was indubitably his amateur, but extraordinarily successful book – *The Foundations of the Nineteenth Century* – that was responsible for spreading racially anti-Semitic notions among the educated middle-classes. He must, moreover, be regarded as one of Hitler's most important preceptors – he was still alive when Hitler came to power and greatly admired the latter's policies. Chamberlain ascribed every important cultural development to the German way of life; in his view anything 'un-Germanic' was *ipso facto* 'unhealthy' and fit only to be discarded, and the Semites, the Jews, were incapable of any creative activity. At the same time he underlined the growing danger of Jewish domination; the Jews were at pains to maintain the 'spotless' purity of their own stock, but on the other hand they did all they could to procure 'the infection of the Indo-Europeans with Jewish blood' – the end-product of which would be a 'herd of pseudo-hebraic half-breeds – a people beyond all doubt physically, spiritually and morally degenerate'. 'Never,' he thundered, 'should man in his apathy' allow the Jews to forget that the laws of nature were holy laws. Because Chamberlain extolled the historical association between the German way of life and Christianity, because he avoided violent anti-Semitic invective, and because he accorded a spiritual value to 'race', his influence on moderate circles was considerable.

Social Darwinism

Meanwhile the intellectual life of the time was being influenced by another trend of thought which was to become significant as the second cardinal principle of the National Socialist 'purification' policy. I am now referring to 'Social Darwinism' – a movement that gained a great deal of support after 1890, and had a profound effect upon Hitler's mind. The 'victory march' of natural science during the nineteenth century had encouraged the notion that, in the final count, all historical development was the result of the self-regulating regenerative powers of the elemental forces of nature. A few years after the publication of Gobineau's book, the English naturalist, Darwin, believed that his study of the origin of the species had laid down the laws of evolution as they affected all forms of life. His premise was that this evolution was part of a long, gradual development through a struggle for existence, in which the stronger and more efficient element always prevailed; the species had continually progressed and improved by a process of natural selection. The revolutionary significance of this theory, supported as it was by careful and detailed research, lay in the fact that it offered a simple mechanical explanation for life's phenomena (that is to say, it showed that these were naturally self-regulating) to replace the earlier acceptance of a supernatural power responsible for the creation of life on earth. Darwin's theory denied the existence of any essential difference in origin between men and animals. Those who came forward to interpret the theory – and there was soon no lack of them – either misunderstood the nature of the difference in quality that had developed between men and animals during the course of evolution or wanted to see the traditional Christian values governing the social behaviour of mankind set aside. Darwin also explained that the biologically superior elements occasionally thrown up during the evolutionary process were, unfortunately, not *ipso facto* of greater value than the rest. As against this, those so-called 'Social Darwinists', who were disciples of the modern creed of 'natural forces' in their political outlook held that human society was also more or less a biological organism, and concluded, therefore, that the *biological factor was the one absolute* in all spheres of life.

'Social Darwinism' – that is to say the adaptation of Darwin's teaching for social and political purposes – was certainly not exclusively, nor even primarily, a German phenomenon. But while the great majority of its foreign adherents adopted it within the framework of practical social politics, its German exponents – stimulated by a prize essay competition on the subject set by the firm of Krupps in 1900 – not only used Darwin's doctrine as the basis of political reform, but gradually raised his theories to the status of a world philosophy. Of particular significance was the fact that German Social Darwinism, in its later form, took as its focal point the theme that 'natural selection' was essential to human progress. This contention led to the conclusion that modern civilization, with its (two-edged) achievements and its humanitarian principles, had to a great extent destroyed the function of natural selection as a 'healthy' and 'proper' regulator of social development. 'Logic' demanded that the community should be reorganized in such a way as to release the beneficial powers of nature and make it easy for them to do their work. The modern State, instead of protecting the weak and helping the sick – that is to say, supporting the 'incapable' elements – should turn its attention to encouraging the healthy, strong and biologically valuable elements in society. It is true that moderate Social Darwinists like Schallmayer refused to accept 'the operation of natural selection as definitive' (although not without emphasizing the 'positive' effects of its cruelties); nevertheless he recommended 'fruitful selection' for breeding purposes as a way of bringing marriage under 'socially hygienic control'. In other words what he proposed was the elimination of physical and mental weaknesses by forbidding the unfit to marry, by the compulsory certification of the insane and by sterilization. He even went so far as to criticize 'traditional human feelings' as being 'inclined to favour the individual unduly', in that, so far, they had rebelled against any sacrifice of the individual in the interests of the community. Yet the 'principle of social usefulness' really carried much more weight as a basis for legislation than the 'untenable idea of human rights'. If the preservation of the species became the cardinal principle of domestic policy, the same argument could be applied to foreign policy. Schallmayer believed, 'in the light of the development by natural selection theory', that the 'power demand' of any individual State governed 'its expansion at the expense of other States', and he therefore urged that every facet of domestic and foreign policy should be geared to ensuring the permanent 'viability 'of the nation: that should be 'the measuring rod'. Exactly what he meant by this was shown by his further appeals – for the subordination of all cultural attainments, all social order and even 'the accepted ideas of good and evil' to the overriding need to arm for the struggle for existence.

That such demands and protestations found their highest datum-point in the nation's sense of its own identity and prescriptive superiority was hardly surprising in that age of nationalism. And when some Social Darwinists went so far as to claim that their 'racially-hygienic' theories accorded with the needs of humanity, then the more radical spirits – Tille is an example – began to champion the 'right' of the stronger races to 'destroy the weaker'; those who could not hold their ground should resign themselves to annihilation. Tille extolled as an 'aristocratic-social' principle the cruelty of the selection process used by nature for the preservation of the species; he declared that innate human rights were incompatible with the doctrine of progress; he glorified self-interest; and he poured scorn on the moral code 'we have brewed up for ourselves out of our weakness', which allowed the incapable to survive.

Hitler (who held that 'in the search for self-preservation so-called humanitarian ideals melt away like snow in the March sunshine') constantly gave expression to very similar sentiments. Seldom did he do so more plainly, however, than in an unpublished speech to a group of officer cadets on 22 June 1944 – although in the state of the war that obtained at that time the futility of the concept behind such theories was never more startlingly apparent.

Nature is always teaching us . . . that she is governed by the principle of selection: that victory is to the strong and that the weak must go to the wall. She teaches us that what may seem cruel to us, because it affects us personally or because we have been brought up in ignorance of her laws, is nevertheless often essential if a higher way of life is to be attained. Nature . . . knows nothing of the notion of humanitarianism which signifies that the weak must at all costs be surrounded and preserved even at the expense of the strong.

Nature does not see in weakness any extenuating reasons . . . on the contrary, weakness calls for condemnation . . .

War is therefore the unalterable law of the whole of life – the prerequisite for the natural selection of the strong and the precedent for the elimination of the weak. What seems cruel to us is from Nature's point of view entirely obvious. A people that cannot assert itself must disappear and another must take its place. All creation is subject to this law; no one can avoid it. . . . Since life on earth began, struggle has been the very essence of existence. . . .

The new doctrine had another consequence, allied to but even more crucially important than, the theory of life's unending struggle – which was used to clothe the naked realities of politics. Those who, 'in the name of scientific knowledge', used the social usefulness or biological capability of the individual as a measure of his worth to society as a whole or who advocated, even in theory, the promotion of eugenics by methods that would result in the elimination of the 'incapable', were men who regarded humanity as merely another species, divested it of all self-respect and dignity, and debased the individual to the material level of an expendable unit in a collective whole. But basically, to be prepared to elevate the theories of a worthless natural science – with the State as its possible instrument – to a position of complete mastery over the individual, and by inference over the whole of his existence and even his personal right to exist, in order to 'steer' the development of society in the direction judged most advantageous to society as a whole, was to invite the total destruction of the image of mankind as it had been fashioned by Greek civilization, Christendom, and the age of enlightenment. Under the influence of nationalist impulses, pretensions and aims a totalitarian design of this kind threatened to engulf all feelings of common humanity between men, and indeed between nations, to cripple the tradition of spiritual opposition to the evil practices of a politically and technically omnipotent authority, and to degrade those who served it to the level of docile tools. For above all a totalitarian system obliterates normal human reactions – as much among the bewildered general public as among those who serve its ends. Evidence is available in many of the National Socialist manifestoes that the biological standard was widely applied in the appointment of the leaders of the movement, in particular of the SS. For instance, Himmler proclaimed that his 'ultimate aim' and one that he had to keep constantly in view since he had become *Reichsführer-SS*, was to create 'an Order of good blood to serve Germany' and to be able to 'draw into our orbit and away from our enemies all those of Nordic blood in the whole world. Unless the blood of leadership in German veins, by which alone we stand or fall, can be increased by the admixture of good blood from elsewhere, we shall never achieve world mastery'. The East would become 'a breeding ground for sound German stock'. But the following observation probably shows, most clearly, Himmler's view of the purpose and method of breeding an élite, and, by inference, his image of mankind:

We are like the plant-breeding specialist who, when he wants to breed a pure new strain from a well-tried species that has been exhausted by too much cross-breeding, first goes over the field to cull the unwanted plants. We, too, shall begin by weeding out the people who, in our opinion, are not suitable SS material . . .[1]

After 1933 National Socialism was publicized as 'the biological will of the German people', and as 'political biology' (see Escherisch and Lehmann). In the present context the ideas and behaviour of the National Socialist leadership can hardly be more pertinently described than in the words of my colleague, Hans Buchheim:

The National Socialists considered that their own people, and during the second world war the people of Europe, had squandered their substance; they looked on them as a plantation overgrown with weeds, which must at all costs be cleared by isolating the 'incorrigible', cutting out the 'canker of decay', propagating the worthwhile elements and letting the less valuable wither away, sterilizing the sick, and either transplanting or suppressing the unstable varieties. The end-product of this policy would be a new, biologically sensible, well-ordered European community. . . . This programme would be carried through by means of euthanasia, deportation, Germanisation and, last but not least, the 'extirpation of all those classes of people considered to be worthless or dangerous'.

The Social Darwinist doctrines – themselves both a symptom and a consequence of contemporary philosophy – had, in that imperialistic age, an influence varying in shade and degree far beyond the circle of those who preached them. The feeling of racial and cultural superiority – strangely mixed up as it was with apprehension about the future – sprang from imperialism together with conscious pride in technical progress. The fact was that a great deal of common ground existed between the theories of Social Darwinism and the more moderate racial doctrines, and each favoured the penetration of the other. It is true that Social Darwinism was not necessarily, nor even innately, anti-Semitic. Several of the exponents of its earlier versions expressly denied that their theories could be given an anti-Semitic, or even a nationalist interpretation; what they recommended would benefit, if not the species in general, at least that part of it represented by the white races. And even the most extreme Social Darwinists never for a moment contemplated wholesale liquidation on Hitler's lines. Furthermore Darwin's doctrine of the self-regulating adaptation and progression of the species was quite contrary to the modern racial theory which saw race as a basic and unalterable fact. In practice, however, the affinities were such – between racialism's denial of the principle of human equality in favour of race improvement through the elimination of the unfit and Social Darwinism's evaluation of the individual (and where possible of the group) in the light of biological standards – that, in the end, the two came to be regarded as 'Siamese twins'. It was not only that Darwinism lent 'authority' to the then imperfectly understood science of anthropology; the synthesis of the biological and the specifically racial ideologies was held to be both necessary and desirable as a mark of nationhood. Eventually the racial doctrine, and the so-called 'scientific' evidence for it, were accepted as absolutes – in the sense of the mythical superiority of the 'particular', the Nordic race or, as Rosenberg later proclaimed, 'of the racially integrated soul of the nation' as 'the standard against which we must finally measure our worth'. As Friedrich Meinecke wrote: 'One would have to embrace the new ethic of national egoism wholeheartedly to be able to give one's blessing to every shift of public opinion [from the rational to the irrational].'

The integration of Social Darwinism and specifically racial concepts was, however, nowhere so clearly reflected as in a thesis – 'An Ethic Revised' – which the geneticist, Lenz, produced for his professor, the Social Darwinist Ploetz, in 1917, and which was published in 1933. In this thesis, which in the author's opinion 'contained all the important features of the National Socialist philosophy', Lenz declared that 'race was the criterion of value', although he conceded that this criterion could not be established in scientific terms. 'In the last resort intellectual acceptance is possible only when the object is one which we are able to approve.' On this basis he was able to discard 'the dogma of the individual' in favour of the racist creed: 'The naïve assumption that all men have equal rights, from a moral point of view,' he wrote,

belongs to an individualistic doctrine. . . . There could be no greater fallacy than the belief that human nature abhors war – the exact contrary is true. . . . Socialist ideas must be made to bear fruit, but in the organically-socialist rather than in the individually-socialist sense. The aim of socialism should be the welfare not of the individual, but of the race. . . . The State is not there to see that the individual gets his rights, but to serve the race. . . . All rights must be compatible with and subordinate to this end. . . .

Lenz was even able to convince himself that 'the moral philosopher', Kant, would, in some respects, have made a much greater impression if 'the principle of natural selection had been discovered in his day'. For if Darwin was right that natural selection through the struggle for existence was the ultimate means by which life progressed, then it followed that this was 'the only means available for the maintenance of racial standards'. A community which ignored the theory of natural selection would inevitably, and through its own fault, become extinct. [Whether the State ought to take a stand 'against a foreign race', Lenz remarked in his foreword to the 1933 edition, 'was a matter of political expediency, which the political leadership would have to decide'.] And he concluded as follows:

Thus we see that everything depends on the racial ideal: culture, progress, personality, happiness, redemption. . . . In this ideal we find the unity of our existence, the unity of life, the unity of Germany in the highest sense. . . . If we deny it, our race is doomed to extinction. The German nation is the last refuge of the Nordic race.

We need only look at the 1933/34 syllabus for the philosophical education of the SS and the police forces,[2] to see how National Socialism made use of the biological racial theory to further both its overall policy and its ambition to breed its own élite. The remarkable thing was that its authors found it necessary to take account of possible theoretical and political objections of other countries (Japan for instance!) by an amplification to the effect that:

it is not appropriate to our way of thinking about the laws of existence to place too much emphasis on the concept of value when considering ethnology and racial history. The vitality and achievements of any race with common ties of heredity and environment merit our respect, as we see in these a manifestation of life willed by nature herself.

In practice such reservations were invalidated by being followed in italics by statements like:

if we stress what Europe owes to the Nordic race, this is not because of some biological evaluation but because the realities of politics have shown that this race, both in the past and in the present, is capable of unifying the whole and of thereby transforming Europe into a single powerful community.

To be sure the statement then went on:

We have never boasted, as the ignorant and hostile have sometimes accused us of doing, that all culture, even that of past ages, stems exclusively from the Nordic race. People of other racial origins, also have cultural achievements to their credit.

But the accent was unmistakably on such assertions as:

The Nordic race in Europe must be recognized as the one which has left its mark on the face of the continent. . . . People of Nordic stock, because of their number, their central position and their achievements, constitute an élite and a unifying element for the rest of humanity.

In spite of the reservations mentioned above, the term 'high-value races' – defined as 'the culminating entities of the biological process' – came into use. These races were the ones who had survived in the struggle for existence, in spite of a low rate of fertility, because of an innate creative ability that had its origin in the particularly harsh conditions of the selective process as it had applied to them. They provided 'the most striking evidence that the basic law of the eternal struggle, in which all the weak and the less valuable must succumb, holds good'.

Mainly because of urbanization – which 'suited the special characteristics of the Jews and gave them a chance to push themselves forward' – the majority of people, and particularly the high-value races, could no longer live in an entirely natural environment. It was because the Nationalist Socialist State appreciated these biological facts – that is to say, the deterioration of the selection process – that it had turned its full attention to 'measures for promoting greater discrimination in reproduction'.

It was then argued, plausibly enough, that in furtherance of the Social Darwinist theories the concept of usefulness to society and ultimately to the State would have to serve as a yardstick in determining human worth and that people would, in consequence, have to be placed unreservedly at the disposal of the State which should be accorded full powers of control.

It is an untenable position when the relationship between the efficient and the ineffective in a State assumes an unhealthy form. The nation has to spend a great deal of energy and money in dealing with the feeble-minded, the criminal and the anti-social. If these examples of poor heredity were eliminated, large sums of money would be saved and could be diverted to other, more productive ends. A responsible State leadership should devote all its attention to plans for maintaining and increasing those of sound stock. In primitive societies, the community rids itself of its weaklings. In so-called civilized nations, a false attitude of brotherly love, which the Church has been especially assiduous in fostering among the broad masses, operates in direct opposition to the selective process.

After all this the significance of the two key sentences in this 'syllabus' was quite unmistakable. These were concerned with the practical application of the accepted theories (to which even so matter-of-fact a man as Reich Marshal Göring paid tribute by declaring that 'the sin against breeding is the hereditary sin of our people').

Two things are essential for the building up and maintenance of a healthy race. Not only must the hereditary factor be unremittingly sustained, but an environment favourable to this 'race' must be established. This can be achieved only if the whole community of the people consciously aligns itself behind this principle (the principle of sound breeding) and if each member of the community conducts his life accordingly.

Hitler's Jewish Policy and the Nazi Party before 1933

There can be no question that the Social Darwinist ideas could serve only to intensify the hatred of the Jews that had been coming to the fore since the eighteen-seventies, nor that the combination of the two must inevitably have the most disastrous consequences from an intellectual point of view. Until 1914 the liberal and humanist traditions of the German middle-classes had been strong enough to prevent organized anti-Semitism from spreading beyond certain small, insignificant groups. In fact, during the years immediately preceding the outbreak of the First World War, it had actually showed signs of decreasing. But from 1916 onwards, as the military and economic situation continued to deteriorate, there was a noticeable change, and after the collapse in 1918 the development of anti-Semitism was complete. The mistaken belief among large sections of the German population that all was well until, so to speak, the eleventh hour, strengthened their conviction that there was 'something fishy' about the sudden, shocking change in the fortunes of the war; and although a study of history shows us that there are no simple explanations, yet we know from experience that in times of crises most people tend to look for a single cause – that is to say, they attribute all their misfortunes and discomfiture to one reason, to one scapegoat. The military defeat, the break-up of the monarchy, the economic depression, the trials of domestic and foreign policy in an 'imported' democracy, the reluctance of a great many people to try to understand the latest developments and to accept them – all this bewilderment and poverty nourished passions and emotions of every kind. After the 'November criminals' [of 1918], the Jew was the favourite scapegoat – people saw in him the source of all their afflictions. The anti-Semitic organizations and publications became surprisingly popular, and Hitler's Nazi Party, along with other pre-war anti-Semitic groups, emerged out of the half-dark.

Hitler himself, whose personality was of such overwhelming and disastrous significance to the Jews in the German-controlled territories, neither invented anti-Semitism nor added anything of importance to the theories on which it was based. He was never so doctrinaire as Rosenberg, for example, or Darré or Himmler, and he was known to have spoken sarcastically about their pan-German cult, even going so far as to question the scientific basis of the race concept as such, as well as the contemporary science of race. Hitler's anti-Semitism was frankly emotional. Yet he seized eagerly on every pseudo-scientific 'doctrine' of modern anti-Semitism – expounded before and after the turn of the century occasionally even in Austria – which provided him with a legitimate justification for his feelings of hatred. In spite of suggestions to the contrary, it seems unlikely that the obscure theories of the Cistercian monk, Adolf Lenz, alias Jörg Lenz von Liebenfels, who contrasted the Aryans with the Jews in the most virulent terms in his principal 'theozoological' work '*Arioheroikern*', and recommended the systematic breeding of the 'culture-bearing' Aryans by such means as sterilization, deportation and elimination of Jews and other inferior races, actually *gave* Hitler his ideas, although he may have spoken favourably of this man and his writings from time to time. It is more probable that Richard Wagner, and in particular Houston Stewart Chamberlain's amateurish 'philosophy' made a stronger impression upon him. The extent to which Hitler adopted the racist theories is shown by his declaration in 1928 (which today has so ironic a ring) that, because of the Russians' racial inferiority, it 'would never occur to anyone' to fear that their vast numbers might lead to a Russian hegemony! 'The size of the Russian population should not be taken as a sign of intrinsic worth nor lead anyone to think that because of its magnitude it could represent a threat to world freedom.'

Hitler combined his passionate hatred of the Jews with a shrewd and penetrating grasp (which he had acquired from his experiences in Austria with Leuger and Schönerer) of the rabble-rousing possibilities of anti-Semitic arguments and propaganda. In his first important speech of 13 August 1920, which was exclusively devoted to the 'Jewish question', he declared quite openly:

We are convinced that scientific anti-Semitism, which clearly recognizes the frightful danger that that race represents to our people, *can only be our guide*; the broad masses, who will always react emotionally, must first be made aware of the Jew as the person who, in daily life, is always and everywhere thrusting himself forward – our task must be to arouse the mass instinct against the Jew, to stir it up and keep it on the boil until it decides to support the movement which is prepared to take the consequences.

Hitler had already explained the 'intellectual basis' of his anti-Semitism and how he intended to reach his objective, in a letter dated 16 September 1919 – that is to say during the previous year. 'Anti-Semitism as a political movement neither can nor should be based on fleeting emotions, but on the acceptance of fact – and the fact is that Judaism is a matter of race and not of religion.' He went on: 'Reasonable anti-Semitism ... must lead to a systematic and lawful campaign for the removal of those privileges which the Jew enjoys – unlike other foreigners living in our midst, who are subject to the law applying to aliens. The final aim of such anti-Semitism must be, unquestionably, the expulsion of the Jews.' In the Nazi Party manifesto of 24 February 1920 Hitler's above-mentioned (which was also the 'official') objective was set out under points 4 and 5:

Point 4 : State citizenship can only be claimed by nationals and only those of German blood, regardless of religious persuasion, can be nationals. No Jew can therefore be a national.
Point 5 : Those who do not possess State citizenship can live in Germany only as guests and are subject to the laws applying to aliens.

In his book, *Mein Kampf*, Hitler wrote: 'If, at the beginning and during the war, someone had only subjected about twelve or fifteen thousand of these Hebrew enemies of the people to poison gas – as was suffered by hundreds of thousands of our best workers from all walks of life and callings on the battlefield – then the sacrifice of millions at the front would not have been in vain.'[1]

When this sentence came to be printed and was seen by the author at proof stage, it was left as it was and remained unchanged in edition after edition, without, apparently, ever rousing the reaction that might well have been expected!

In the so-called National Socialist 'world philosophy', the Nordic race – personified in the Führer – typified the principle of the good, while the Jew was the 'anti-race' – the principle of evil endowed, like the devil, with almost supernatural powers. And even when anti-Semitism was temporarily soft-pedalled for tactical reasons, it remained the core of a National Socialist ideology which denied the Jew his right to the status of a human being.* Scarcely anyone realized what a terrible threat such ideas and slogans represented when they were adopted by a political group which first proclaimed the nation as morally of the highest value and then made itself and its leader into the embodiment of that nation, thereby claiming sovereignty for the standards of its political behaviour – that is to say, a group which, having made

*The statement of the chief Nazi judge, Walter Buch, is an example: 'National Socialism has recognized that the Jew is not a human being. He is nothing but an agent of decomposition.'

itself master of the conscience of its supporters, then accorded itself limitless rights over the destiny of its fellowmen.*

Anti-Semitism also had an important part to play in Hitler's foreign and European policy. It is true that the race concept in its absolute form conflicted with the concept of nationhood and with that of the association of peoples in nations with similar ways of life and interests. Clearly Hitler, with his pronouncements about the race concept as a supra-national concept, intended to toss a propaganda slogan of the first importance into Europe and thus lay a bait for potential fifth columnists – in short, to use the theoretical supra-national race concept to initiate a practical 'disintegration process' among the European nations, which would serve and further the power aims of a supernational Germany. 'As though by a magnet,' as he expressed it later, 'the best elements of Germanic stock ... must be drawn into our orbit.' In the meantime, however, the Jews had been unearthed as visible *internal* enemy No. 1 – the exaggerated threat they were supposed to represent making it easy for Hitler first to concentrate all means of propaganda in the desired direction and then to build up and vindicate the totalitarian power structure of which he had dreamed in the guise of national defence, security and well-being. There he was – the enemy: a concept which, evidently, no totalitarian system ever seems able to do without. It was he who was the object of and the justification for the hate campaign [at no time taken seriously enough by those who opposed the Nazi Party or by its members] which resulted in countless isolated instances of malevolence, and sometimes exploded into actual persecution even before the seizure of power.

The First Years of Persecution

On 30 January 1933 Adolf Hitler was nominated Chancellor of the Reich by the President of the Reich, von Hindenburg. This

*'A world philosophy can only be created and maintained by fanatics who are willing to sacrifice their identity for their faith' – thus Rudolf Höss summed up the repeated admonitions of Himmler and Eicke, who even drew upon the attitude of the Jehovah's Witnesses to illustrate their point. 'The SS-man must believe with just such fanaticism in the National Socialist idea and in Adolf Hitler.' *Commandant at Auschwitz : Autobiographical Notes of Rudolf Höss.*

meant that the anti-Semitic prejudices of the National Socialist Party were immediately transformed into official government policy. In furtherance of these inclinations, the new Reich Chancellor had at his disposal all the resources of power and propaganda attaching to his own dominant Party, and, in addition, those attaching to the State, over which the Party had gained ascendancy with such astonishing speed. The new régime's first 'Jewish action' – the boycott of 1 April 1933 – proved this beyond all doubt.

The reason given by the Party for this boycott of the Jews in Germany was the 'atrocity campaign' which the Jews abroad had allegedly been carrying on for weeks against the new régime. In reality the outward signs of the critical attitude shown by large sections of the foreign public (and by no means only by the Jews) was merely an echo of those expressions of disapproval that had been heard already before 1 April 1933 in Germany itself from the so-called 'enemies of the new State', who included the Jews. It is true that, in general, the National Socialist organizations had kept themselves somewhat in the background until the general election of 5 March 1933. But after the election all this changed – in spite of strenuous attempts made in the interests of foreign policy either to keep the numerous outrages against the Jews out of the press or to minimize or conceal the part played by the Party in allowing and encouraging them. For example, on 11 March 1933 Alpers the *SS-Führer* in Braunschweig, a lawyer by profession and later Braunschweig's Minister of Justice, ordered a group of SS men to break into two Jewish warehouses disguised as a band of robbers and, at a signal from him, to do all the damage they possibly could. The National Socialist Minister of the Interior had in the meantime taken care to withdraw the regular police patrols from the area. After the operation had been carried through successfully, Alpers, in full SS uniform, addressed a public meeting that same afternoon, condemning the occurrence and putting it down to communist disturbances. Exactly the same happened in Göttingen before 1 April, when the display windows of almost all the Jewish-owned shops were shattered – whereupon the uniformed SA, SS and regular police forces appeared, but 'could do nothing to prevent' the destruction of a synagogue as well, according to the report of the incident in the

Göttingen Tageblatt. On 13 March, in Breslau, the SA went so far as to picket the entrances to the district and county courts and to refuse admission to all Jewish lawyers and judges. The police did nothing, and the Chief of Police sent a petition, which made mockery of the legal position, to the Department of Justice, in which he requested that consideration should be given, in accordance with the wishes of the people, 'to limiting the influence of Jewish organs of judicial administration'. In the event the Department of Justice capitulated and on 16 March 1933 reduced the number of Jewish lawyers attached to the Breslau courts to seventeen (and these were provided with special police passes) in order, so it pleaded, 'to pacify public opinion'. From 15 March 1933 onwards the Polish consul in Leipzig was obliged to intervene almost daily, as even Jews who were Polish citizens were being subjected to ill-treatment.[1] During this period, too, a synagogue in Dresden was wrecked and Jewish shops were damaged in Chemnitz and elsewhere. Moreover by the middle of March 1933 a totally illegal 'weeding-out' of Jewish personnel from local government, law courts and colleges was in full swing in central Germany. In many places Jews who were arrested were obliged, before orders were given for their release, to sign a declaration to the effect that no physical violence had been offered them.

There is no doubt that events of this kind aroused sharp criticism abroad and that this, of course, was both embarrassing and annoying to the National Socialist government. Denials were fruitless. And so 'the Nazi Party leadership' decreed the boycott on 1 April 1933 against Jewish shops, Jewish goods, Jewish doctors and Jewish lawyers, declaring (quite unjustifiably in fact) that it was 'in answer' to the atrocity campaign instigated by the Jewish community abroad. It is possible that, even then, this explanation was chosen in order to be able to present the operation in the guise of 'reprisals', that is to say, to provide added pretexts for anti-Jewish measures that might otherwise meet with opposition. Be that as it may, a number of 'action committees' were set up under the direction of one of the most violent Jew-baiters of the party, the *Gauleiter* of Franken and editor of the scandal sheet *Der Stürmer*, Julius Streicher – a man whose corrupt practices and other offences finally led to his being retired into the background in 1939. The function of these committees was to popularize the boycott and to organize tens of thousands of mass meetings (which in the event never took place) for the purpose of demanding that the relative strength of the Jews employed in all professions 'should be fixed according to the proportion of Jews in the German population as a whole'. This demand was to be concentrated in the first instance on three objectives: (*a*) attendance at German schools and colleges, (*b*) the medical profession, and (*c*) the legal profession. Point 5 of the decree of the Party leadership contained threats against any newspaper which failed to support the operation, and press notices appeared, with photographs of people who continued to patronize Jewish shops – all with the idea of popularizing the boycott. Significantly, Hans Kerrl, the National Socialist Reich Commissioner of Justice in Prussia – hence a government official – explained in a broadcast on 31 March 1933 that, having regard to the anticipated 'self-help actions' of the population, it was the duty of all those in authority ... to suggest to all Jewish judges holding office that they should at once tender their resignation or to find some other way of preventing them from entering the law court buildings. Jewish public prosecutors should be sent on leave immediately, and Jewish lawyers admitted only in such numbers as were proportionate to the size of the Jewish population. On 1 April, Kerrl – again without any legal basis – placed a ban on any Jewish notary engaging in official business, and on 4 April ordered that no Jewish lawyer should be allowed to practise in Prussia. After all this – and the stricter passport control instituted on 4 April 1933 – the American consul was not anticipating events to any great extent when, on 8 April, he declared that the National Socialists had, for all practical purposes, taken away from the Jews two fundamental civic rights: the right to a free choice of profession, and the right to freedom of movement.

If Hitler himself believed that he would be able effectively to further the solution of the Jewish problem in the sense that he wished by operations of the kind represented by the boycott of the 1 April, and that activities of this sort would be acceptable in terms of foreign policy, he was to learn his mistake from the reaction to the boycott. Significantly, the American consul in Leipzig remarked in his report: 'In fairness to the German people it must be said that the boycott was unpopular with the working classes and with the educated sections of the middle-classes.' Presumably the extreme anti-Semites of the Nazi Party had overestimated the extent to which the ordinary German was hostile to the Jews, and they must have been disappointed by the indifference to the boycott shown by large sections of the population. On the other hand the Party leadership could hardly shut its eyes to the obvious disadvantages of such practices where foreign political relations and foreign trade were concerned. At the same time their action and the illegal measures connected with it had created a situation which called for 'regulation by statute', and had thus provided them with a favourable basis for the government measures they desired. However little such law-creating regulations could be said to represent 'justice' in the true sense of the word, they did show up to advantage in a number of ways as being much less radical than those originally demanded by the Party press. And this was of value from more than a psychological and propaganda point of view. The 'pseudo-legality' of the whole procedure was just as effective in paving the way to totalitarian control as it was in meeting the inescapable demands of foreign policy, and in establishing the concept of the majority will of the people at a stage when the National Socialist régime had not yet completely consolidated its position. For in many circles of the German middle-classes there still existed an instinctive dislike of the violence and lack of restraint of the Nazi anti-Jewish campaign, particularly as it affected the individual Jew. Nevertheless the measures to implement the official government policy of 'restricting Jewish influence in German life' (dressed up as they were in the threadbare garments of formal legality) did find acceptance – and not only because of the new régime's 'energy in the national interest', at which some were inclined to look askance. There were anti-Semitic circles, even among the educated middle-classes, where the 'exclusion laws' were regarded as necessary, or at least as 'expedient' and therefore tolerable; the majority ignored the fact that they undermined the very foundations of the idea of equality before the law. If we look at what followed from an overall point of view, we can see that the Nazi Party never renounced noisy demonstrations and provocative incidents, let alone their rabble-rousing propaganda. The focal point of the government's Jewish policy until

1938 was to be found on the one hand in the so-called 'legal exclusion' of the Jews, and on the other – and this corresponded to the growing power of the SS – in the régime of suppression and terror administered by the police – a régime which developed gradually but systematically and was all the more effective for being relatively unpublicized. In this way public opinion in general became attuned to the Party's continuous and officially tolerated moral denigration of and discrimination against the Jews.

The beginning of the first main stage of the National Socialist persecution of the Jews was marked by the promulgation of an Act of 7 April 1933 (for which preparation had been made for more than a week!) with the resounding title of 'The Re-establishment of the Career Civil Service' [*zur Widerherstellung des Berufsbeamtentums*]. Under this Act 'public servants not of Aryan stock' (which meant, according to the first executive order under the Act of 11 April 1933, those who had *one* Jewish grandparent and were therefore quarter Jewish) were dismissed from office. As it happened, after the Reich President, von Hindenburg, had protested against the comprehensive nature of the new Act, a number of 'non-Aryan' public servants – those who had held office since 1 August 1914, those who had fought at the front for Germany or her allies, and those whose fathers or sons had been killed in action – were excluded from its provisions; but these exemptions remained in force for barely two and a half years. Under the Act more than 2,000 'non-Aryan' scientists and professors, including a number of world-famous scholars, were driven out of office, in direct contravention of their well-earned rights.

Acts, ordinances and executive orders similar to the Career Civil Service Act (and to begin with containing the same exemptions) excluded Jews from the professions (in particular the legal profession and that of patent agent), and from unpaid public service, for instance, jury service. In many cases the coordinated (*gleichgeschaltene*) organizations in German public life demanded 'of their own volition' the expulsion of their Jewish members. The following announcement in the *Gross-Berliner Ärtzeblatt*[2] of 20 May 1933 is an example: 'We, the German doctors, demand that no Jew should be permitted to undertake the medical care of German citizens.'

A ruling to the effect that 'non-Aryan doctors' were no longer to work in hospitals, and that those who were newly qualified were not to be regarded as such had been passed a month earlier (on 22 April 1933); a similar ruling was applied to dentists and dental technicians. Following an Act for 'Preventing Overcrowding in German Schools and Colleges' [*Gesetz gegen die Uberfüllung von deutscher Schulen und Hochschulen*] of 25 April 1933, the number of 'non-Aryan' Germans in relation to the total attendance at each school and college must no longer exceed the proportion of 'non-Aryans' to 'Aryans' in the German population as a whole. The appointment of Jews to the office of assistant judge was forbidden by a circular issued by the Prussian Minister of Justice on 28 April 1933. Under the second executive order of the Civil Service Act (4 May 1933), any civil authority could revoke its contract of employment with its 'non-Aryan' workers and employees. Under the third executive order, honorary professors, university lecturers and notaries were included in the provisions of the Civil Service Act, and the exemption rules applying to 'ex-combatants' were considerably tightened up. Following an Act of 6 May 1933, 'non-Aryan' tax experts were no longer admitted, and after a ruling by the Reich Finance Minister on 5 July 1933 marriage loans were stopped, even if only one of the couple was 'non-Aryan'. Under an Act of 14 July 1933 naturalization papers taken out between 9 November 1918 and 30 January 1933 were cancelled in cases where naturalization was no longer considered to be 'desirable'. In accordance with a long-standing aim of the Party, this was directed principally at Jews in the eastern provinces (executive order of 26 July 1933), and no consideration was given to whether they had committed any offence or not. Under an Act of 26 September 1933 'non-Aryan' notaries could be refused admission, even if they were ex-combatants. Under the Act of 29 September governing the entail of farms in the Reich [*Reichserbhofgesetz*] only those farmers could inherit who could prove that there was no Jewish blood in their forebears as far back as 1800. A regulation of 17 May 1934 laid down that from henceforth 'non-Aryan' doctors and doctors with 'non-Aryan' wives or husbands would be allowed to join the medical insurance scheme on qualification only in specially 'favourable' cases. The legal education order of 22 July 1934 made Aryan origin a condition for admittance to legal examinations; a similar order of 8 December applied the same condition to pharmaceutical examinations. Finally, under the Compulsory Service Act [*Wehrgesetz*] of 21 May 1935, 'Aryan' origin was made a 'basic' condition of being called up for military service, although there were certain exceptions. But in no case could 'non-Aryans' rise to commissioned or non-commissioned rank. Following an ordinance of 25 July 1935 the drafting of 'non-Aryans' for active service came under a total ban.

The exclusion of the Jews (albeit with the exceptions already mentioned) from all branches of public life in Germany was matched by their exclusion from the cultural life of the country. This was achieved by means of an Act [29 September 1933] setting up a Reich Chamber of Culture, under the provisions of which Jews were excluded from the faculties of literature, art, theatre and film, established by the Act. Instead they were assigned to cultural and artistic organizations of their own, which were amalgamated into a 'Reich Association of Jewish Cultural Unions' [*Reichsverband jüdischer Kulturbünde*] by an order issued by the President of the Reich Chamber of Culture on 6 August 1935, and were put under the control of a special representative of the Reich Ministry of Propaganda. Before this the Editors Act [*Schriftleitergesetz*] of 4 October had laid it down that no Jew and no Aryan married to a Jew could be appointed as an editor, although at this time there were still certain exceptions on the lines of those provided in the Civil Service Act (executive order 19 December 1933).

The exclusion of the Jews from 'German sport' on the grounds that they did not fulfil the Aryan requirements followed naturally from all this. But matters were not allowed to rest there. Before long the officially recognized Jewish sporting organizations, like the Reich Association of Jewish Ex-Combatants and the German Maccabi Circle found their activities curtailed in various ways by local authorities who banned or restricted their use of playing fields and swimming baths.

Police practice under SS direction left no doubt that the aim at this period was the emigration of the Jews as speedily and on as large a scale as possible. One way in which this was shown was in the preferential treatment secretly and indirectly accorded to Jewish organizations willing to emigrate as opposed to that accorded the more German-orientated groups. The former were given special passes, and in their case certain of the restrictions ordinarily imposed were relaxed. Jewish emigration was to some extent made easier by the Haavara Agreement drawn up between the Zionists and the Reich Ministry of Economics in September 1933. Under this agreement German Jewish emigrants paid their liquid assets into the 'Palestine Trust Company for the Assistance of German Jews, Inc.' [*Palästina Treuhandgesellschaft zur Beratung deutscher Juden GmbH*]. The funds thus acquired were used from time to time to pay for half the German exports to Palestine, Palestine paying for the other half in foreign currency. From their sale of German exports the Haavara in Palestine reimbursed the immigrant German Jews for the payments they had made to the Trust Company in Germany. According to internal regulations wealthy emigrants were required to hand over part of their assets to those without means, so that the latter could also emigrate to Palestine. Only some 170,000 Jews had emigrated under this scheme by November 1938, as apart from the German foreign currency regulations, this solution was made more difficult by the narrow professional stratification of the Jewish community and the overloading of the Jewish relief organizations with non-German emigrants. Apart from the fact that German Jewish emigrants, as well as having to surrender their business interests, were as a rule also deprived of the greater part of the rest of their property and in any case had to be prepared to face a highly uncertain future abroad, many of them could hardly bring themselves to believe that they would come to be regarded as outcasts, and would eventually find their very lives threatened, in a Germany which they looked upon as their homeland. In the event many emigrants returned to Germany between 1933 and 1935. On the other hand a large number of Jews who saw the situation as it was and were either unable or unwilling to emigrate, chose to commit suicide.

The fact was that the so-called 'legal' exclusion of the Jews and the terror methods adopted by the police, although occasionally varying in the severity with which they were applied, were developing steadily. Public opinion was likewise hardening against the Jews and finding new ways of expressing its contempt and dislike – a turn of affairs which was, without doubt, extremely distressing to its victims. Everything possible was done through continuous incitement to represent the Jews as pariahs among the nation. The subordinate ranks in the Party were particularly assiduous in this respect, as was the press, led by *Der Stürmer* which displayed its notorious placards in nearly every town and village. The number of posters carrying insulting or threatening announcements was already legion. Holiday resorts, spurred on by local Party officials, vied with one another in proclaiming themselves 'free of Jewish taint': in addition to the almost universal 'Jews not wanted here' notices, it was not uncommon to find such announcements as 'Bathing Prohibited to Dogs and Jews'. The point was reached when even the Bavarian political police (that is to say, the Gestapo) deemed it prudent to order the removal of such notices as, for instance: 'Jews come here at their Own Risk', 'Get out, Jews, or else . . .' and so forth, as 'being, or coming very close to being offences punishable at law'. By 1935 the municipal authorities had so far exceeded their statutory powers as to forbid the Jews access to public parks, swimming baths or playing fields, and temporarily even to public transport. Similarly illegal (and in practice unenforceable) regulations were drawn up in the provinces to prevent Jews from engaging in certain trades by forbidding them the use of the local public utilities in marketing their goods. The Party's Central Department for Local Government Policy [*Hauptamt für Kommunalpolitik*] actually authorized demonstrations in favour of a stricter interpretation of these regulations.

Besides all this the Party, systematically and without meeting any criticism, pursued a policy calculated to destroy the fellow feeling of the German people for the Jews. So as to procure a general outlawing of the Jews, Party officials never failed to bring pressure to bear (directly and indirectly and sometimes accompanied by threats) on anyone who continued to patronize Jewish shops, to trade with Jews, or to have friendly social relations with individual Jews. The action of one municipal authority in south Germany, which ordered its officers, employees and workmen to break off all social relations with Jews as 'a moral and patriotic duty' and required from them a signed statement in confirmation, was certainly no isolated incident. The social boycott of Jews was naturally more effective in the villages and small towns. In spite of this, it obviously required 'high up' intervention – as can be seen from the number of appeals, warnings and threats issued to Party members and to those who were outside the Party – to ensure that the desired goal was reached and the position maintained, even after the suppression of the Jews had become an accepted fact of everyday life in Germany.

The Nuremberg Laws and their Consequences

After a propaganda campaign lasting for several months, Hitler released the Nuremberg Laws: 'The Reich Citizenship Act' [*Reichsbürgergesetz*] and 'The Act for the Protection of German Blood and German Honour' [*Gesetz zum Schutze des deutschen Blutes und der deutschen Ehre*] known in its shortened form as 'The Blood Protection Act' [*Blutschutzgesetz*]. The date was 15 September 1935 and the occasion the Party rally at Nuremberg. The German public as a whole was taken completely by surprise.

The Reich Citizenship Act introduced what was called 'Reich citizenship' alongside nationality (to which those who had hitherto been nationals of the State still had a right). To acquire the former status, it was supposed to be necessary to obtain 'a certificate of Reich citizenship'. [In the event it never came to this, although as a precaution all non-Jewish Germans were provisionally classified as Reich citizens, in accordance with the provisions of the first order under the Act, and remained so classified until the Third Reich came to an end.] Only Reich citizens were to be allowed 'full political rights under the provisions of the Act', and only those nationals of 'German or related blood' could become Reich citizens. Clause 4 section 1 of the 'first order under the Reich Citizenship Act (1 November 1935)' included the supplementary statement:

'No Jew can be a Reich citizen. The right to vote on political questions is not extended to him and he may not be appointed to any office of State.'

Section 2 of Clause 4 of the above order revoked that part of the Civil Service Act (see p. 44) exempting Jewish ex-combatants and Jews who had been in public service since 1 August 1914 from its provisions. The section laid down that Jewish ex-combatants were to be superannuated as from 31 December 1935 and (temporarily) to be granted a pension. All the others lost their pension rights, as had the Jewish officials dismissed in 1933.

The Blood Protection Act mentioned above prohibited marriage and extra-marital relations 'between Jews and nationals of German or allied blood' in the interest of the so-called 'survival of the German race'. It further provided – adding insult to injury – that no Jew might 'employ a female national of German or allied blood under 45 years of age . . . in his household'.

A superficial examination of the position of the Jews under the Nuremberg Laws might lead one to suppose that they did little more than give official sanction to an existing situation. Moreover the effect of their implementation (after serious differences of opinion within the Party) was restricted to a limited number of those against whom they were directed, in so far as they were not immediately applied to people who were half or quarter Jewish ['half-breeds'] – unlike the Civil Service Act. This meant, of course, that those who were three-quarters or wholly Jewish were so much the worse off. The end-result of the Nuremberg Laws was to turn the Jews and 'persons accounted as Jews' into persons with lesser rights in the community (to put it mildly) and to give permanent force to what many Germans had hitherto preferred to believe was some sort of provisional arrangement – a view which had made it easier for them to ignore the Party's injunction to regard every individual Jew as an outcast. There can be no doubt from an historical point of view that the social isolation and moral condemnation of the Jews, on which the seal of legality and official approval was now set (purely on biological grounds), gave a psychological boost to the later, more extreme forms of persecution instituted by the Party leadership, who regarded the Nuremberg Laws as merely a stage in the fulfilment of their Jewish policy. Yet there were some people at that time, and among them high-ranking government officials, who inclined to the view that the new laws represented both the culmination of this policy and a legal settlement which, however unsatisfactory, would regularize a situation 'that had got thoroughly out of hand' through 'incitement and encroachments'. The Nazi intention to deny the Jews the status of German citizenship and to make them subject to the laws applying to aliens had been set out clearly in the Party manifesto. Suitable legislation to this effect had been under consideration for a long time and had been put on one side time and again. At the last minute it was drafted in great haste and presented to Parliament so that it looked (as Hitler meant it to look) as though it were merely implementing the Party programme. Without exactly admitting this, even Hitler's remarks about his measures were, for obvious tactical reasons, intentionally ambiguous. The government's action, he told Parliament fatuously, 'was based on their conviction that some "once-for-all" secular solution could perhaps ... lead to the establishment of a workable arrangement with the Jews'. Frankly, he added (hinting at things to come), it might be necessary 'in case of repeated breakdowns' to pass a law 'handing the problem over to the National Socialist Party for eventual solution'. Hitler's real intentions as regarded future developments were revealed by certain remarks that he made about the Jews to his closest colleagues after the Party rally: 'Out with them from all the professions and into the ghetto with them; fence them in somewhere where they can perish as they deserve while the German people look on, the way people stare at wild animals.'[1] Nothing perhaps betrayed Hitler's innermost feelings about his Jewish policy and its dreadful consequences as clearly as did the text and tone of his hitherto unpublished address to the Party *Kreisleiters* on 29 April 1937. Referring to an article in a provincial newspaper, in which the editor had asked that some means of distinguishing Jewish firms should be introduced, Hitler observed: 'From whom is he demanding this? Who can give the necessary orders? Only I can give them. The editor, in the name of his readers, is asking me to act. First, I should tell you that long before this editor had any inkling about the Jewish problem, I had made myself an expert in the subject. Secondly, this problem has been under consideration for two or three years, and will, of course, be settled one way or another in due course. My point is then this: the final aim of our policy is crystal clear to all of us. All that concerns me is never to take a step that I might later have to retrace and never to take a step that could damage us in any way. You must understand that I always go as far as I dare and never further. It is vital to have a sixth sense that tells you, broadly, what you can do and what you cannot do. Even in a struggle with an adversary it is not my way to issue a direct challenge to a trial of strength. I do not

51

say "Come on and fight, because I want a fight." Instead I shout at him (and I shout louder and louder): "I mean to destroy you." And then I use my intelligence to help me to manoeuvre him into a tight corner so that he cannot strike back, and then I deliver the fatal blow.'

It was in line with this attitude and with the lack of restraint shown in discrimination against the Jews [this had even been extended to Jewish children in German schools] that a decree was promulgated in the autumn of 1935 whereby the names of Jews who had given their lives in the First World War were to be omitted when new war memorials were erected. 'Out of a spirit of generosity', it was added, it had been decided 'not to order the removal of these names from existing memorials.' This was quite enough to cause several officials to show their zeal by 'erasing' the names of the Jewish fallen, as no less a man than Theodor Heuss testified in the case of his own home town:

'It shocked me beyond words when I realized that respect for the dead – for the dead who had simply given their lives in the war – had vanished, while men were already contemplating a new war.'[2]

In general, however, a certain amount of soft-pedalling followed the passing of the Nuremberg Laws. There were significant reasons for this. Parts of the foreign press had been demanding a change of venue for the coming Olympic Games, and approaches made by interested foreign circles to the National Socialist Reich sports leader seemed to indicate that another capital city might be chosen. Since Hitler desired that 'the Olympic Games of 1936 should take place in Berlin whatever happens', the Secret State Police [*Geheime Staatspolizei*] issued an order to the effect that 'as few obstacles as possible' were to be placed in the way of the participation of Jewish sporting bodies affiliated to the sports organizations of the Reich Central Committee 'until after the conclusion of the Olympic Games'. Assurances had been given to the International Olympic Committee on 7 June 1935 that no differentiation would be made between Aryans and non-Aryans in the field of sport. Anti-Jewish inscriptions and *Stürmer* placards largely disappeared. At the same time a flood of 'legal' discriminatory measures followed the Reich Citizenship Act, in the guise of consolidating measures. After taking into account the results already achieved under the first order, the second order (21 December 1935) under the Reich Citizenship Act also required the resignation from their appointments in the public and voluntary hospitals of senior Jewish doctors. The order, which took effect on 31 March 1936, also applied to Jewish official medical consultants, and in addition contained provisions regarding the dismissal of Jewish officials and those who had official status of any kind. [Jewish officials who were ex-combatants, but who had not earned a pension under general insurance regulations or who were not entitled to a pension, *could* be paid 'a maintenance allowance' subject to cancellation without notice, in accordance with their worth to society and their needs.] Both before and after this date, the professional activities of Jewish doctors, veterinary surgeons, and the holders of public offices such as members of arbitration boards, stamp collectors, slaughter-house inspectors and tax assistants were subject to far-reaching restrictions or total prohibition. Moreover, licences were refused to chemists and a ban was placed on the recruitment of Jews to the provincial police forces or for active defence duties.

Further proscriptive orders were issued (especially after the Olympic Games). These affected chartered accountants, auditors, the restaurant trade, the tuition of Germans by Jews, Jewish teachers in German schools (provided this did not cause shortages!), game licences, the attainment of doctorates, adoption, the engagement of experts by Chambers of Industry and Commerce, children's allowances, the appointment of chemists (8 October 1937), the right of succession and legacies, passports, changes in surnames, dental surgeons and dentists, surveyors and auctioneers, tax reductions, subsidies, the manufacture and acquisition of firearms, ground rent relief, rent subsidies, foreign currency regulations, marriage witnesses, tax exemptions, Jewish schools, visiting university lecturers, jury service, employment in banks, billeting, Jewish street names, admittance as patent agents, the nursing profession, and tutelage and guardianship.

Because of the time factor there were some omissions from this apparently comprehensive list, but the steady drive to perfect the disbarment rules was obvious even before the pogroms of the autumn of 1938. Within the framework of a new bout of persecution, the idea of distinguishing Jewish firms was put into effect by the third order (14 June 1938) under the Reich

Citizenship Act. Under this order Jewish firms had to be registered as such, and the Reich Minister for Economics was empowered to introduce a special trade mark for Jewish firms – clearly a portent of things to come. The fourth order under the Reich Citizenship Act, issued on 25 July 1938, barred all Jewish doctors from practising, as from 30 September 1938. With the approval of the Reich Minister of the Interior, which could be revoked at any time, they were allowed to treat Jews, but as medical orderlies only, not as doctors. The fifth order under the Reich Citizenship Act (27 September 1938) closed the legal profession to Jewish lawyers. From 30 November, when the order became operative, they were permitted to act only when 'strictly' necessary (and this provision was revocable) and merely as 'consultants', mainly where Jews were concerned. These 'consultants' were required to pay up to 70 per cent of their fees into a 'compensation fund', so that disqualified Jewish lawyers, who were ex-combatants, could, if necessary, be paid 'a maintenance allowance, subject to cancellation without notice, in accordance with their worth to society and their need'.

The sixth order under the Reich Citizenship Act, issued on 30 October 1938, with effect from 30 November 1938, barred Jews from practising as patent agents and made no provision for the appointment of persons to represent the Jews in applications for patents.

In the meantime an announcement had appeared in the *Reich-gesetzblatt* [Government Gazette] on 23 July 1938, stating that all Jews were to apply to the police for an identity card before 31 December 1938, that they were to show this card on demand at any time, and that they were to produce it, whether or not they were asked to do so, in all dealings with the administration. In conjunction with this, an order was issued on 5 October 1938 requiring Jews to surrender their travel permits within fourteen days; passports issued for foreign travel would be valid only if clearly marked with the letter 'J', so that their holders could be identified as Jews.

Previously, an order dated 17 August 1938 had laid down that male Jews were to add the name 'Israel' and female Jews the name 'Sara' to their non-Jewish first names by 1 January 1939, and that they were always to use these Jewish names in any legal or business dealings.

On 12 June 1937, Heydrich, the Chief of the Security Police [*Chef der Sicherheitspolizei*] had already issued a confidential decree to the effect that 'Jews guilty of race pollution . . . who had served their sentences should invariably be re-examined to determine whether protective custody (*Schutzhaft*), i.e. removal to a concentration camp, should be ordered. Jewish women who had committed the offence of racial pollution with Germans were to be taken into protective custody as soon as the judicial proceedings had been completed.'[3]

The Pogrom of 9–10 November and the Destruction of the Economic Existence of the Jews

It is frequently stated that the position of Jews in the German economy was almost unaffected until 1938. But as more recent studies have shown, this was simply not the case. The discriminatory measures and the boycott must, in general, have had a directly harmful effect on the economic activities of the Jews. In addition to the professional restrictions described in the last chapter, there were also the commercial restrictions, illegal directives and measures affecting various branches of trade (such as the special trade marks for distinguishing Jewish firms and so forth) that carried with them either direct or indirect economic disadvantages for the Jews. The majority of Jews were no longer able to earn their living; they had no jobs and had to exist, more or less precariously, on their capital; the Jewish charitable organizations were overwhelmed. Open or veiled threats had already forced many Jews, particularly in the provinces, to sell their businesses – nearly always, of course, on unfavourable terms. The ban on Jews occupying positions of profit (the legality of which was highly doubtful) and the breaking of business contracts was not affected by the fact that the 'Aryan clause' did not apply to economic affairs. Not that anyone had any practical objections to new laws to restrict the economic activities of the

Jews; it was simply that the uncertainties of the existing law sufficed.

Towards the end of 1937 the trend towards the 'Aryanization' of the economy, from which Göring hoped to find the means of financing the armaments programme, was openly stepped up. [This was stimulated by the totally unjust expropriation policy carried out after the *Anschluss* in Austria, where the proprietors of Jewish undertakings had been removed and replaced by completely unqualified Party officials.] Corrupt practices of the worst kind were rife, so much so that *Reichskommissar* Bürckel found it difficult to carry out the Aryanization of the larger undertakings (at any rate) without corruption creeping in. To stop Jews handing over their firms to Aryans on a nominal basis, an 'Order (22 April 1938) for the Prevention of Camouflaged Assistance to Jewish Undertakings' [*Verordnung gegen die Unterstützung der Tarnung jüdische Gewerbebetriebe*] threatened any German national who lent himself to such practices with imprisonment or a fine. The way in which the position of the Jews in the economic life of the country was going to be dealt with was clearly foreshadowed by the 'Order for the Disclosure of Jewish Assets' [*Verordnung zur Anmeldung des Vermögens von Juden*] of 26 April 1938 – especially when Göring decreed that a deposit (representing a proportion of the assets) was to be paid as a 'guarantee', in the interests of the German economy. Simultaneously it was decreed that special authorization was to be obtained for every sale or lease of land, of an industrial undertaking or of forestry concessions in which Jews were involved, as well as for the opening of any new factory or workshop by a Jew. Jewish industrial undertakings already had to be registered and identified under the provisions of the third order (14 June 1938) of the Reich Citizenship Act. The 'Changes in the Industrial Code (German Reich) Act' (6 July 1938) [*Gesetz zur Änderung der Gewerbeordnung für das Deutsche Reich*] finally placed a complete ban on Jews engaging in certain occupations, such as dealing in real estate, acting as caretakers and negotiating loans.

In October 1938, after the Munich Conference, there was a marked increase in Göring's activities. In a speech on the 'Four-Year Plan' in the Reich Ministry of Aviation on 14 October 1938, he demanded that the Jewish problem 'be tackled energetically and forthwith', as the Jews 'must be driven out of the economy'.* This was now a burning issue for the extreme anti-Semites in the Party. It was difficult to see how a decisive blow against the economic position of the Jews could be struck within the framework of the existing disbarment laws. Yet while they were still active in the economy the total exclusion of the Jews from German life could never be achieved. After Munich the decision on what action to take hung fire; some outside pretext was awaited.

This was supplied by the assassination of the legation secretary, von Rath, by the 17-year old Jew, Grünspan, in Paris on 7 November. 'Obviously', wrote the *Völkischer Beobachter* on the very day of the incident, 'the German people will be able to draw their own conclusions from this new outrage.' On the evening of 9 November, the Reich Minister for Propaganda, Dr Goebbels, lit the fuse. In a rabble-rousing speech to the Party and SS leaders assembled in the *Altenrathaus* in Munich for their annual celebration of 9 November 1923, he unleashed the Jewish pogrom. Known as the *Reichskristallnacht* [Crystal Night] – a title which today has a somewhat euphemistic ring, but was intended as bitter irony by the Berliners who invented it – this has been a stain on the name of Germany ever since. The cunning way in which Goebbels kindled the flame without giving any direct orders can be seen from the official report of the Party High Court [*Obersten Parteigerichts*] to Göring,[1] in which it was stated: 'The words of the head of the Reich Ministry of Propaganda left the assembled party leaders in no doubt that they were not to appear openly as the instigators of the demonstrations, although, of course, they were to organize them and see that they were carried through.' Hitler himself also knew what was happening – more, he was actually responsible for the ostensible 'spontaneous reaction of the German people' – although he remained strategically in the background. That Hitler's was the

IMT, vol. xxvii, p. 163. It is of interest to note that Göring added that it was essential to stop 'the uncontrolled Commissar economy' that was being established in Austria; the solution of the Jewish problem was not intended 'as a welfare scheme for inefficient Party members'. The Austrian Minister, Fischbock, observed in this context that, to start with, there were 2,500 Commissars in Austria; today there were 'over 3,500 – most of whom had no qualification for the job'. In spite of this the party in Austria claimed that Aryanization was their concern, and that it must be allied to the compensation of Party members of long-standing.

intellect behind the outbreak has not only been testified by the then head of the Reich press and others in the know; the support that he gave to Goebbels's hints to the Party and the SS points in the same direction. And there is clear evidence in the further statement in the Party high court report: 'After listening to his [Goebbels's] speech the Führer decided that the demonstrations to which he had referred ought neither to be prepared nor organized by the party. On the other hand, if they occurred spontaneously, nothing was to be done to break them up.' Thereupon synagogues throughout the length and breadth of Germany were burnt to the ground and over 7,000 Jewish shops were destroyed. On top of that a fine, originally of one billion, but eventually amounting to a total of one and a quarter billion marks, was imposed on the Jews and the insurance payments to which they were entitled in compensation for the damage caused was confiscated by the State. On 11 November Heydrich sent a telegram to Göring reporting the death of 36 Jews[2] – a later reckoning by the Party high court made the total 91 dead. The perpetrators went scot free – unless they had committed 'race pollution' or had overstepped the bounds of 'discipline'. The explanation given by the Party courts for this kid-glove treatment was that a remark by Goebbels had forced them to the conclusion that the individual perpetrator 'had acted in accordance with the real wishes of the leadership, however vaguely this may have been expressed'. The lie was also given to the pretence of spontaneity in the demonstrations by a teletype message sent at the time by the SS,[3] who were involved only as supplementary control forces in the disturbances organized at the instigation of Goebbels by the Party and the SA, and on the whole had very little to do; they were critical of Goebbels and his machinations in private, but only because noisy outbreaks of this kind were in direct contradiction to their well-tried practice of silent, bureaucratic terror. Because of this they dedicated themselves with that much more zeal to the business of arrests (which came exclusively within their sphere of jurisdiction), the aim and outcome of which was the incarceration of some 30,000 particularly wealthy Jews in concentration camps. The result was a speeding-up of the emigration programme, since when these Jews were (relatively quickly) released, they left Germany in much greater numbers than before. 'I have not yet met a single German from

58

any walk of life,' wrote the British Chargé d'Affaires in Berlin on 16 November 1938, 'who does not disapprove to some degree of what has occurred. But I fear that not even the unequivocal condemnation of professed National Socialists and senior officers in the armed forces will have any effect on the gang of madmen who are at present in control in Nazi Germany.'[4]

At a conference held at the Ministry of Aviation on 12 November 1938[5] and attended by all those ministers and civil servants responsible for putting into effect (in accordance with Hitler's instructions) the policy for excluding the Jews from the economy, Göring, as chairman, explained that he had been instructed by Hitler, both verbally and in writing, to 'centralize the decisive step now to be taken' in regard to the Jewish question. In his speech he referred to the regulations already in operation and to the final plans for the Aryanization of, first of all, retail shops and then of factories and partnerships. Göring said that he was 'displeased' with the demonstrations, and must condemn 'senseless physical destruction' in all its forms. He then brought up the question (he had already mentioned it on 14 October) of forcing the Jews into ghettos. Heydrich, while suggesting 'restricted areas' and hinting that the Jews might be made to wear some distinguishing mark, showed that he really preferred the idea of a massive emigration programme. Goebbels put forward the idea of banning Jews from the theatre and cinema as well as from holiday resorts, swimming pools and so forth. Very little was heard during all this from the 'middle-class' Ministers and State Secretaries.

A veritable torrent of discriminatory orders then began to flow over the heads of the Jews. In addition to provisions for the closing and compulsory sale of Jewish undertakings [wholly or in part against government stock!] and of real estate belonging to Jews, these included the exclusion of all Jews from German schools and universities, the designation of restricted areas, the ban on visits to theatres, concert halls, museums, sports stadia, swimming pools and so forth, and the withdrawal of driving licences and licences for commercial vehicles. The seventh order under the Reich Citizenship Act, issued on 5 December 1938, reduced the pensions payable to compulsorily retired Jewish officials; the eighth order (17 January 1939) barred their professions to Jewish dentists, veterinary surgeons and chemists, degrading the first-named into 'dental orderlies' qualified only to treat Jewish patients. Finally an order of 21 February 1939 required Jews to surrender all the gold and silver objects in their possession (with the exception of wedding rings) as well as all their precious stones and pearls 'for sale by public auction' within a fortnight. A further order of 30 April 1939 revoked the law for the protection of tenants, and it became common practice to force the Jews into what were called 'communal Jewish houses'. Jews who were fit for work were more and more frequently conscripted for forced labour. After the outbreak of war came the curfew* and the confiscation of radio sets (without compensation, of course). This was followed in 1940, among other things, by the withholding of clothing coupons and the severing of telephone connexions. Daily it became more and more obvious that the anti-Jewish regulations were increasingly motivated purely by spite. To what depths of depravity the Party press had sunk since the *Kristallnacht* can nowhere be seen more clearly than in an article in the *Schwarze Korps* of 24 November 1938. After observing scornfully that the 'desperate straits' in which the Jewish 'parasites' would find themselves would probably mean that 'they would turn, as one man, to crime', it concluded with self-righteous hypocrisy: 'If this should happen we shall be faced with the stern necessity(!) of rooting out the Jewish underworld in the interest of law and order, just as we root out ordinary criminals: with fire and the sword. Then we shall see the final and utter collapse of Judaism in Germany – its total destruction.'

The Road to the 'Final Solution'

The ultimate purpose of future Jewish policy – up to the 'solution' – had in the meantime been outlined several times in speeches by Göring and Hitler. At the conference of 12 November 1938 mentioned in the last chapter, Göring had declared: 'Should the German Reich come into conflict at any time in the foreseeable future with a foreign power, the first thing we Germans would obviously think of would be our final reckoning with the Jews.'[1]

*By order of the local police [*örtlichen Polizeistellen*] 1 September 1939 – in summer after 21 hours, and in winter after 20 hours.

Hitler's intentions and plans were brought into the open on 24 November in the course of a noteworthy discussion with Pirow, the South African Minister for Economics and Defence. Pirow had suggested to the dictator, as a matter of urgency, that he should offer some workable solution to the Jewish problem in the interest of an understanding with England and to show his support for the Chamberlain–Halifax Cabinet. Hitler countered with heated arguments about the Jewish 'invasion' from the East and the scale of their assets in Germany ('even now from 4–6 times higher per head ... than their hosts'!), adding, according to the official records: 'But the problem would soon be solved. On this point his mind was irrevocably made up . . . One day the Jews would disappear from Europe. Many nations already felt indignant about Jewish activities within their frontiers.'

Pirow (according to his own version of the interview) then made the official suggestion that:

1 Germany should raise an international loan for the emigration and resettlement of the Jews. The interest on the loan should be paid for in goods, so that no foreign currency should be required,
2 Germany should put one of her former colonies at the disposal of the Jews for resettlement purposes.

Hitler's reply to this was that even if he were willing, he would never be able to persuade the German people to hand over to Germany's bitterest enemies areas 'for which the blood of so many German heroes had been shed, and for which men like Lettow-Vorbeck had fought'. The Jews would never work as settlers in East Africa in any case; all they wanted was 'to live off the country and trade'. When Pirow pressed the point, Hitler burst out: 'The last thing that world Judaism wants is to see the Jews disappear from Europe. On the contrary it looks on the Jews in Europe as the advance troops for the bolshevization of the world.' In conclusion Hitler made a remark which betrayed his intentions as nothing else could and confirmed earlier evidence. He was, he said, 'exporting only one idea, and that is not the idea of national socialism. It is the idea of anti-Semitism.' The fact that Hitler was now ready to state his aims publicly and without reservation (a thing that he had never done before, although, of course he had been hoping for a long time that they would be realized) was due to the events of 1938, which had won for him freedom of action in the field of foreign affairs.

Exactly how he felt and what he meant to do, Hitler explained even more plainly on 21 January 1939. According to the German official records, he told the Czechoslovakian Foreign Minister, Chvalkovsky, quite frankly: 'We are going to destroy the Jews. They are not going to get away with what they did on 9 November 1918. The day of reckoning has come.'

The same ideas emerged from a prophecy made by Hitler in his speech to Parliament on the sixth anniversary of his coming to power – 30 January 1939.

And there is one thing that I should like to say on this memorable day – memorable, perhaps, to others besides ourselves. During my lifetime I have often made prophecies, and people have laughed at me, more often than not. In my struggle for power the Jews always laughed louder when I prophesied that, one day, I should be the leader of the German State, that I should be in full control of the nation, and that then, among other things, I should find the solution to the Jewish problem. I imagine that the Jews in Germany who laughed most heartily then are now finding that their laughter chokes them. Today I am going to make another prophecy: If the Jewish international financiers inside and outside Europe succeed in involving the nations in another war, the result will not be world bolshevism and therefore a victory for Judaism; it will be the end of the Jews in Europe.

Hitler, who privately visualized a much more extreme solution, may well have disliked the emigration policy (which was now taking a form that could more suitably be described as expulsion), but for the time being it was the only practical way. Göring therefore turned back to Heydrich's suggestion of 12 November 1938, which was based on what the then *SS-Obersturmführer* Eichmann, had done in Austria.[2] This man, who had first been the official responsible for Jewish questions at the head office of the SD [*Referent für Judenfragen in dem SD-Hauptamt*], then assistant to the *SD-Führer* of the *SS-Oberabschnitt* [main region] Danube, and later (in August 1938) the organizer of the Central Office for Jewish Emigration [*Organisator der Zentralstelle für jüdische Auswanderung*] in Vienna, had worked out a method of expelling the Jews (either encouraged by Heydrich or on his own initiative)[3] which combined deportation with extortion. Wealthy Jews wishing to emigrate (most of these were in concentration camps) were obliged to sacrifice part of their assets to provide foreign currency for paying the immigration charges (in the form of 'bearer bonds') of the less well-off as well as their own. Anything left over after these payments had been made was confiscated by the Reich. The success of this scheme was due to the help given by the Jewish charitable organizations, which even supplied the necessary foreign currency. Germany, as Heydrich explained in February 1939, did not have to provide 'any return service whatsoever, not even in the shape of increased exports'. Göring, in his capacity as Administrator [*Beauftragter*] of the Four-Year Plan (and using the plenary powers bestowed on him by Hitler after the *Kristallnacht*) sent instructions along these lines to Frick, the Minister of the Interior, in the following terms:[4]

From: The Administrator of the Four-Year Plan, Berlin,
          24 January 1939
          Field-Marshal Göring
To: The Reich Minister of the Interior, Berlin
The emigration of the Jews from Germany will be promoted by every possible means.
A Reich Central Office for the Emigration of the Jews [*Reichszentrale für die jüdische Auswanderung*], composed of members of the departments concerned, will be set up within the Ministry of the Interior. This office will be responsible, uniformly, throughout the whole of Germany, for

1 all measures to be taken in preparation for the intensification of the emigration of the Jews. Under this heading it will be required to create an appropriate Jewish organization for the uniform preparation of emigration applications; to take all possible steps to ensure that funds are available, both in this country and abroad, and that these funds are put to a proper use; and, in consultation with the Reich Office for Emigration, to decide to which countries emigration should be directed;
2 the co-ordination of emigration. This should include plans for giving preference to Jews of the lower income groups;
3 the expedition of emigration in *individual cases*. By centralizing the procedure for emigration applications, individual emigrants will be able to get the necessary official passes and certificates more easily and with less friction. Centralization will also provide a check on the execution of the emigration programme as a whole.

The *Reichszentrale* will operate under the direction of the Chief of the Security Police [*Sicherheitspolizei*], who will appoint the executive director [*Geschäftsführer*] and control the work of the Office.

Reports on the work of the Office will be regularly submitted to me. My approval will be required before any important measures are put into effect. In addition to the members of the departments concerned, Ambassador Eisenlohr will be appointed to the Board to be in charge of matters of international interest and Ministerial Director Wohlt(h)at will be in charge of matters relating to the Rublee-Plan.

(signed) Göring*

The tenth order under the Reich Citizenship Act (4 July 1939) provided that the Jewish organization mentioned in Göring's minute should be created by requiring all Jews ordinarily resident in Germany, whether German nationals or stateless, to combine in a 'Reich Union of German Jews' [*Reichsvereinigung*

*In connexion with the conference at the Ministry of Aviation on 19 November 1938, the Austrian Minister for Economics, Labour and Finance, Dr Fischböck, had suggested, with the agreement of the Reich Ministers for Economics and for Finance, and that of the Under-Secretary of State in the Ministry of the Interior, Stuckart, that a solution of the Jewish problem might be found in taking advantage of an offer made by the Chairman (the American, Rublee) of the International Committee for Political Refugees, set up by the International Conference held in Evian in the summer of 1938. The Rublee Plan was based on the idea that the emigration of the Jews from Germany should be linked with the promotion of German exports in such a way that it would be possible for the Jews to transfer their ledger credits abroad. Ribbentrop, who was basically against working with other countries on anything connected with the German (!) Jewish question and had opposed Rublee's visit to Berlin, finally agreed (as did Göring) to private negotiations with Rublee, provided that they did not take place either in London or in Berlin. Without Ribbentrop's knowledge, but with Hitler's approval, the President of the Reich Bank, Dr Schacht, went to London to discuss the matter. As a result of these discussions, the Fischböck–Schacht Plan was accepted as the basis for negotiation. Ribbentrop, who did not approve of Schacht's activities and said so, nevertheless appointed Ambassador Eisenlohr to represent the Foreign Office on the council to be established on the German side for putting the plan into effect. At the same time he issued instructions that the terms agreed with Mr Rublee were not 'to be signed with a flourish' and that 'there were to be no more promises to Mr Rublee about the future treatment of the Jews in Germany'. In the middle of January 1939, an 'exchange of ideas' took place between Schacht and Rublee in Berlin, which had as its object the emigration of some 150,000 Jews (or some 400,000 counting wives and children), whose 'age (15–45) and state of health would make it possible for them to earn their living abroad', within three or, at the most, five years. Twenty-five per cent of Jewish assets would have to be put into a 'cash fund' and transferred by increased exports and seventy-five per cent would accrue to Germany, in so far as it was not needed for the support of the Jews until they emigrated or 'died'. After Schacht's dismissal on 20 January 1939, Göring appointed Ministerial Director Wohlthat (from the Office of the Administrator of the Four-Year Plan) to carry on the negotiations. Later Wohlthat, and Göring himself, had fresh discussions with Rublee and his agents about a plan, similar to the Schacht Plan, but which 'did not go so far'. Further negotiations, undertaken with reluctance on the German side, were interrupted by the outbreak of war.

der Juden in Deutschland]. The aim was clearly to promote emigration. At the same time the Reich Union was made financially responsible for Jewish schools and Jewish welfare services. *SS-Gruppenführer* Heydrich, as Chief of the Security Police, was put in control of the Reich Central Office for Jewish Emigration – in spite of the fact that this was officially part of the Reich Ministry of the Interior – itself formally under the control of Himmler, the *Reichsführer-SS* and Chief of the German Police. Heydrich appointed the head of Division II of the secret State police, *SS-Standartenführer Oberregierungsrat* Heinrich Müller (the notorious 'Gestapo Müller'), as executive director; Eichmann, who had built up a central office for Jewish emigration in Prague after Hitler had marched in in March 1939, did not take over the appointment until October 1939 – by which time emigration on a large scale was obviously no longer practicable. It was, however, because of his past career that Eichmann, after the establishment of the Reich SS Security Department [*Reichssicherheitshauptamt* or RSHA] in September 1939, and following his transfer to Division D of the RHSA's *Amt* IV (*Geheime Staatspolizei*) in December 1939, took over first, in January 1940, *Referat* IV D 4 Emigration and Evacuation [*Auswanderung und Räumung*] and later *Referat* IV B 4 Jewish Affairs and Evacuation [*Judenangelegenheiten, Räumungsangelegenheiten*]. At the first meeting of the *Reichszentrale*, which took place on 11 February 1939, Heydrich issued general instructions along the following lines: As it was 'by no means certain' that the Rublee Plan would be put into effect, it was essential 'to act without regard to it and to promote emigration with all other available means'. Executive responsibility 'would in general be vested in the State police services'.

Heydrich then proposed the establishment of central offices (similar to that which existed in Vienna) not only in Berlin, but also in Breslau, Frankfurt-am-Main and Hamburg, as 'these are the places where there is the greatest concentration of Jews'. The task of the *Reichszentrale* would be 'to co-ordinate all previous procedures (which had often been contradictory in their effect) and to make them as simple as possible for the Jews'. This 'simplification' was based on the Vienna 'model' to the extent that it speeded up the completion of the necessary formalities by centralizing them in one office. As far as the individual Jew was concerned, it meant, for all practical purposes, that he had to leave Germany virtually without visible means of support, apart from the 'bearer bonds' without which he would not be allowed to enter the 'receiving country'. Nevertheless the system worked in a very large number of cases, so intolerable had life become for the Jews in the Third Reich.

The latest twist that had been given to the persecution of the Jews by the pogrom of 9 November 1938 (and this was only a foretaste of things to come) was reflected in a decree circulated to all German diplomatic missions and consulates on 25 January 1939 by the Foreign Office and its newly constituted 'Special German Section' [*Sonderreferat Deutschland*]. This widely circulated memorandum, couched in unusually brutal and unpolished terms, revealed the secret link between the new Jewish policy and the successes of the Third Reich's foreign policy in 1938 – the 'Year of Destiny'. It made no mention of the fact that several governments had sent notes of protest about the treatment meted out to their Jewish nationals in Germany since the *Kristallnacht*, but instead referred with satisfaction to the official anti-Semitic trends in Italy, Hungary, Poland and (particularly) Roumania. 'Now at last the success of our foreign policy at Munich is beginning, like the tremors that precede an earthquake, to shake the centuries-old impregnable position of the Jews, even in far distant lands.' The memorandum laid particular emphasis on the need to 'speed up the emigration of all Jews living in the territories of the Reich', as this was 'the ultimate aim of German Jewish policy'. The notorious reluctance of foreign governments to admit Jews without means was, of course, an obstacle to the practical realization of this aim. But the author of the memorandum pretended that the reluctance stemmed from 'international Judaism' which was unwilling to countenance a 'mass emigration of its members' from Germany unless a 'Jewish State' was established, adding for good measure: 'Activities in the international field that we have seen so far make it clear that Jewish tactics are aimed less at mass emigration than at the transfer of Jewish assets out of the country.' [In fact, of course, the scale of such transfers was strictly limited to the minimum immigration requirements laid down by the various receiving countries.] The 'impossibility' of allowing 'even a fraction of Jewish assets to be transferred in foreign currency' was, according to the author of the memorandum, 'quite obvious'. [He even claimed that all such assets really belonged to Germany.] Because of all this, Germany would have to use her own initiative to find a way to solve the problem – but on the lines suggested by Alfred Rosenberg, that is to say not by helping to found a Jewish State, but by establishing Jewish 'reserves'. Through the Haavara Agreement, against which the German section of the Foreign Office and the foreign affairs committee of the Nazi Party had been inveighing for years and which was now finally abrogated, the German people had contributed 'significantly' to the establishment of a Jewish State in Palestine. Instead of encouraging world Judaism 'to increase its power internationally' Germany should be working, in her own interest, for the 'break-up' of Judaism. In accordance with Hitler's desire to 'export' anti-Semitism, the author of the memorandum went on to hope that emigration on so massive a scale would stimulate anti-Semitic tendencies in the receiving countries and would make it easier for them to understand German Jewish policy. 'The poorer the immigrant Jew and the more of a burden he is to the receiving country, the more strongly will this country react and the more favourable will be the effect from the point of view of German propaganda.'

On 1 September 1939 Hitler, by attacking Poland, unleashed the war, which in his 'prophecy' of 30 January, he had already attributed to the Jews. This meant of course that plans for the emigration or expulsion of the German Jews had to be cancelled – or virtually so, although the routes via Sweden, Soviet Russia and Japan were still open during the first few months. But what the war did do was to give the tendencies inherent in National Socialism a unique opportunity to develop. The fact that so many nations were involved relieved the dictators of the tactical need to consider world opinion, while their military successes afforded them hitherto unimagined scope for planning and acting on a vast scale. As things turned out it depended very largely on the attitude of the German army whether or not the National Socialist dictators were to have complete freedom of action. Within the framework of his decision to conduct the war from a 'world philosophy' point of view, Hitler entrusted his SS and the 'task forces of the Security Police and the Security Service' [*Einsatzgruppen der Sicherheitspolizei und des SD* – as they were later known[5]] – with what, in official language, was described as 'special political police duties'. After having been employed at the time of the *Anschluss* with Austria, during the annexation of the Sudetenland, and in the elimination of the rest of Czechoslovakia, these field formations were now employed for the fourth time on the Polish battlefield. They were special motorized units, whose officers belonged to the SD, the Gestapo and the *Kripo* (the two last comprising the *Sicherheitspolizei*); and their duties were outlined, briefly, as 'the suppression of all elements hostile to the Reich and to Germany behind the fighting line'. They were required therefore – as a decree issued later by the CSSD significantly expressed it – 'to carry out essentially the same duties as the State police within the Reich'. During the Polish campaign the *Einsatzgruppen* were legally subordinate to the army to a higher degree than later in the war. However, as they received their so-called 'technical' orders from the *Reichsführer-SS* or from the CSSD the practical possibility of the army being able to control them was, from the outset, remote. Nevertheless, in the early days, the army was in a relatively strong position *vis-à-vis* the *Einsatzgruppen,* and, as long as it remained in complete control in the operational zone, it frequently took advantage of this fact.

During the Polish campaign no general orders to shoot the Jews were issued to the *Einsatzgruppen*. In any case, there were too few of them to deal in this way with the millions of Polish Jews. Afterwards the original five, later six, *Einsatzgruppen* were re-grouped into fifteen *Einsatzkommandos,* each 100-150 strong to which a *Sonderkommando,* subsequently an independent sixteenth *Einsatzkommando,* was attached. In addition, the systematic extermination policy ordered by Hitler was, for tactical reasons, at first directed more against the Polish ruling classes than against the Jews. The *Einsatzgruppen* were, of course, active in seizing, liquidating and confiscating Jewish organizations in Poland. There was also a marked increase in the anti-Jewish outrages (atrocities, degradations of the worst kind, and the burning down of synagogues) perpetrated by the armed formations of the SS – and even by some members of the armed forces, although senior officers were still intervening, with considerable severity, in cases of this kind. [Hitler's secret Amnesty Decree of 4 October 1939 put an end to the practical effect of such interventions.] Summary executions ['mass shootings' as they were called in the evidence of the military authorities] were carried out to start with in Galicia by an *Einsatzgruppe* 'with special duties', under *SS-Obergruppenführer* von Woyrsch, but it was subsequently withdrawn at the urgent request of the army.

The worst outrages of all were perpetrated during the last ten days of September by an *SS-Totenkopf Standarte* in Wloclawek where on 24 October 1939 the Jews were forced to wear some special distinguishing mark for the first time in the twentieth century. It was here that 800 Jews were arrested for no reason and that a number of them were shot 'while trying to escape'. The *Standartenführer*'s original plan had been to arrest all the male Jews in the locality. 'They will all be shot in any case', he had commented. Whereupon the local military commander, who succeeded in imposing a limit on the number of arrests, had expostulated: 'The Führer can hardly intend us to shoot all the Jews'![6]

On army orders a large number of Jews were then driven eastwards over the river San (which formed the demarcation line along part of its course); and others who tried to cross back from the Russian zone into the German zone of occupation suffered appalling casualties.[7] Finally, in the middle of October 1939, the SS began the systematic shooting of the Jews in various localities in the areas annexed by the Reich, for instance, in Bromberg.[8]

In the meantime Heydrich had started to implement the 'Jewish policy' in real earnest. He informed the head of his department and the commanders of the *Einsatzgruppen* on 21 September 1939 that Hitler had approved the deportation of the Jews from the recovered German territories into the remaining part of Poland, and that this operation was to be completed within a year. To achieve this objective Heydrich issued the following 'concise order':

1 Jews to be moved to the towns as quickly as possible;
2 Jews to be moved out of the Reich into Poland;
3 The remaining 30,000 gypsies also to be moved into Poland;
4 Jews in the German territories (that is to say those previously held by Poland) to be systematically deported by goods train.[9]

On the same day (21 September 1939) Heydrich sent a despatch to the leaders of the *Einsatzgruppen* confirming his order that Jews in the rural areas (in particular those living in what was later to be known as the '*Generalgouvernement*') should be rounded up and concentrated in a few of the larger towns with good railway connexions, in which ghettos would 'probably' later be established. A Jewish 'council of elders' was to be appointed at the earliest possible opportunity in each Jewish district and was to be charged with seeing that all future orders were scrupulously obeyed – on pain of 'the most severe penalties if sabotage should occur'. Significantly Heydrich referred to the concentration of Jews in large towns as a first 'interim measure' (*sic*) pending the realization of the 'top secret "final objective", which would take rather longer to achieve'.[10] It is not impossible, although it cannot be proved, that the words 'final objective' in this context actually meant the 'final solution', that is to say, the physical destruction of the Jews, and not the creation of a vast 'Jewish reserve' – although nothing in Heydrich's despatch so much as hinted at this. Be that as it may, the fact that Heydrich specifically ordered that there was to be *no* concentration of Jews in a narrowly confined area in West Galizia (between Wisloka and the San) suggests that this was the locality planned for the creation of a 'Jewish State under German control near Cracow' – the expression used in the minutes of a conversation that took place between von Brauchitsch, Commander-in-Chief of the Army, and Heydrich.[11] Von Brauchitsch had taken this opportunity to ask that the displacement of the population should be discontinued for the time being and that it should, in any case, be carried out under the direction of the military, and not of the civil, authorities. In spite of this, Heydrich ordered the leaders of the *Einsatzgruppen* on 21 September to carry on with the concentration operations in co-operation with the German civilian and competent local military authorities with all possible speed – although the special interests of the army and the German economy were to be taken into account. Subsequently a copy of the order was forwarded to the Commander-in-Chief for his information. When von Brauchitsch protested, Heydrich's order was countermanded by a new order, issued by Himmler himself, to the effect that Heydrich's order should, for the time being, be taken to mean that 'large-scale preparations' should be made, but that its 'execution in the fullest sense of the word' should be 'postponed to a later date'.[12]

On 7 October Himmler was appointed 'Reich Commissioner

for the Strengthening of Germanism' [*Reichskommissar für die Festigung deutscher Volkstums*] and was charged with the duty of 'eliminating the destructive influence of those alien sections of the nation which represent a danger to the Reich and to the German community'. In addition, from 26 October 1939, Hitler took most of the responsibility for the administration of Poland out of the hands of the OKH – which meant that the National Socialists virtually had a free hand.

Already at the end of October Himmler proposed that the postponed deportation of the 550,000 Jews (nearly 450,000 of them Poles) from the new German territories should now go ahead. In December the first large-scale mass deportations – from the *Reichsgau* Posen – were organized by the RSHA and carried out by the *Sipo*. In this operation over 87,000 Poles and Jews were deported in eighty goods trains. Earlier in the same month *SS-Hauptsturmführer* Eichmann (*Referat* IV D 4) had been appointed Special Adviser on the Evacuation of the Jews and Poles [*Sonderreferent für die Evakuierung von Polen und Juden*]. The actual operation, however, was carried out under the aegis of the regional office of the Office for the Resettlement of the Poles and Jews [*Amt für die Umsiedlung der Polen und Juden*] – later known as the 'Deportee Centre' [*Umwandererzentralstelle*] – under the direction of *SS-Obersturmbahnführer* Rapp of the SD *Abschnitt*, Posen, who, according to his own reports, often encountered opposition from the armed forces and railway personnel when putting his measures into effect.

The transfer of population from the assimilated territories continued throughout the winter in appalling conditions, but was temporarily interrupted in January 1940 in response to representations made by the civil administration of the Government General as well as by the OKW Economics and Armaments Office [*Wehrwirtschafts- und Rüstungsamt*]. On the other hand some 6,000 Jews from Vienna, Moravia, Teschen and Stettin (in addition to those 'illegally' driven over the demarcation line) had been deported by 13 February 1940. The deportations from Teschen and Stettin had been carried out in a particularly brutal manner and had thereby attracted considerable attention, even in the foreign press. This seems to have caused Göring to ban the deportation of the Jews from the *Altreich* [Germany as it was before the outbreak of war]. Frank, the Governor of the assimilated territories, had also begun to protest with increasing vigour (although mainly for economic reasons) against the deportation of Jews to the Government General. Not that this had prevented him from instituting his own deportation measures to move the Jews out of Cracow which he intended should be 'clear of Jews', except for an enlarged ghetto, by the end of 1940.

The main reception area at that date was the district around Lublin, which was the site designated (after the demarcation line had been redrawn on the Bug) for the creation of the Jewish reserve.[13]

However, the project (which was probably never taken seriously by the highest authorities) was abandoned within a few weeks (by April 1940 at the latest), according to a report from Kruger, the HSSPF. On 12 March Hitler himself had told Colin Ross that 'even the creation of a Jewish State in and around Lublin would never solve the problem', adding unctuously that 'the Jews would have to live in such overcrowded conditions that it would be impossible for them to attain a tolerable standard of living'.

Immediately after the victory in France the Jewish Sub-Section III of the German Division [*Judenreferat III der Abteilung Deutschland*] of the Ministry of Foreign Affairs – more precisely *Legationsrat* Rademacher – proposed a plan[14] that had already been considered in regard to Poland though on a far less grandiose scale. On 3 June 1940 Rademacher suggested three possibilities in regard to the 'precise definition of Germany's basic war aims': '(*a*) the deportation of all Jews from Europe, (*b*) the separation of eastern Jews from western Jews – the former (to whose regenerative powers and devotion to the Talmud the Jewish intelligentsia owed their continuing existence) to remain as hostages in German hands (possibly in Lublin?) in order to tie the hands of the American Jews, and the latter to be deported from Europe (possibly to Madagascar?), and (*c*) the establishment of a Jewish National Home in Palestine (danger of a second Rome?)'.[15] Apparently the RSHA started preparatory work on the Madagascar project almost immediately, for on 24 June Heydrich asked Ribbentrop to let him know about 'any impending discussions on the subject of the solution of the Jewish problem' in case 'the Ministry of Foreign Affairs ought to know about them'. In explanation he added that: 'The very size of the problem – and we have to consider that there are about three and a quarter million Jews in the territories now under German control – means that it can no longer be solved by emigration; some *territorial* solution will have to be found.' Himmler himself wrote a memorandum on 'The Treatment of Alien Elements in the East' at the time of the French campaign in May 1940, in which he observed: 'The possibility of a large-scale emigration of the whole Jewish people to Africa or some other colony leads me to hope that we may have found a way of loosening the grip of the Jews once and for all.' Rademacher's plan, when worked out in greater detail, envisaged France handing over Madagascar as part of the peace treaty, and evacuating and compensating the French inhabitants. That part of the island not needed by Germany as a military base would then become a vast ghetto of four million Jews, administered by a police governor appointed by Himmler – in other words, by the security police who were the only people with the 'necessary experience' in this field. Rademacher believed that by this means Germany would be able, on the one hand, to use 'the four million Jews as hostages for the good behaviour of their racial brethren in America', and on the other 'to turn to her advantage, propaganda-wise, the generosity she was showing towards the Jews by allowing them a substantial measure of self-government'. An inter-European bank could finance the operation from Jewish property seized by the SS – the additional funds that would certainly be necessary could be extracted from the Jews; each individual Jew would be allowed to take with him one 'fair-sized' suitcase.

This fantastic project was seized on by the RSHA 'with delight' – according to the records – and every detail was worked out by Eichmann's department. 'As a way of avoiding lengthy contact between the Jews and other peoples,' Eichmann declared, 'a solution involving deportation overseas, to an island, is preferable to any other.' And because all Jews deported to Madagascar would lose the nationality of the country which had previously given them shelter from the moment of their deportation – so Rademacher averred – the possibility of the Jews being able to found their own Vatican State in Palestine and exploit 'Jerusalem as a value symbol' to further their objectives, would likewise be avoided.

Himmler gave his approval to the project, and in August 1940 it was directly passed on to Ribbentrop by Heydrich. At about the same time Hitler, too, is supposed to have defined his objective as 'the collective evacuation of the Jews from Europe'; and Frank had already expressed his relief in July that, within the foreseeable future, the Jews would be exiled to Madagascar instead of being transported, endlessly, into the Government General. Needless to say – with peace as far away as ever – the plan was stillborn. In spite of this, two years later when the extermination programme had already started, Hitler still acted as though he meant to deport the Jews to Madagascar after the end of the war.

In the meantime deportations from the Reich continued. On 22 and 23 October 1940 – apparently at the instigation of Hitler himself* – *Gauleiters* Bürckel and Robert Wagner ordered the transportation by nine goods trains of more than 6,500 Jews from the *Gaue* of Baden and Saarpfalz into the unoccupied zone of France 'without warning the French authorities'. With the sole exception of the Jewish partner in mixed marriages no one was spared and the victims even included men who had fought at the front and the inmates of old people's homes – one of them a 97-year-old man from Karlsruhe. They were given between a quarter of an hour and two hours to get ready – depending on the locality – and were, of course, forbidden to take their possessions with them; these were confiscated by the competent *Regierungspräsident*. The *Staatspolizeileitstellen* in Karlsruhe, Neustadt an der Hordt and Saarbrucken 'prepared and carried out the operation' in secret by order of the *Reichführer-SS*. 'The population hardly realized what was happening', it was stated with barely concealed satisfaction in a note drafted by Eichmann (who was responsible for the organization of the transfer) and signed by Heydrich. The repeated representations of the French government, who asked that the deportees should be sent back and expressed its willingness to make itself responsible for reimbursing the costs incurred, were treated by Ribbentrop in a 'most dilatory fashion'. They did not achieve their purpose –

* 'Hitler ... ordered the deportations', wrote Heydrich in a draft note to the Ministry of Foreign Affairs on 29 October 1940. Two Foreign Office entries (by Rademacher and Luther) of 31 October and 25 November confirm. Also Nuremberg Document(s) NG 4933 and 4934.

although they may have contributed to the fact that the further deportation of German Jews (from Hesse, for instance) into unoccupied France which had apparently been planned (as a first step to Madagascar?) did not actually take place. In the autumn of 1942 when the whole of France was occupied, the survivors of 'Operation Bürckel', who had been interned in camps at Les Milles near Aix-en-Provence, Gurs and Rivesaltes by the Vichy government, were sent to Auschwitz.

In February and March 1941 over 5,000 Jews from Vienna were deported into the Government General where it had already been found impossible to concentrate the Jews in ghettos in the way that Heydrich had originally ordered, and especially not within the time limit prescribed. This was certainly not due to any lack of 'statutory' or 'administrative' orders. For instance, the principle of *forced labour* for all Jews between the ages of 14 and 60 (even though there was only enough work for some of them) was introduced on 26 October and confirmed on 12 December 1939; on 23 November 1939 a general order directed that all Jews (and all Jewish undertakings) should be distinguished by 'the Star of David' [*Zionsstern*]; and on 28 November an order was issued for the establishment of 'Jewish councils' in every district. On 11 December severe restrictions were imposed on freedom of movement, and on 26 January 1940 Jews were forbidden to use the trains.* It was not until 13 September 1940 (and then only because some pioneering work had been done in one or two places) that Frank issued a general order for 'residence restriction', that is to say, for the creation of ghettos.

Responsibility for their establishment and supervision was at first vested in the civilian authorities: the chief government official at the town or district level [*Stadthauptmann* or *Kreishauptmann*] or the head of the Internal Administration Division (*Abteilung Innere Verwaltung*) in the Governor-General's Department, according to the legal status and area of the place to which each particular order applied. 'Ghetto Administrative Offices' [*Ghettoverwaltung*] were set up under the civilian authorities for executive purposes [in Warsaw these functions were entrusted to the 'Commissar for the Jewish Residential District' (*der Kommissar für den judischen*

* The ban on travel by train proved impossible to enforce.

Wohnbezirk)], and the members of the 'Jewish councils' were subordinate to them. What happened was that instead of the Jews from the rural areas being concentrated in the larger towns speedily and, as far as possible, in one operation, a few 'greater ghettos' were created one by one – evidently delayed in Warsaw owing to the plans for 'reservations' in Lublin and Madagascar. The first ghetto to be established in the former Polish areas and the one that lasted longest (until the summer of 1944 strangely enough) was the one in *Lodz-Litzmannstadt*, which was annexed by the Reich at the end of April 1940. Other greater ghettos were created in the Government General during October–November 1940 in particular: Warsaw (where over 400,000 Jews were finally interned), followed by Cracow in March 1941; Lublin and Radom in April; and Lemberg in December. This last was also the first to be closed, in so far as there could be any question of 'closing' ghettos. Internal resettlement programmes within the Government General reduced the number of inmates of the greater ghettos here and there, but the population figures in most of them – despite the appalling death rate* – swelled rapidly at first. A great many smaller ghettos (before, but mainly after Warsaw) were also created – sometimes simply by 'isolating' villages in which there was a preponderance of Jews; most of these, as well as countless Jewish labour camps, remained in existence for some time.

Efforts to make the sentences served in concentration camps more 'economic' (that is to say, more productive) had been mounting since 1938, and were now augmented by the activities of Globocnik, the SS and Police Chief in the Lublin district, who, exercising the special powers conferred on him in connexion with the Jewish question, began to take an active part in the management of the forced labour camps run independently by the SS. There had been signs, even as early as May 1940, that the security police of the Government General – to whom the 'unregulated' employment of Jews in German firms was a thorn in the flesh – were striving to bring the Jewish councils, and thereby manpower management, under their exclusive control.

*In Warsaw (470,000 inmates) 44,630 died in 1941 and 37,462 in the first nine months of 1942; in Lodz, 29,561 of the original 160,000 inmates died between 1 May 1940 and 30 June 1942; in all the ghettos and forced labour camps probably one-fifth of all the Polish Jews, that is to say, over 500,000 people, died (Hilberg, *op. cit.* p. 173).

The Final Solution

1   The decision and how it was put into effect in the occupied zone of Soviet Russia

The exact moment at which Hitler made up his mind that the Jews must be physically destroyed cannot be precisely determined from the evidence available. According to Felix Kersten, Himmler's Finnish masseur, whose recollections of conversations with his patient must be treated with some reserve, Hitler, encouraged by Goebbels and Bormann, had issued instructions to Himmler about the progressive destruction of the Jews immediately after the French campaign in the summer of 1940.[1] However, the fact that it was Hitler who, in all probability, initiated the deportation of the Jews from Baden Baden and Saarpflatz into unoccupied France in October 1940, makes it seem likely that the first definite decision took place at a later date. What is certain is that the nearer Hitler's plan to overthrow Russia as the last possible enemy on the continent of Europe approached maturity, the more he became obsessed with the idea – with which he had been toying as 'a final solution' for a long time – of wiping out the Jews in the territories under his control.

It cannot have been later than March 1941, when he openly declared his intention of having the political commissars of the Red Army shot, that he issued his secret decree – which never appeared in writing though it was mentioned verbally on several occasions – that the Jews should be eliminated. In practice what happened first was that the *Einsatzgruppen* of the *Sipo* and the SD which followed closely behind the army – there were four of them, A, B, C, and D, composed as usual of *Einsatzkommandos* and *Sonderkommandos* – themselves shot the Jews whom they unearthed in the occupied territories. As already stated, their commanders were drawn from members of the SD and the *Sicherheitspolitzei* (i.e. the Gestapo and the *Kripo*). The total strength of an *Einsatzgruppe* varied between 500 and 1,000 men who included, apart from the headquarters and the technical personnel (such as drivers, interpreters, wireless operators and so forth), members of the ordinary uniformed police [*Ordnungspolizei*] and the *Waffen-SS*. In the autumn of 1941 *Einsatzgruppe*

A, for instance, had a strength of 990 men, of whom 133 had been seconded from the *Ordnungspolizei* and 340 from the *Waffen-SS*.[2] Locally recruited militia were used as support troops.

On Hitler's orders, the official duties of the *Einsatzgruppen* were formally set out by Field Marshal Keitel, Chief of OKW, in 'Instructions on Special Matters attached to Directive No. 21 (Barbarossa)' of 13 March 1941, Paragraph 2 (*b*), dictated by Hitler himself,[3] read as follows:

In order to prepare the *political and administrative organization the* Reichsführer-SS *has been given by the Führer certain special tasks* within the operations zone of the army;[4] these stem from the necessity finally to settle the conflict between two opposing political systems. Within the framework of these tasks the *Reichsführer-SS* will act independently and on his own responsibility. This is, however, without prejudice to the over-riding plenary power hereby accorded to the Commander-in-Chief, Army, and the authorities to whom it may be delegated by him. The *Reichsführer-SS* is responsible for seeing that military operations are not affected by any measures necessary to carry out his task. Details will be settled direct between OKH and the *Reichsführer-SS*.

During the final discussions on 26 March between Wagner, the *Generalquartiermeister*, and Heydrich, the CSSD (representing Himmler), a draft order from OKH on the duties of the *Einsatzgruppen* in the operations zone was drawn up. This order was issued, unchanged, on 28 April 1941 by Field Marshal von Brauchitsch, C-in-C Army.[5] There cannot, therefore, have been many further discussions on the subject, and the evidence given by *SS-Führer* Schellenberg of *Amt* VI of the RSHA (who was present during the discussions) that they did not take place until May, must be incorrect.[6]

According to the text of the order, the *Einsatzgruppen* in the operations zone were to carry out their 'special' security police duties on 'their own responsibility'; they were also empowered 'within the terms of reference of their own responsibility to take executive measures against the civilian population'. The operations zone was divided into (1) the combat zone [*Gefechtsgebiet*], (2) behind this, the L. of C. area [*rückwärtiges Armeegebiet*], and (3) behind this, the rear army area [*rückwärtiges Heeresgebiet*]. In the L. of C. area the *Einsatzgruppen* were subordinate to the army 'in regard to movement, rations and billets', but to the CSSD (i.e. Heydrich) for discipline, jurisdiction and technical matters (in other words, in regard to the actual functions they were required to perform). The same proviso applied to the rear army area, except that here it was made even plainer (than in the L. of C. area) that the *Einsatzgruppen* would be subordinate to the representative of the CSSD attached to the commander of the rear army area – that is, the officer commanding the *Einsatzgruppen*. The military authorities inserted a 'reserved right clause' into the arrangement which provided that in L. of C. area nearest to the front, the respective army commander was entitled to give the *Einsatzgruppen* 'any necessary directions to prevent interference with (military) operations'. The commander of the rear army area could only issue 'limited' instructions, and then only 'when danger was imminent'. In the event, the military authorities made very little use of this right during the months to come.

That the duties of the *Einsatzgruppen* would include the shooting of all Jews was not stated anywhere in the order issued by von Brauchitsch in agreement with Heydrich. (It is not within the scope of this work to examine whether and if so, how far, the military authorities guessed or knew what was going to happen.) When the *Einsatzgruppen* were being formed in May 1941, their leaders, according to the evidence of those present, were, however, told about the *secret decree on shooting by word of mouth*.[7] According to the testimony of Ohlendorf, who was in command of an *Einsatzgruppe*, the 'liquidation order' (as he called it) meant 'putting to death all racially and politically undesirable elements among the prisoners, where these might be thought to represent a threat to security';[8] and it came out at the trial of the *Einsatzgruppen* at Nuremberg that the order was finally extended to cover four main groups: communist officials, so-called 'second-class Asiatics', gypsies and Jews.

In a written minute of 2 July 1941, which has only recently come to light, to the four *Höhere SS und Polizeiführer* – Jeckeln, von dem Bach-Zelewski, Prützmann and Korsemann – Heydrich 'summarized' the 'basic instructions' that he had already issued direct to the *Einsatzgruppen* and *Kommandos*, as follows:

4 *Executions*
The following will be executed:
all officials of the Comintern (most of these will certainly be career politicians);

Officials of senior and middle rank and 'extremists' in the party, the central committee, and the provincial and district committees; the Peoples' Commissars;

Jews in the service of the Party or the State;

other extremist elements (saboteurs, propagandists, snipers, assassins, agitators, etc.);

in so far as in individual cases they are not required, or are no longer required for economic or political intelligence of special importance, for future security police measures, or for the economic rehabilitation of the occupied territories. . . .

No steps will be taken to interfere with any purges that may be initiated by anti-Communist or anti-Jewish elements in the newly occupied territories. On the contrary these are to be *secretly encouraged*. At the same time every precaution must be taken to ensure that those who engage in 'self-defence' actions are not subsequently able to plead that they were acting under orders or had been promised political protection. Special care must be taken in regard to the shooting of doctors and others engaged in medical practice. . . .

There can be no doubt, in spite of the emphasis on the execution of Jews 'in the service of the Party or the State' in this *written* memorandum to the four HSSPF commanders, that the *Einsatzgruppen* had *verbal* orders to shoot *all* Jews. According to the testimony of a commander of a *Sonderkommando* (and other witnesses), already by June 1941 Heydrich himself had explained to the commanders of the *Einsatzgruppen* and *Einsatzkommandos* (in small groups) that 'Judaism in the east was the source of Bolshevism and must therefore be wiped out in accordance with the Führer's aims'. The draft instructions to the CSSD *Kommandos* earmarked (in agreement with OKW) for the *Stalags** of 28 June 1941 – which was issued without amendment as CSSD Operational Order No. 8 on 17 July – had already laid down that, in addition to communist officials, 'all Jews' were to be included among those Soviet Russian prisoners-of-war segregated for execution.[9] The general report submitted by *Einsatzgruppe* A on 15 October 1941 stated that the security police, '*in accordance with instructions received*', were resolved 'to solve the Jewish problem decisively and by all available means'. A further statement in the same report on the effect that 'the cleansing operations being carried out by the security police, *in accordance with* basic instructions, have as their objective *the*

*Prisoner-of-war camps.

total elimination of the Jews' was even more conclusive.
[Whereas Heydrich had given orders that 'local anti-Semitic
outbursts in the form of pogroms against the Jews' were to be
encouraged 'from the first hours of the invasion', even in the
'unlikely event of this proving difficult in the initial stages' –
without, of course, 'letting it be known that the Germans were
in any way involved'.[10]]

In the final analysis events speak for themselves. For instance,
according to a document recently come to light, *Einstaz-
kommando* 3 of *Einsatzgruppe* A stationed in Lithuania caused
Lithuanian partisans to shoot 416 Jews (including 47 women) in
Kowno (Fort VII) on 4 July 1941† – only two days after the
Kommando had begun operations and two days after Heydrich's
written decree to the HSSPF's concerning the classes of persons
to be executed. From 15 August 1941 the *Einsatzkommando*
(according to its own 'general report') was also shooting Jewish
children almost daily: for instance, in the operation carried out in
Moletai and Utena on 29 August 1941, '1,469 Jewish children'
were put to death in addition to 582 Jewish men and 1,731
Jewish women. Under the heading 'Executions up to 1 February
1942' [they had actually been 'carried out' by 25 November
1941], the following figures were given: communists, 1,064;
guerrillas, only 56; mentally unsound, 653; Poles, 44; Russian
prisoners-of-war, 28; gypsies, 5; Armenians, 1; Jews, 136,421!
These figures were reported by *Einsatzgruppe* A, which had
already executed 229,052 Jews.[11] *Einsatzgruppe* B reported
45,467 shootings by 14 November 1941; *Einsatzgruppe* C,
95,000 by the beginning of December 1941; and *Einsatzgruppe*

IMT, vol. XXXVII, pp. 672 and 687 [my italics]. Also the general report of
Einsatzgruppe A at the beginning of 1942: 'Systematic cleansing operations
are being carried out – in accordance with the principles laid down in orders
concerning the relentless elimination of Judaism. Certain difficulties may be
encountered in regard to the final and complete extermination of the Jews left
in White Ruthenia after the German invasion.' [Some of them had to be
spared for essential work; severe frost impeded 'mass executions'; the Jews
were widely 'dispersed' over the countryside. In spite of this, it had proved
'possible to shoot some 41,000 Jews'] (*ibid*. vol. XXX, pp. 76 and 79).
†The commander of *Einsatzkommando* 3, *Standartenführer* Jäger, said: 'The
executions carried out by the Lithuanian partisans on my instructions and by
my orders. . . .' That this was not one of the local pogroms referred to by
Heydrich is obvious from the final statement in Jäger's general report:
'Before the security police tasks were undertaken by *Einsatzkommando* 3, the
partisans had liquidated 4,000 Jews by pogroms and executions.'

D, 92,000 by 8 April 1942. To these figures must be added a further 363,211 shootings carried out during the months August to November 1942 in the Ukraine, South Russia and the province of Bialystok, as reported to Hitler by Himmler himself. It must therefore be reckoned that by this date over one million Jews had been murdered by the *Einsatzgruppen* and their support troops (the police and locally recruited 'militia') alone. It is hardly surprising that a member of a German military economics office in the Ukraine, writing about the combined operations of the *Einsatzgruppen*, described them as 'unparalleled in the intensity of their effect by any other measures instituted in the Soviet Union'. And all this in spite of the fact that, according to the writer, 'terrified as the whole Jewish population is', and much as 'the Jews hate the German administration and the army', there was no evidence that they were 'widely engaged in sabotage and similar acts', nor that they could be considered 'to represent a threat to the German *Wehrmacht*'.[12]

From time to time mention is made of the 'position as regards liquidation' in the individual situation reports of the *Einsatzgruppen* that have been preserved. The figures increase from report to report – by tens of thousands and then by hundreds of thousands – until the sum of the separate figures reaches a total which, incredible as it may seem at first, has to be accepted as correct, and from which human imagination recoils.

A spontaneous remark made by Hitler during the course of a planning conference with Rosenberg, Lammers, Keitel, Göring and Bormann on future occupation policy on 16 July 1941 betrays how closely the summary executions carried out by the *Einsatzgruppen* corresponded with his desires. After stressing the importance of *camouflaging* his intention never to give up the conquered Russian territories, Hitler went on: 'Nevertheless we are taking all the necessary measures – shootings, deportations and so on – and so we should. ... The whole vast area', he added, referring to measures for 'the protection of the administration', 'must of course be pacified as quickly as possible – and the best way to do that is to shoot anyone who so much as looks like giving trouble.' Even the guerrilla warfare which the Russians had initiated, he went on, was 'not without its advantages as far as we are concerned, since it gives us a chance to wipe out anyone who gets in our way'.[13]

As a result of this conference, two Führer decrees were issued on 17 July: one on police security in the occupied territories in the East,[14] and the other to provide for the eventual transfer of the administration of the occupied territories of Soviet Russia from the military to the civil authorities. The use of the term 'security' afforded Himmler a position of special authority in matters of civil administration (and, for all practical purposes, *vis-à-vis* Alfred Rosenberg, the Reich Minister for the Occupied Territories) similar to that he already enjoyed in the military sphere, and gave him complete freedom of action in regard to the executive bodies under his control. This decree reads:

1 The *Reichsführer-SS* and Chief of the German Police will be responsible for police security in the newly occupied territories.
2 As soon as the civilian administration has been established in these territories, the *Reichsführer-SS* is empowered, in discharging his responsibility under 1 above, to give instructions to the Reich Commissioners. Where these instructions are of a general kind, or where they have some basic political significance, they will be issued through the Reich Minister for the Occupied Territories. In cases involving preventive measures in the face of some immediate threat to security, an exception to this ruling may be made.
3 For executive purposes in the sphere of police security an HSSPF will be attached to each Reich Commissioner, and will be directly and personally responsible to him. An SSPF will be attached to each General, Chief and District Commissioner, and will be directly and personally responsible to them.

The way in which Himmler interpreted his 'security functions' and the extent to which he expected co-operation from other departments may be seen from looking ahead to a minute that he sent to the Reich State Secretary for Transport, Dr Ganzenmüller, on 20 January 1943. The minute read as follows:

The *deportation of suspected partisans and those who may be helping them* is an essential prerequisite to the pacification of the Government General, Bialystok, and the Russian territories. In this connexion the deportation of the *Jews* is of the first importance. The deportation of the Jews *from the west* is likewise essential, or we shall have to reckon with an increase in terrorist activities. I need your help and your co-operation in this matter. It is absolutely necessary that additional goods trains should be placed at my disposal if I am to carry out these tasks with the speed required. I am well aware of the strain at present being placed on the transport system, and of the many demands with which you are faced. Nevertheless I must ask you to come to my assistance and provide me with more trains.'[15]

How little Hitler's order to wipe out the Jews actually had to do with security in the occupied territories can be seen from what happened in the case of two sects in the Crimea. Whereas the *Karaimen,* all of whom were practising Jews, were spared, the *Krimtschaken,* as Ohlendorf discovered from inquiries in Berlin, were eliminated as being 'unquestionably of Jewish race', although they did not, or had long ceased to, adhere to the Jewish faith. Security could hardly be said to be an important consideration when the life and death of some particular sect was dependent on the answer to some complicated racial riddle – especially when the question of whether this or that sect represented any sort of threat to the German occupying power was never even discussed.

In the following pages the principles of the policy of extermination and the ideas that inspired it will be discussed, but only the most important stages in its development will be described. What may be called 'the point of no return' in the evolution of the 'final solution' was reached when the RSHA (IV B 4*b*) issued a decree to all *Staatspolizeistellen* and to the representatives of the CSSD in Belgium and France on 20 May 1941. This stated that, 'according to a communication received from Reich Marshal Göring', Jewish emigration from the Reich and from the Protectorate of Bohemia and Moravia was to be 'stepped up in spite of the war, in so far as this was humanly possible'.

The Jews in France or Belgium were not, however, to be allowed to emigrate, since this would overstrain the already inadequate resources needed for getting the Jews out of the Reich; the *'certain final solution of the Jewish problem'* had also to be borne in mind.[16] Moreover – so ran the decree – even if Jews from the Reich were to be permitted to emigrate to unoccupied France, as might happen 'for some special reason – for instance, to get rid of the Jews without means' – there could be no compensatory immigration of Jews 'into territories occupied by us' in view of 'the certain final solution of the Jewish problem'.

If Göring's note is taken at its face value, it would seem that it was still possible – although only just – for German Jews to emigrate. But if we consider that reference had twice been made to the 'final solution', that, at about this time, orders concerning the summary execution of Jews were being issued to the *Einsatz-*

gruppen, and that effect began to be given to these orders as soon as the invasion of the Soviet Union was under way, we are forced to the conclusion that Hitler had already made up his mind, early in the spring of 1941, that the 'final solution' was to be the biological annihilation of the Jews.

Göring's memorandum to Heydrich – written in his capacity as Controller of the Four-Year Plan with reference to the decree which he had promulgated on 24 January 1939 (see p. 63) – cannot for this reason be considered as a turning-point in the history of the 'final solution'. What it did was to set the seal of official approval on the procedure – to 'legalize' it, so to speak, in order to implicate other (mainly government) administrative departments. The memorandum read as follows:

Berlin 31.7.41

From: The Reich Marshal of the Greater German Reich, Controller of the Four-Year Plan
Chairman of the Reich Defence Council [*Ministerrat für die Reichsverteidigung*]
To: The Chief of the Security Police and the SD
SS-Gruppenführer Heydrich
Berlin

To complete the task with which you were entrusted in my decree of 24.1.39 regarding the solution of the Jewish problem by emigration or evacuation to be carried out in the way best suited to the prevailing conditions, you are hereby now charged with making all necessary preparations in the organizational, technical and material fields for a total solution of the Jewish problem in all territories under German control.

You are further requested to send me, as soon as possible, a draft setting out details of the preliminary measures taken in the organizational, technical and material fields, for the achievement of the final solution to which we aspire.

(signed) Göring.[17]

Once it had been decided to exterminate the Jews, it was logical enough to discontinue all half-measures and to prohibit any further emigration. On 23 October 1941, Müller, the Chief of the Gestapo, briefed *Sipo* stations by circular that Himmler had issued an order 'banning all further Jewish emigration, with immediate effect'. To avoid all possibility of error (in view of the private instructions that the annihilation of the Jews was to be camouflaged!), Müller added in brackets 'existing regulations concerning deportation will remain in force'. The final sentence in the circular – '*Only in quite exceptional cases*, if, for instance, a positive advantage to the Reich would be likely to accrue therefrom, will the emigration of individual Jews be permitted with the prior approval of the RSHA' – made virtually no change in the existing regulations, to which the attention of 'the civil authorities concerned' also had to be drawn.[18]

The fact that Himmler did all he could to discourage any limit being placed on the number of his victims by means of a more precise definition of the term 'Jew', is yet another sign of the thoroughness with which he was determined to carry out his task. In spite of the agreement reached in earlier discussions held at the Ministry for the Eastern Territories about an extension of the Nuremberg Laws (under which [at least] all those persons who had ever belonged to the Jewish religious community or either of whose parents could be said to be Jewish were to be counted as Jews) Himmler wrote to his representative in the Ministry – *SS-Gruppenführer* Gottlob Berger – on 28 July 1942 in the following categorical terms:

I must ask you urgently to see that no definition of the term 'Jew' is published. We are simply tying our own hands by dogmatizing in this stupid way. The occupied territories will be cleared of Jews. The Führer has charged me with carrying out this very difficult task. No one can relieve me of the responsibility. I cannot allow myself (*sic*) the luxury of discussing it.[19]

It is clear that Hitler had already made his wishes known in regard to the stages by which the 'final solution' was to be achieved. Or so it would seem from a memorandum that Himmler sent to Greiser, the *Gauleiter* and *Reichsstatthalter* in *Gau* Wartheland, on 18 September 1941.

It is the Führer's wish that the Altreich and the *Protectorates should be cleared of Jews from west to east*. I am therefore doing all I can to see that the deportation of the Jews out of the Altreich and the Protectorates into the territories assimilated into the Reich during the past two years is completed during this year *as a first stage*, preparatory to their being sent further east early in the new year.'[20]

The first phase of mass shootings in the occupied territories of the Soviet Union was completed during the months that followed, although the exact date varied from region to region, according to the date when military occupation came to an end. To facilitate these lethal operations – and in particular the murder of women and children – the RSHA eventually put gas trucks at the disposal of the *Einsatzgruppen*; gas trucks were also brought into use at about this time as an instrument of the 'final solution' in Poland and Serbia. According to existing witnesses the execution squads in Russia 'were against' the use of gas trucks, because they found the unavoidable cruelty 'morally intolerable' from their own point of view.

In spite of the large numbers of victims, by no means all the Jews were wiped out in this first phase. And so the Polish pattern was repeated: survivors had to wear the yellow star (on their chests and backs); 'Jewish councils' were set up and forcibly required to help in the compilation of registers; and subsequently the Jews were concentrated in the larger towns. Later ghettos were established (where the *Einsatzgruppen* had not already provided them) and these too were administered, initially, by the civil authorities. According to the secret 'instructions' issued by Lohse, the Reich *Kommissar* for the Ostland (which adopted the Nuremberg interpretation of the term 'Jew' as did the military in the vast zone of operations) the inmates of the ghettos were to receive 'only the amount of food that the rest of the population could spare and in no case more than was sufficient to sustain life'. Lohse then went on to announce – and his official style did not obscure his meaning – that 'any *provisional* instructions I may have issued' were not intended to obstruct 'additional measures, in particular those initiated by the security police'. His object had been 'merely to safeguard the minimum measures taken by the General and District Commissioners until such time as the more intensive measures for the final solution can be put into effect'.[21]

There was, of course, no lack of regulations concerning the notification and transfer of Jewish assets (although in a communist State these scarcely ever amounted to more than a few personal possessions), nor of those conscripting Jews for forced labour – in 'work parties' *outside* the ghettos, *inside* the ghettos, in work camps, in armament factories, and even 'individually, in private firms' where, according to Lohse's instructions, there was to be no question of 'paying the rate for the job'. Even the *Einsatzgruppen* were occasionally obliged to admit (although with considerable reserve) that 'it is not always possible – in the present situation of acute labour shortage – to avoid sparing the lives of Jewish manual workers temporarily, if essential and urgent repair work is to be put in hand'.[22] Himmler could hardly suspect passive resistance in the face of the undeniable need for skilled labour, even though the widespread employment of Jews (who proved to belong in this category) in important positions (not least in the *Wehrmacht* ordnance factories) threatened to develop into an obstacle to the achievement of the 'final solution' about which an irrevocable decision had been made. Yet, in spite of all this, several Field Marshals issued detailed written appeals to the troops explaining that 'the German soldier must *fully* understand the necessity for the harsh, but just, atonement required of Jewish sub-humanity'.[23] Appeals like these, whatever else they may or may not have achieved, at least succeeded in stopping overt criticism. And it was a rare, although not an isolated occurrence, when a staff officer of Army Group Centre, who had been posted to the front, stated in an *official* report of December 1941 that everyone now knew 'what is going on', and that 'the officer corps, almost to a man, is against the shooting of Jews, prisoners and commissars', as they saw in it 'a stain on the honour of the German army'.[24]

In view of the demands made by the war even Himmler was obliged to consent to advantage being taken of the Jewish labour force available, in so far as the various stages of the 'final solution' allowed. This had already happened in the Government General, and especially in Lublin, where the *SS und Polizeiführer* Globocnik was running the SS industrial undertakings with the help of his 'own' Jewish labour camp. Nothing, however, was to be allowed to interfere with unimpeded progress towards the 'solution', which was to be carried out 'uncompromisingly' and with all possible speed. Those Jews who found themselves the possessors of the coveted 'work permits' hoped in vain that their 'expertise' would make them indispensable.[25] In December 1941, in part answer to Lohse's question whether 'all Jews, regardless of age and sex, or their usefulness to the economy (for instance, skilled workers in the *Wehrmacht*'s ordnance factories) were to be liquidated', the Ministry for the Eastern Territories (to which the question had been addressed) replied: 'The rules relating to the problem require that the demands of the economy be ignored.'[26]

Nor was this all. In all the prisoner-of-war camps in the areas under German control where there were Soviet prisoners, the 'unreliable elements' (and especially the Jews) were, with the approval of the OKW Prisoner-of-War Department [*Abteilung Kriegsgefangene*] of the OKW under General Reinecke, being segregated for execution by the *Einsatzkommandos*[27] (in spite of various counter-suggestions put forward by Admiral Canaris, the Head of the *Abwehr*).

In the meantime the situation in the crowded ghettos of occupied Russia was naturally being 'eased' by the 'additional measures' referred to by Lohse – in other words, by the second series of mass shootings. They were carried out to some extent by the *Einsatzgruppen* and *Einsatzkommandos* now attached to the 'commanding officers' and 'the local commanders [*Kommandeure*] of the security police and the SD', but principally by units of the ordinary uniformed police [*Ordnungspolizei*] and locally recruited militia. Army units were instructed in principle 'to hand the Jews over to the SD'.*

The mass shootings of the Jews at this stage were described as 'anti-partisan operations' – a psychologically useful gambit in view of the growing threat behind the front lines. [In fact, only a very few Jews had actually fled to the forests and marshlands, and of these by no means all had become guerrilla fighters – but this in itself made it easier to represent them as 'helping the partisans' or even as 'suspected partisans'.]† The principal target of the 'operations' was the ghettos which were decimated and 'cleaned out' one after another: one has only to look at Himmler's reckoning of 363,211 Jews shot in four months (see p. 82) to see precisely what this meant. The indescribable horror that was a normal part of the proceedings caused Reich Commissioner Lohse to ask, on one occasion: 'What is Katyn in comparison to all this?'‡

*See, for instance, the instruction pamphlet on 'use of troops against partisans' issued by the anti-partisan staff (intelligence section) of 11th Army on 15 December 1941. Nuremberg Document NOKW 52. (Photocopy in the Institut für Zeitgeschichte, Munich.)

†In his report No. 51 to the Führer, of 20 December 1942 (Document No. 511) on the results of the 'anti-partisan operations' since August 1942 in South Russia, the Ukraine and Bialystok, under para. 2 'Persons helping the partisans or suspected of being partisans', Himmler used three headings: (*a*) captured . . ., (*b*) executed . . ., and (*c*) Jews executed. . . .

‡When the General Commissioner for White Russia, *Gauleiter* Kube, requested that two secret reports should be forwarded to the Minister for the Eastern Territories, Rosenberg – 18 July 1943. *IMT*, vol. XXXVIII, p. 371.

On 27 October 1942 Himmler ordered the destruction of the last Ukrainian great ghetto – at Pinsk. The order provided that if it were possible to intern 1,000 male workers in a 'maximum security camp', this number might be spared and 'handed over to the army for use in the construction of wooden huts'; if not, they were to be 'liquidated along with all the others'.[28] On 21 June 1943 (here I am anticipating events) he issued the following general and definitive order in regard to Ostland [one of the areas under a Reich Commissioner] in line with his usual technique in the Government General:[29]

1 The *Höhere SS und Polizeiführer*, Ostland,
2 The *Chef des Wirtschafts – Verwaltungshauptamtes*
   I hereby give orders that:
   i all Jews still in ghettos in Ostland will be transferred to concentration camps;
   ii as from 1. 8. 1943 no Jews will be released from concentration camps for outside employment;
   iii a concentration camp will be established near Riga to which the *Wehrmacht* is to transfer its existing outside clothing and armament factories. Private firms will not be admitted. The undertakings will be exclusively concentration camp undertakings. *Chef* WVHA will be responsible for ensuring that no delay in the supplies required by the *Wehrmacht* results from this reorganization:
   iv in order to reduce the number of Jews in the Olschifier area, as many Jews as possible from the area will be removed to the Olschifier concentration camp;
   v all those inmates of the ghetto not required will be evacuated to the East;
   vi the reorganization of the concentration camp will be completed by 1. 8. 43 at latest.

It proved impossible to carry through this order – which for many of those affected meant death in the gas chambers at Minsk – in the time stipulated, but when all was finished only some ten thousand Jews were left in the forced labour-cum-concentration camps. As the Red Army advanced some of these were transferred to concentration camps in the Reich itself; all but a few died during the last months of the war.

It is common knowledge that from June 1942 onwards *Sonderkommando* 1005, under *SS Standartenführer* Blobel, was engaged, on Himmler's orders, in exhuming and burning the corpses of the victims of the mass shootings in an attempt to remove all traces of the crime. In vain!

Parallel developments within the Reich itself and in the Protectorates of Bohemia and Moravia included a police order of 1 September 1941 with effect from 19 September, under which all Jews were required to wear the 'Star of David' (a star about the size of a side plate made from yellow material outlined in black, with the word 'Jew' in black across it). Anyone defying the order was liable not only to arrest and fine, but also to 'any police security measures that might be thought necessary'. On 14 and 24 October 1941 the deportation of the Jews from the Greater German Reich began on a vast scale under two deportation orders signed by Daluege, head of the *Ordnungspolizei*. Goods trains belonging to the German railways, each carrying some 1,000 people, steamed out of the Reich – the principal towns affected being Berlin, Hamburg, Hanover, Dortmund, Düsseldorf, Cologne, Frankfurt-am-Main, Kassel, Stuttgart, Nuremberg, Munich and Breslau, and also Vienna, Prague, Theresienstadt, Brünn and Luxemburg. The destination of the first deportations – between 16 October and 13 November – was Lodz; in the second wave – 14 November to end January 1942 – the reception points were Warsaw, Kowno, Minsk and Riga. On several occasions in Kowno and Riga, the human freight was dragged out of the trains by the *Einsatzgruppen* and, together with the inmates of the local ghettos, was either shot on the spot or shortly afterwards. The Reich Union of German Jews, formed in 1939, was, as were the 'Jewish Councils' in the occupied territories, forced to help in organizing the deportations and to provide 'overseers'.

2 The total deprivation of rights and the deportation of German Jews

In conjunction with the 'final solution' policy the deportation regulations were extended under the provisions of the eleventh order of the Reich Citizenship Act of 25 November 1941, to include those Jews who were also German nationals. The idea behind the new ruling stemmed from the device originally thought out by Himmler, in his capacity as 'Reich Commissioner for the Strengthening of Germanism', for the Polish territories annexed by the Reich, which entailed the preparation of a comprehensive 'List of German Nationals' [*Deutsche Volksliste*], divided under four headings. By this means residents in the erstwhile Polish territories could acquire Reich citizenship in one of four grades. What made this device 'impossible' in the context that now applied was that the 'alien Jews' of the *Altreich* (as German nationals, which they *still* were) were in a better position under the law than the Poles who, though 'racially allied', could not be 'Germanized' and therefore did not qualify to be included in any one of the four grades in the 'List of German Nationals'. The Poles could not become German nationals in the full sense, but only 'protected members of the German Reich', without any rights as nationals. Since Hitler was 'entirely opposed' to the idea of Jews being 'protected members' under any Act or order, it was eventually decided, after tedious discussions among the senior authorities [the Reich Minister of the Interior was in favour of designating the Jews as 'stateless' from the start, as this would make their deportation 'legal'] to apply paragraph 2 of the order.

Under the provisions of this paragraph any Jew normally 'domiciled abroad' lost his nationality from the date when the above order came into effect; and any Jews who later became domiciled abroad from the date at which this occurred. The wishes of the Jews affected were totally disregarded. Paragraph 1, clause (ii) of the order (which stated that 'a Jew will be accounted as normally domiciled abroad if he is living in a foreign country in circumstances that do not indicate temporary residence') reads like the purest mockery. Since it was 'not intended' that the Government General 'should be treated as a foreign country in terms of the order', the Reich Minister of the Interior sent a confidential minute to the senior authorities on 3 December 1941, in which he made it clear that the aforementioned provisions were also to apply to those Jews 'who are normally domiciled in territories occupied by German troops or under, or about to be under, German civil administration, in particular the Government General, and the Reich *Kommissariats* of Ostland and Ukraine'.[30] The assets of those Jews who lost their German nationality on transferring their domicile abroad were confiscated, under paragraph 3 of the order, and assigned to the Reich. To ensure the efficient working of this provision, it was laid down that those persons whose assets were assigned to the Reich under paragraph 3 could not inherit from a German national, and that any German national making gifts to such persons would be liable to imprisonment and fine. A special ruling was required when one of the planned deportation centres, namely Lodz/Litzmannstadt, became part of the zone of the interior, following its assimilation into the Reich. To find a way round this, reference had to be made to 'the relative provisions concerning devolution to the German Reich of all assets owned by enemies of the people and the State'.[31] The total assets thus assigned were to be used, according to paragraph 3, clause (ii), 'for the furtherance of all existing aims connected with the solution of the Jewish problem': a formula which the Reich Minister of the Interior claimed in all seriousness was dictated 'by the needs of foreign policy'[32] (as though some acceptable solution to the Jewish problem and one likely to meet with international approval were being sought!), but which, in the context of the 'final solution', had a sinister ring. The Reich Minister of the Interior also made it his business to point out in addition that the provisions of the order ... 'would greatly facilitate the task of those civil servants who had to deal with the Jewish question (expatriation and confiscation of property in individual cases)'. Characteristically the order linked what might be called 'legal issues', like nationality and loss of assets, with deportation – for which there was no sort of legal justification. Paragraph 8 stated unambiguously that 'responsibility for deciding in which cases confiscation of assets is appropriate will be vested in the *Chef der Sicherheitspolizei* and the *SD*'. Officially the costs involved in the deportation of the Jews were also his responsibility, but the security police lost no time in getting round this by levying an 'emigration tax' – as the Jewish contribution towards deportation costs[33] – which had to be paid by the victims in acknowledgement of receipt of the precise instructions issued to them in regard to loss of nationality and surrender of assets.

One final point: in discussions about the order the Reich Minister of Justice had not overlooked the point that once Jews were 'stateless persons' (which the Reich Minister of the Interior had wished to make them without delay) they would be liable to less severe penalties at law for treachery, for instance, than the Germans – since foreigners and 'stateless persons' owed 'no particular loyalty to the Reich'. A further executive order had already been drafted, under which any Jew engaging in any act in which it would be unlawful for a German national to engage, or committing a criminal offence 'against the German nation' would be liable to imprisonment or the death penalty, except where such act or offence committed by a Jew was directed solely against Judaism. Hitler, however, rejected the suggestion, as he had others put forward by the Reich Minister of the Interior 'favouring the privileged half-breed', partly on the grounds that it was 'absurdly complicated'; but mainly (as Lammers, the Head of the Reich Chancellery wrote in confidence to Martin Bormann) 'because he does not think there will be any Jews left in Germany after the war, and it seems to him, therefore, unnecessary to pass a law now that may be difficult to enforce, will tie up manpower and would not, in any case, provide a basic solution'.[34]

As long as there were still Jews in Germany, however, the régime had no difficulty in finding new ways to discriminate against and harry them. From 1 May 1942 Jews were forbidden to use public transport without local police permits – which in the event were issued only for 'travel to work' where this involved a journey of more than seven kilometres (not counting the return journey) or to school involving a journey of more than five kilometres (also not counting the return journey); and they were not allowed to sit down unless there was some overriding need, and were completely banned from sleeping and dining cars. Jews were forbidden to use public telephones and automatic ticket machines; access to the countryside was barred to them; they were not allowed to visit restaurants, to use station waiting-rooms, or to go to an 'Aryan' hairdresser. Jews (and in cases of mixed marriages, the husbands or wives of Jews) were forbidden to buy newspapers or periodicals, to sell their books, or to buy books from a bookseller; from May 1942 they were no longer allowed to keep domestic pets of any kind. The issue of 'smokers' cards' to Jews was stopped after June 1942; on 19 October 1942, their rations of eggs, meat, meat products, cereals, full milk and (for those over six years old) skimmed milk were cancelled. In Berlin Jews had been issued with ration cards stamped with a 'J' to distinguish them from the rest of the population since June 1941: since July 1940 their shopping hours had been restricted to between four and five o'clock in the afternoons. The cost of air-raid precautions was not refunded to

Jews and they were not entitled to compensation for war damage [as against this, third parties could put in claims to the Reich, which were met from 'claims for restitution which the Reich was entitled to bring at any time against the Jew who had suffered damage'].[35]

Besides all this Jews were required, under an order issued by the Board of Control [*Aufsichtsbehörde*] on 10 January 1942, to hand in any furs and woollen articles they possessed [if they had only one coat and it had a fur collar, this had to be ripped off]; under an order of 9 June, 'any inessential articles of clothing', and under an order of 19 June, any electrical or optical apparatus, bicycles, typewriters, gramophone records and so forth in their possession had likewise to be surrendered in good condition. From 15 April 1942 Jews were required to paint the Star of David on their houses. A confidential decree issued by the Reich Minister of the Interior on 18 December of the previous year (1941) denied Jews disabled on active service the right to possess identity cards. Under a similar unpublished decree issued by the Reich Minister of the Interior (Reich SS Security Department) to the Reich Union of German Jews on 20 June 1942, all Jewish schools were to be closed and all other forms of education for Jewish children discontinued as from 1 July 1942, 'having regard' (in the words of the memorandum sent by the Reich Minister of Education to the President of the Administrative District) 'to the greatly accelerated transfer of the Jewish population that has occurred during the last few months'.

The rights of German Jews in industry during this phase were governed by paragraph 1 of the 'Order concerning the Employment of Jews', issued on 3 October 1941. This paragraph stated briefly: 'Special conditions will be applied to Jews employed in industry.' After considerable deliberation an executive order was issued on 31 October, revealing exactly what this meant. An introductory statement that 'the Jew ... as an alien cannot be a member of a German trade association' was followed by a provision that Jewish employees were to be paid only 'for work actually done'. The cancellation of the payment of bonuses was not all; subsidies, children and family allowances, extra payment for Sunday and holiday work, and even sickness benefits were also cancelled. Unpaid free time to be granted at the discretion of employers, who had the right to refuse requests for time off, was substituted for negotiated holiday periods. Jewish employees could be given notice at any time, with effect from the evening of the next working day. Unemployment benefits were limited to 'the minimum necessary to sustain life'; and the regulations governing the hours of work for adults were extended to cover young persons. From then on there was virtually nothing to prevent the exploitation of Jewish labour – which certain specified firms were required to employ.

The provision that the Jews (where practicable) were to be employed 'in groups' was of particular importance in the light of the 'final solution'. For this meant in practice that Jews employed in the war economy – and there were a great many of them by this time – were temporarily safe from deportation. Even before the issue of the order, the armaments firms and the OKW *Wehrwirtschaftsamt* [Military Economy] Department had been doing their best to keep their Jewish employees – and clearly not always in the interests of the war effort! They managed to get Heydrich to agree that 'Jews in certain specified employment' were to be deported 'only if the heads of armament firms and the labour offices consider their deportation will have no adverse effect on the interests of the war effort'. [The dependants of such employees were also to be exempt.] However, the Security Police must have continued to seize Jews working in armament factories in individual cases, as in March 1942 Göring issued overriding instructions to the effect that 'Jews working in industries vital to the war effort are not, in principle, to be deported until further notice'. In spite of this, Hitler decreed in the autumn that even Jews employed in armaments factories must be deported.

Finally there was the effect of the policy of the 'final solution' on the right of Jews to 'protection under the law'. On 12 June 1940 an order to give effect to the fifteenth order under the Reich Citizenship Act (under which Jewish lawyers were no longer free to exercise their profession) laid down that Jews could be barred by the court from appearing as defence counsel in cases 'where this seems desirable in regard to the nature of the proceedings' – in the event mainly in political trials or when cases of 'racial pollution' were being tried. An ordinance issued by the Reich Minister of Justice on 20 November 1941 required that the names of all Jews serving prison sentences should be forwarded, six weeks before the expiry of the sentence, to the Gestapo in order that the latter could make arrangements to take them away. The order for 'The Administration of the Criminal Law in regard to Poles and Jews in the Eastern Territories assimilated into the Reich' of 4 December did not go quite so far as to hand over penal justice in its entirety to the police [which was what Himmler wanted] although it did restore to a limited extent the police courts-martial. But the slide towards injustice and despotism was quite apparent: not only were penalties of extreme severity imposed (the slightest expression of hostility against the Germans, even in the case of young people, was punished by death or imprisonment in a punishment camp), but the protection afforded by legal rights and normal procedure was steadily withdrawn. The text of Article II of the above order – 'Poles and Jews will be liable to punishment . . . if they commit any act contrary to the basic principles of German criminal law as interpreted in the light of the requirements of the State in the assimilated eastern territories' – is a case in point. The order (which applied only in the eastern territories) also included provisions which the Minister of Justice would liked to have seen included in the eleventh order under the Reich Citizenship Act: namely that Jews [and Poles, that is to say 'protected members of the State'] could not refuse to be tried by German judges on the grounds that the latter would not be impartial, and were no longer to be sworn-in as witnesses in criminal proceedings. [The rules governing perjury and false oaths continued to apply, however, if the evidence given was untrue, even though it had not been given on oath.] In the situation in which they found themselves, there was virtually nothing the Jews could do in face of this fresh order. And what Himmler did not manage to achieve by it (in the way of oppressing the Jews and Poles), he accomplished later, throughout the whole of the Reich, by measures directed solely against the Jews.

To begin with, the new National Socialist Minister of Justice, Thierack, made an arrangement with Himmler (on 18 September 1942) to hand over the 'anti-social' elements among the prison population to the *Reichsführer-SS*, so that they could be 'worked to death'. These elements were to include Poles serving sentences of over three years, Czechs or Germans serving sentences of over eight years, and 'others' (political prisoners, Jews, gypsies, Russians and Ukrainians) regardless of the length of sentence to be served. Thierack later arranged with Himmler (subject to Hitler's approval) that 'in future, Jews, Poles, gypsies, Russians and Ukrainians convicted of offences should not be sentenced by the ordinary courts, but would be executed by the *Reichsführer-SS*[36] in view of the leadership's plans for settling the eastern problem'. Thierack's justification for such a procedure was – as he wrote to Bormann with unequalled frankness – that, 'in spite of the harsh penalties imposed [on these four categories], there is little that the law can do towards exterminating them. . . .* My idea is that we shall get better results if we hand them over to the police, who can then carry out their measures untrammelled by the niceties of criminal law'.†

There can be no doubt that five or six contingents of so-called 'anti-socials' were handed over to Himmler – and that political prisoners were certainly included.‡ But Thierack's plan for 'handing over' convicted Poles to the police miscarried – officially, at least – despite Hitler's approval because of objections voiced by the Prefects [*Oberpräsidente*] and Governors [*Reichsstatthalter*] of the assimilated territories.[37] And Himmler himself, who had not advocated the arrangement, was less than enthusiastic about it. In the event the Poles continued to be dealt with under the provisions of the penal order of 4 December 1941. As for the Jews, on the other hand, the thirteenth order under the Reich Citizenship Act, issued on 1 July, finally gave 'legal' form – so stubbornly pursued by Himmler – to his activities.

* That is to say, Jews, Poles, gypsies, Russians and Ukrainians.

† In this letter, dated 13 October 1942, Thierack also asked Bormann to let him know 'if the Führer approves of my idea'. If he did, Thierack would 'take the matter up officially with Dr Lammers' – always, of course, with the idea of relieving 'the German body politic' of its Poles, Russians, Jews and gypsies, and making the 'assimilated territories in the east fit for colonization by the German people'. Nuremberg Document NG 558. (Microfilm in the Institut für Zeitgeschichte, Munich.)

‡ In April 1943 Pohl, Chief of the SS Economic and Administrative Department, told Thierack that, out of a total of 12,658 political prisoners sent to concentration camps, 5,935 had died 'in the meantime' (in other words, in about six months). This 'alarmingly high mortality rate' could only be due to the fact that the prisons were 'getting rid of prisoners suffering from every imaginable kind of disease'. In the interests of the war effort he must ask that only those political prisoners who were in good health be sent in future. Nuremberg Document NO 1285. (Photocopy in the Institut für Zeitgeschichte, Munich.)

Paragraph 1 of the order stated: 'Criminal offences committed by Jews will be punished by the police.' The penal order applying to the Poles was 'no longer to be applied to the Jews', as it provided too many loop-holes. Under paragraph 2 any assets remaining to a Jew after his death were to accrue to the Reich. For the Jews, this was the end as far as 'protection under the law' was concerned – the whole process of deprivation of rights was accomplished in the guise of a 'law'. As it happened, apart from the fact that it also affected the Jewish partner in a mixed marriage, this latest order did little more than give legal sanction to an existing situation. The RSHA had already taken steps to complete, or at least to accelerate the process by issuing instructions on 11 March 1943 to the effect that, on completion of their prison sentence (regardless of its length), all Jewish offenders were to be sent, for life, to the concentration camps in Auschwitz or Lublin;* and on 21 April Thierack issued a similar order.

3 The Wannsee Conference

While the *Einsatzgruppen*, in pursuance of the policy of the 'final solution', had been shooting the Jews in the zone of operations since the beginning of the Russian campaign, the first large-scale deportations of the Jews out of the Reich and the Protectorate did not begin, as we have seen, until the autumn of 1941. Before the machinery of destruction (which was not yet, technically, in full working order) could be brought into operation, it occurred to the organizers of the extermination programme that they should discuss and co-ordinate the overall plans for its execution with the State departments concerned, in order to ensure administrative cooperation. It was not only that decisions had to be reached on such matters as how to treat people of mixed blood, which classes of people were to be the principal target of the measures, whether or not Jewish armament workers should be deported and what was to be done about

*On the other hand, Poles, on completion of prison sentences of over six months, were sent to concentration camps for the duration of the war. *IMT*, vol. XXVI, p. 259.

foreign Jews in Germany – there was also the more important question of procedure in the occupied territories and in the allied, friendly and satellite countries to consider. For the National Socialist leadership had no intention of confining its plan to exterminate the Jews within the narrow confines of the areas controlled by the Reich: it was to extend throughout the whole sphere of German influence, and this, in particular, required the support of the Ministry of Foreign Affairs.

This was the purpose of the so-called Wannsee Conference which Heydrich – on the pretext that the evacuation of the Jews was gathering momentum – originally called for 29 November 1941, and then postponed to 9 December,[38] and which finally took place on 20 January 1942 in the Headquarters of Interpol (International Criminal Police Commission), at No. 56/58 Grossen Wannsee. Exercising the plenary powers conferred on him by Göring on 31 July 1941, Heydrich had invited the 'competent' officials to a ministerial conference. Those present included, in addition to officials from the SS departments and the Party Chancellery, the appropriate representatives of the Reich Ministry for the Eastern Territories, the Reich Ministry of the Interior, the Office of the Controller of the Four-Year Plan, the Reich Ministry of Justice, the Ministry for Foreign Affairs, and the Reich Chancellery. Heydrich took the chair. The minutes of the meeting, kept by Eichmann, have been preserved,[39] and their contents may be summarized as follows: after again calling attention to Göring's instructions (which would require 'parallel lines of action' on the part of 'all departments directly concerned' for their implementation), Heydrich announced that 'central responsibility for working out the final solution of the Jewish problem would, regardless of geographical boundaries, lie with the *Reichsführer-SS und Chef der Deutschen Polizei* (the Chief of the Security Police and the SD)' – for all practical purposes, therefore, with Heydrich himself. Turning to the 'stages' in the 'struggle' against the Jews he pointed to the fact that 'they had been driven out of the various areas inhabited by Germans', and thus 'from the German nation's living space'. This was how he saw the emigration measures that had been applied 'systematically and on an increasing scale' against the Jews. They had had obvious disadvantages, of course, but these had had to be accepted in the absence of 'any possible alternative solution'.* With reference to the ban which Himmler had in the meantime placed on emigration, 'having regard to the possibilities offered by the eastern territories', Heydrich explained:

Instead of emigration, there is now a further (*sic*) possible solution, to which the Führer has already signified his consent – namely deportation to the east.

Although this should be regarded merely as an interim measure, it will provide us with practical experience which will be especially valuable in connexion with the future final solution.

This euphemistic speech may have been intended to conceal the idea of using some of the Jews condemned to be deported in an experiment in extermination by speedy and unobtrusive technical methods which had already been considered (according to the testimony of a witness not yet mentioned) in the Riga district and which might prove useful for the large-scale liquidation plans. According to the (exaggerated) estimate of the RSHA, the 'final solution of the European Jewish problem' would involve about 11 million 'practising Jews', including significantly those in England, Ireland and Turkey.

The most pertinent paragraph in the minutes read as follows:

In pursuance of the final solution, special administrative and executive measures will apply to the conscription of Jews for labour in the eastern territories. Large labour gangs of those fit to work will be formed, with the sexes separated, which will be directed to these areas for road construction and undoubtedly a large part of them will fall out through natural elimination. Those who remain alive – and they will certainly be those with the greatest powers of endurance – will be treated accordingly. If released, they would, being a natural selection of the fittest, form a new cell from which the Jewish race could again develop. [History teaches us that.]

Either Heydrich did not say what was to happen to the Jews who proved unfit for work, or it was left out of the minute as being insufficiently veiled. However, it must have been perfectly clear to everyone – and not only to those who presumably knew

* At this point, according to Eichmann's minute, Heydrich observed that the Jewish finance houses abroad (at the instigation of the Jewish organizations of the interior) had refrained from 'demanding foreign currency for bearer bonds and immigration charges' and that this had 'protected the value of German foreign currency'. Up to the end of September 1941, they had 'made about 9,500,000 dollars available by way of gifts'.

all about it already, like Dr Bühler,* for instance, State Secretary for the Government General, who asserted that the situation might be less difficult than anticipated, since 'most of the Jews we are talking about' would be 'unfit for work'.

The words 'treated accordingly' used in regard to 'those with the greatest powers of endurance' could likewise have left no one in doubt about what the final solution was to be and how it was to be achieved. The penultimate sentence in the conventionally worded minute – 'agreement has been reached on the various possible solutions that have been under discussion' – was hardly less unequivocal. According to the minute, this would involve both *Gauleiter* Dr Meyer (Ministry for the Eastern Territories) and Dr Bühler in a certain amount of preliminary work, in the execution of which every possible precaution was to be taken to avoid upsetting the local population in the territories concerned. At his trial at Jerusalem in 1961, Eichmann, who had been present at the conference, told the court that the term 'possible solutions' referred to 'possible methods of putting people to death'. In this connexion it is perhaps hardly necessary to look further than the warning against 'upsetting the local population in the territories concerned'.

Turning to the 'classes of person' to be earmarked for deportation and extermination, Neumann, the State Secretary in the Office of the Controller of the Four-Year Plan, stated that Göring's view and that of the Ministry of Economics and Supply was that 'those Jews employed in essential war work should not be deported – or at least not until some substitute for them has been found'. Heydrich then confirmed – with almost as many provisos – the agreement he had made in the previous autumn (of 1941), that is to say, 'that the instructions he had issued about the deportation of that particular class of Jew were to remain in force'.

Heydrich also told the conference, in the same evasive and ambiguous way, about a regulation that had been drawn up for another class. This, which was apparently not discussed in detail

*Before the Wannsee Conference (see his evidence of 23 April 1946; *IMT*, vol. XII, p. 79) Bühler had had a private conversation with Heydrich, in which, so he asserted, it was not made clear to him what was meant by the 'final solution' and 'resettlement'. On the other hand his comment, as summarized in the minutes of the Wannsee Conference, would seem to prove that he had been fully informed.

at the conference, was to apply to Jews over the age of 65, who were not to be evacuated (that is to say, killed), but to be *transferred** to an Old People's Ghetto in Theresienstadt in the Protectorate. In addition to old people, Jews who had been severely wounded at the front and those who had been awarded war decorations – Iron Cross Class I and above!† – would also be considered for Theresienstadt. . . . 'This highly suitable solution', added Heydrich, 'should serve to silence all criticism at one stroke.' In October 1941 he had already expressed the opinion that, in order to avoid friction in carrying out the deportations, it would be necessary to counter, in good time, any objections that might be raised by 'senior government departments', by some *tactical* proposal, such as the establishment of this 'relief camp' in Theresienstadt. The same note of cynicism was apparent in Eichmann's remark during a meeting at the RSHA – held after several serious blunders during deportation had come to light. He suggested that, 'to avoid trouble' individual Gestapo posts should be spared the 'disagreeable task' of 'dragging off elderly people' who would in all likelihood be transferred to Theresienstadt, in any case, by the summer or autumn of 1942 at the latest. 'That should disarm our critics from outside,' he added. And in furtherance of this objective, Jews subsequently evacuated to Theresienstadt included those who had world-wide connexions, those who were internationally famous, those who had 'Aryan' relations and so forth.

The sudden 'disappearance of well-known' Jews (even if they were transferred to the camp as such) could have caused such a sensation that the cover story ('resettlement' instead of forced labour in the east), considered so important to the success of the extermination programme, might have been in danger of being exposed! To counter 'atrocity propaganda', therefore, the inmates of the camp were permitted, from September 1942, to

*My italics. It is interesting to note that Heydrich differentiated between 'deportation' and 'transfer'. The term that came into use later was 'change of address'.
†The question of what was to be done about those Jews who had received war decorations had already been discussed at a private meeting in Prague between Heydrich, Karl Hermann Frank, Eichmann and others on 10 October 1941. Referring to 'certain limitations' that had been agreed with the OKW, Heydrich said, baldly: 'We can't keep all these Jews in the Reich whatever happens; a proportion of them will have to be evacuated.'

write harmless-sounding letters to their relations both at home and abroad, and the camp was given an air of spurious respectability as a 'Jewish settlement'. After extensive preparations and precautions, it was finally opened to representatives of the German and International Red Cross and to a Danish Commission.

The transfer of almost all the Jewish community of Bohemia and Moravia (75,661) to Theresienstadt began in November 1941. As against this the deportation of the selected categories from Germany (41,900) and Austria (15,226) did not begin until June 1942, while the evacuation of those from other countries (in particular, 4,894 Jews from Holland, most of them German refugees) came even later, and was not completed until 28 October 1944.

In the meantime, in addition to over 60,000 of the Czechoslovakian Jews – for virtually all of whom Theresienstadt turned out to be nothing more than a transit camp for the death camps in the east – over 16,000 German and over 7,500 Austrian Jews – that is to say, a total of more than 83,000 of the inmates of Theresienstadt – were deported in the autumn of 1942, but mainly in May and September/October 1944, in defiance of all agreements reached, to Riga, Minsk, Lublin or Auschwitz; and of these only some 3,500 survived. Of the grand total of 140,937 persons transferred to Theresienstadt up to 20 April 1945, no less than 33,521 died in the camp itself. Survivors therefore numbered only about 23,000 as against 118,000 who died or disappeared – a balance sheet which reveals the true nature of the 'relief camp'.

The picture would be incomplete without mention of the unparalleled fraud perpetrated in the guise of a 'home purchase scheme' by the RSHA and the Central Office for Jewish Emigration (to an even greater extent) against the Jews condemned to exile in Theresienstadt. There was admittedly a precedent for this fraud, which incidentally reveals a good deal about internal State affairs in the Third Reich. During *Amt* IV B 4's meeting on 6 March 1942 Eichmann had announced with regret that 'under the eleventh order [of the Reich Citizenship Act of 25 November 1941], Jewish assets could no longer be considered as accruing to the RSHA' (because, under that order, they were to accrue to the State). However, according to his evidence at his trial at Jerusalem, the 'device' of the emigration tax had at once occurred to him – that is to say he had caused the victims of the deportation orders to be 'invited' through his agency, the Reich Union for German Jews, to surrender 25 per cent of their liquid assets to the Union before deportation as a contribution to the cost of supplying the transports with food and other necessities of life. The sums paid over in this way were to be placed in a 'Special Account W' which (as Eichmann had explained to the meeting on 6 March) would be 'put to the credit of *Referat* IV B 4 of the RSHA'.

In the event, Eichmann was far from satisfied with the results of this probably all too well camouflaged 'device', for he was soon exhorting his colleagues 'to urge the Jews to pay more into Account W. Up to the present – *presumably because of a mistaken belief that the fund is to be used exclusively for the benefit of the Jews* – contributions have been coming in too slowly'.* Meanwhile the 'Vienna Emigration Fund' established by the Central Office (by this time Eichmann and Heydrich) in Austria, and the 'Bohemian and Moravian Emigration Fund' under the control of the local commanders of the Security Police and the SD in the Protectorate were 'taking over' almost all the assets of the Jews affected by deportation orders by insisting that these, as 'persons authorized to dispose of their property' should surrender their power of attorney or make some correspondingly suitable offer, even before the orders became effective.

The directors of these funds could use 'the assets acquired in this way' (as it was phrased in the Reich Minister of Finance's memorandum of December 1942) either at their own 'discretion' or according to 'the instructions of the Chief of the Security Police and the SD' – namely to finance 'those costly measures

*A memorandum of Ministerial Counsellor Maedel of the Reich Ministry of Finance of 14 December 1942, which, in spite of its many reticences, is nevertheless revealing enough, refers to the text of a circular issued by the Central Office of the Reich Union on 3 December 1941: 'The district offices of the Reich Union of German Jews are the bodies authorized to dispose of these funds. ... It must be assumed, however, from what has emerged in the course of several meetings with the representatives of the Reich SS Security Department, that the police departments will, to a large extent, be responsible for how the money is to be spent (payment of transport costs, etc.). The Chief of the Security Police and the SD is exclusively responsible for the supervision of all payments made by the Reich Union.' [My italics.]

... for which no budget was previously available'.

As though this were not enough, the RSHA hit upon the idea of the 'home purchase scheme', whereby the Reich Union of German Jews was required to inform those designated for Theresienstadt that their transfer would mean 'the surrender of all their assets', but that when the time came to emigrate the Reich Union 'both could and would arrange contracts similar to those drawn up in connexion with the home purchase scheme for inmates of old people's homes' – and would, moreover, see to it that the contracts were arranged without delay. Under the scheme the Reich Union would assume financial responsibility for the 'provision of accommodation and welfare facilities, for life'. Against this the emigrants would have to assign the whole or part of their liquid assets (ready money, bank balances, investments and debts owing to them) as 'security'. The RSHA were at pains to insert into the 'declaration of assets for home purchase' form a proviso to the effect that all Jews signing such contracts should be aware that the statement they made as regards their assets in this connexion would not exempt them from providing the *official* declaration of assets required before emigration. Thus the SS, which had so generously renounced its claim to 'a budget' for 'its measures', used its power to steal a march on the responsible State finance department – by plundering those Jews who were still *relatively* wealthy, that is to say, those designated for Theresienstadt.

The form of contract, which as an example of successful deception could hardly be bettered, has been preserved in sufficient numbers to serve as illustrative material. The text of one such contract is given below:

Home Purchase Contract H
No............/............
Between the Reich Union of German Jews
and
Herr Siegfried Israel Klein
the following contract will be binding.

1 *a* Herr Klein, Berlin W 15, Joachimstaler Str. 12, acknowledges:
    That because the Reich Union is under an obligation to defray the costs of communal accommodation in Theresienstadt, including costs incurred on behalf of those with slender means, it is the duty of all persons with disposable assets, who are involved in the communal accommodation scheme to pay to the Reich Union by way of purchase money not only the cost of their own accom-

modation, but such additional sums as are possible to enable assistance to be given to those of slender means.

b Herr Klein......................
Purchases from .... for communal accommodation for the sum of approximately 53,070 RM (Fifty-three thousand and seventy RM)

2 Payment of the purchase money will be made:
  a in cash: DM............................
  b by completed transfer of bank credits and investments – transfer document enclosed herewith.

3 Only objects may be taken into the communal accommodation which are in accordance with official instructions.

4 *a* On completion of the contract the contracting party will, for the duration of his life, be relieved of his liability to pay for accommodation or welfare; laundry facilities, medical care, drugs and medicine, and hospitalization when necessary.
  b The right of the Reich Union to provide accommodation in some other place is reserved.
  c No claim in respect of any change in the form of accommodation provided will be entertained.

5 If, in the event of physical or mental illness on the part of the contracting party(s) or for some other reason, his/their continued participation in the communal accommodation scheme becomes impossible and accommodation in some other place appears desirable, the Reich Union is entitled to take the necessary steps. Similar power may be exercised in cases of serious breaches of the rules of the communal accommodation scheme.

6 *a* On completion of the contract the purchase money becomes the property of the Reich Union.
  b No legal claim for the repayment of the purchase money is permissible even following the death of the contracting party or because the contract is cancelled for other reasons.

(Place) 1943	(Place) Berlin, 7 June 1943
	Siegfried Israel Klein
Reich Union of German Jews	Signature of the contracting
District Office	Party(s)
....	
Jewish Union of Public	Code Word: Berlin
Worship and Instruction	
	Registration number: A 480 318
....	Address: W. 15, Joachimstaler
	Str. 12
....	....
(Signature) (Signature)	

It is easy to imagine the feelings of those who had signed

contracts like this in good faith when they saw with their own eyes in Theresienstadt what their purchase money – often amounting to several hundred thousand Reichsmarks – had actually bought in the way of accommodation (paragraph 4c!) which the Reich Union expressly 'reserved' the right to change for something worse.

The problem of what to do about 'half-breeds and mixed marriages' was also exhaustively discussed at the Wannsee Conference, but no definite conclusions were reached. Although the extremists in the Party inclined to the view that even 'half-breeds of the first generation' and the Jewish partner in a mixed marriage should be included in the extermination programme, further discussion yielded 'suggestions for compromises' – such as 'voluntary' sterilization of half-breeds (or the threat of deportation to, at least, a 'half-breed settlement'), and obligatory divorce in the case of mixed marriages.* In the event, as much because of the far-reaching consequences and technical difficulties involved in enforcing them during the war, as because of the opposition to them voiced by some sections of the civil service, all the suggestions (deportation, sterilization and obligatory divorce) were dropped. There were certain exceptions, of course, particularly in the concentration camps where any half-Jews, who happened to be among the inmates, were expressly included by the RSHA in November 1942 in the liquidation programme.†

As far as the achievement of the 'final solution' in the countries occupied by Germany or within the German sphere of

---

*To the argument put forward by von Stuckart and Losener that if half-Jews were deported, the half of them that was German in origin would turn against Germany, the Minister for the Eastern Territories objected (on 16 July 1942) that fears of this sort were wholly unjustified as far as the occupied territories in the east were concerned, since he had given instructions that half-Jews were to be treated in every respect in the same way as the wholly Jewish – that is to say, they were to be subjected to the same anti-Jewish measures. (Nuremberg Document NG 2586.)

†The circular issued by Müller on 5 November 1942 repeated Himmler's instructions that all Jews in concentration camps in the Reich were to be transferred to the concentration camp at Auschwitz or the prisoner-of-war forced labour camp at Lublin. ... 'In this context half-breeds of the first generation will be treated as Jewish.' (Nuremberg Document NO 2522 – see also PS 3676 5th October 1942. Photocopy in the Institut für Zeitgeschichte, Munich.)

influence* was concerned, it was agreed at the Wannsee Conference that there should be close cooperation between the RSHA and the Ministry of Foreign Affairs, in particular with the latter's German Section. The more violently anti-Jewish the National Socialist leadership became, the more it strove to bring its satellites and 'friends' to the same way of thinking – so much so that the severity of anti-Jewish measures adopted in these countries came to be regarded as the measure of their loyalty. Every effort was made, through the offices of the diplomatic representatives of the Reich, to drive them along the path of persecution by the usual stages – discriminatory laws and definitions (the term 'Jew'), distinguishing marks, confiscation of property, and, if possible, concentration camps – until the time was ripe to ask the particular government in power whether it would prefer 'to recall its Jewish nationals from the Reich, within a given time limit' or 'to agree to have them removed to ghettos in the east'. If these tactics were successful and it was practicable to arrange the 'resettlement of the Jews' (as it was still euphemistically called) from the countries in question,† Eichmann came into the picture. Through the agency of the 'Jewish specialists' [*Judenberater*] seconded from his department to the relevant German embassies – and in the occupied territories, through the 'Jewish Desks' [*Judenreferenten*] attached to the BdS – Eichmann himself, together with his transport specialist, Novak, and the competent traffic control officials, set the deportations in motion. Eichmann, who was certainly a conscientious official but was obsessed with his mission to fight the Jews, developed within

*Listed roughly in the order of the extent to which German influence or diplomatic pressure governed their attitude to the Jewish question, these were – at the beginning of 1942: Croatia, Slovakia, Roumania, Vichy France, Bulgaria, Hungary and Italy (the chief opponent of the liquidation of the Jews).

† In the case of Slovakia – as a 'second' step to which the most careful consideration had been given – it fell to the RSHA,'on instructions from the *Reichsführer-SS* to the Foreign Office', to request the Slovak government to make available 20,000 strong young Slovak Jews ['for labour assignments'!]. When the Slovak government 'gladly agreed' [before the episcopate had protested and 35,000 Jews had received 'special exemption'], the *Reichsführer-SS* suggested that the remaining Slovak Jews 'might be deported to the east so that Slovakia could be cleansed of Jews'. (Report of Under State Secretary, Luther, of 21 August 1942. Nuremberg Document NG 2586.) Also Hilberg, *op. cit.* pp. 345 *et seq.*

the framework of his widespread powers a high degree of personal initiative not least in the form of deception tactics of the most evil kind.

4   The final solution in Poland

The chronological order of the 'final solution' in the regions was also discussed at the Wannsee Conference. No sooner had Heydrich proposed that priority should be given, at least as far as deportations were concerned, to Reich territory including the Protectorate (as Hitler wished),[40] than State Secretary Bühler intervened, suggesting, as a matter of urgency, that it would be better to begin with the removal (elimination) of the Jews from the Government General. His reasons were instructive: 'first, the transport problem would not be so serious there', so that difficulties about 'the deployment of labour (so important to the war effort, as State Secretary Neumann had stressed) would be less likely to obstruct the smooth running of the operation! Moreover, most of the Jews were "unfit for work", and for this reason – in the Government General anyway – they could represent a real danger (packed into the ghettos as they were) as carriers of disease or exponents of the black market.'

Exactly five weeks earlier, on 16 December 1941, the authorities in the Government General had been discussing the outbreak of spotted fever around Warsaw, and had come to the conclusion that the large number of cases must be due to 'lack of resistance' ... particularly among the Jews, and that this in turn must be ascribed to the fact that they were undernourished and crowded together in ghettos ('a blessing in itself'!). The only way out was a simplification of the 'far too lengthy' procedure of the special courts in imposing 'liquidation' for 'leaving the ghettos without permission'.[41] This had given Frank an opportunity to make the following observations about the introduction of the 'final solution'.

'Something will have to be done, one way or another – and I make no bones about it – to settle this business of the Jews ... I know that many of the present anti-Jewish measures in the Reich are being criticized and I am aware from the reports on morale that there is repeated talk of cruelty, harshness and so forth. I want to ask you to join with me now, before I say anything else, in one formula – basically our sympathy lies with the German people alone and with no other in the world. I ask nothing of the Jews except that they should disappear. They will have to go. I myself have been involved in the business of deporting them to the East. A full-scale conference on this subject is taking place in Berlin in January to which I am sending State Secretary Bühler. The conference will be held in the office of *SS-Obergruppenführer* Heydrich in the *Reichssicherheitshauptamt*.' [Frank was referring to the Wannsee Conference of 20. 1. 42.]

The least we can expect is that a large-scale Jewish migration will begin.

But what is going to happen to the Jews? Do you really believe they are going to be quartered in settler's villages in the Ostland? In Berlin people have said to us: Why do we go to all this trouble? There's nothing we can do with them in the Ostland or the *Reichskommissariat* either – let the dead bury their dead! Gentlemen, I must ask you to arm yourselves against all considerations of pity. We must destroy the Jews wherever we meet them and whenever opportunity offers so that we can maintain the whole structure of the Reich here. . . . The Jews batten on to us to an exceptionally damaging extent.* At a rough estimate we have in the Government General about 2.5 million people with Jewish connexions, and on top of that – and this is the point – we now have 3.5 million Jews.† We can't shoot these 3.5 million Jews, and we can't poison them, but we can take steps which, one way or another, will lead to extermination, in conjunction with the large-scale measures under discussion in the Reich. The Government General must be as free of Jews as the Reich itself.

In view of the number of Jews still living in what was formerly Poland – where a greater number of them had settled than anywhere else in Europe – shooting would certainly have been inadequate. It would also have been impractical if, as Bühler had been warned, care was to be taken 'to avoid upsetting the local population'. The search for ways of achieving 'the desired

*As opposed to this, at a government session [*Regierungssitzung*] on 9 December 1942, Frank said: 'The disappearance of our old-established Jewish community has divested us of not inconsiderable labour forces. There is no doubt that our production programme will suffer if, in the middle of it, an order comes through that the Jews are to be removed for extermination. But we in the Government General are not responsible for this. The order for the extermination of the Jews comes from higher up.'

†This figure was greatly exaggerated. Hilberg, *op. cit.* p. 309; Reitlinger, *op. cit.* p. 274.

result' led in the first instance to the idea that it might be possible to profit from the experience gained in getting rid of the mentally sick in the *Altreich*, using the methods adopted at the time of what was called the 'Euthanasia Programme'. This exercise (which involved the use of gas chambers filled with carbon monoxide gas) was directed from the 'Führer's Chancellery' by Philip Bouhler – whose office at *Tiergartenstrasse* 4 was known as the 'Euthanasia Centre' ['T4'] – and organized by Bouhler's deputy, *Oberdienstleiter* Brack. It is significant that already in the first operations against the mentally ill in institutions the registration forms sent to those concerned required them to state their 'race' and the 'nature of their employment' as a means of identification.

Owing to the failure to keep the true nature of the exercise a secret, and because of courageous opposition – particularly on the part of the Church – Hitler, who shied away from the idea of issuing a statutory order, allowed the proceedings to lapse in August 1941. After a while, however, its place was taken by a 'Euthanasia Operation' – known as 14f13 – launched in the concentration camps against the mentally sick (a term which was interpreted in a fairly broad sense),* other chronically sick prisoners and, in particular, those 'unfit for work', as selected by a medical commission. After some sort of a preliminary check inside the camp, the selected prisoners were given 'registration forms' and taken before visiting members of the medical commission for further examination. Then – after a final selection had been made at the commission's headquarters in Berlin, they were allocated to one of the 'Euthanasia Stations in the Reich' (Bernburg, for instance). Priority was given to 'politically undesirable elements'† and, in particular, to the Jews‡ – since this tied up with the 'final solution' which was already under way.

Later Jewish prisoners considered 'fit to work' were given a

*Brack's testimony in the Doctors' Trial, Nuremberg, Case I.
†In a report sent in by the camp commandant on the total number of prisoners dispatched by the head of the maximum security section of the concentration camp, Gross Rosenburg, in one transport (to Euthanasia Stations), a number of Poles and Czechs were also included. Nuremberg Document PS 1151. (Photocopy in the Institut für Zeitgeschichte, Munich.)
‡A letter accompanying the above report stated: '70 prisoners from the camp area and 104 from the special blocks were selected.' But as regarded Jewish prisoners, simply 'Jews – 119 prisoners'.

short reprieve and no longer executed out of hand,* but what happened to them in the early days under Operation 14f13 is shown in a letter written from Buchenwald by one of the doctors on the selection panel – Dr Mennecke – to his wife on 25 November 1941:

> 'The next contingent consisted of about 1,200 Jews, who were not put through any preliminary test. All we had to do was to copy the reasons for their arrest (plenty of them, as a rule) from the reports on to the forms. Simply paper work. . . .'[42]

It was not only the methods and technical contrivances that had been developed during the euthanasia campaign in the Reich that were turned to good account in putting the 'final solution' in the East into effect; the personnel who had gained useful experience were also recalled. The first time this happened was in the extermination camp Chelmno [Kulmhof] am Ner, sixty kilometres north-west of Lodz, where operations started in December 1941: here a *Sonderkommando* under the command of *SS-Hauptsturmführer* Lange – and later under *SS-Hauptsturmführer* Bothmann [until March 1943 and again during several months of 1944] – murdered at least 152,000 Jews (probably considerably more) from the *Warthegau* and the ghetto at Lodz (Litzmannstadt), 'helped' by a Jewish labour squad who were subsequently shot. The murders were carried out by 'exhaust gas' in gas trucks (mobile gas chambers) into which the victims were enticed with false promises – or driven with whips, if the first device failed.† *Kriminal Kommissar* [eventually *Polizeimajor*] Wirth was another who had participated in the implementation of the euthanasia programme in the Reich and was subsequently given a senior appointment in the extermination camps in the Government General.[43] 'On *Reichsleiter* Bouhler's instructions,' wrote Brack to Himmler on 23 June 1942, 'I transferred some of my men to *Brigadeführer* Globocnik in connexion with his special duties some time ago.

---

*The medical commission selected 81 of the 119 Jewish prisoners sent forward in January 1942 – and spared 38. In March the camp authorities themselves took '42 Jews fit for work' out of one contingent. On the other hand, at the beginning of 1942, Himmler issued an order that 'all the concentration camps in the Reich are to be cleared of Jews'.

†According to witnesses in the Kulmhof Trial, held in Bonn in 1963.

At his request I have now transferred additional personnel.'* Globocnik's own report to the head of the SS Personnel Department [*SS-Personalhauptamtes*] of 29 October 1943 stated that a total strength of 92[44] had been put at his disposal by 'the Führer's Chancellery for the execution of Operation Reinhard' – the name given to the mass measures directed by Globocnik for the extermination of the Jews in the Government General. Before Wirth's special sections were despatched, Himmler (according to the testimony of the SS judge, Dr Morgen) is supposed to have asked each of them, personally, to swear an oath of silence and to have told them: 'I have to expect of you superhuman acts of inhumanity. But it is the Führer's will.'[45]

The draft of a ministerial memorandum of 25 October 1941, written by a senior official in the Ministry for the Eastern Territories, *Amtsgerichtsrat* Dr Wetzel, provides a particularly clear picture of the relationship between those engaged in the practical execution of the 'final solution' and the administrative departments, as well as of early discussions on the subject and preliminary plans. The memorandum was written to the Reich Commissioner for Ostland (Lohse) and reads as follows:[46]

From: The Reich Minister for the Occupied Eastern Territories
      Controller: *AGR* Dr Wetzel
Ref. The solution of the Jewish Question.
1 To: The Reich Commissioner for Ostland
    Ref. Your report of 4. 10. 41 concerning the solution of the Jewish question.
With reference to my letter of 18 October 1941, I have now to inform you that *Oberdienstleiter* Brack of the Führer's Chancellery has agreed to collaborate in the manufacture of the necessary buildings and gas apparatus. The latter is at present in short supply, and production must be stepped up. As Brack is of the opinion that the manufacture of the apparatus will lead to much greater difficulties in the Reich than on the spot, he considers that it would be most useful to send some of his people – in particular his analytical chemist, Dr Kallmeyer – to Riga immediately to assume responsibility for all further developments. *Oberdienstleiter* Brack points out that there will be a certain amount of danger attached to the future proceedings and that special safety precautions will be required. In these circumstances I would ask you to apply to *Oberdienstleiter* Brack at the Führer's Chancellery,

*In a letter to *SS-Gruppenführer* von Herff [Head of the SS Personnel Department] of 13 April 1942, Globocnik describes Wirth as 'the inspector responsible for the camps at Belzec, Sobibor and Treblinka'. (Original in the Document Centre, Berlin.)

through your *Höhere SS und Polizeiführer* for the secondment of Dr Kallmeyer and such other assistance as you may require. In this connexion I have to inform you that *Sturmbannführer* Eichmann, who is in charge of the Jewish question at the *Reichssicherheitshauptampt* is in agreement with this procedure. He tells me that camps for Jews are to be established in Riga and in Minsk, to which Jews from the Altreich will eventually be sent. For the present Jews from the Altreich will be evacuated to Litzmannstadt and other camps, and those who are 'fit for work' subsequently transferred further east for use as labour.

In our present position we cannot afford to have scruples about taking advantage of Brack's facilities for the elimination of Jews who are not fit for work, as these will provide a way of avoiding any possible recurrence of the events which occurred, according to a report I have in front of me, at the shooting of the Jews in Vilna. Incidentally, I see from the report that the shootings took place in public, which can hardly have been approved.

Jews fit for work, on the other hand, are to be transferred further east for use as labour. It goes without saying that the men are to be separated from the women.

Please forward a report on your latest measures.

N[ame] of the M[inister]

In the meantime, extermination operations were in full swing in the Polish territories, although not in the Baltic States. The establishment of the camp at Chelmno was followed in the middle of March 1942 by the opening of another extermination camp at Belzec in the then Lublin district. This was the first camp to be equipped with *permanent gas chambers* – although, as always, every possible precaution was taken to conceal the fact.

Until December 1942 (possibly with an interruption of several weeks, due to technical difficulties) hundreds of thousands of Jews were despatched to this camp – in large contingents from the ghettos in the Lublin, Galizia and Cracow districts and in smaller parties, mainly from the Protectorate. They were murdered by exhaust gas from internal-combustion engines. According to Kurt Gerstein, whose well-known report on Belzec is in our possession, one of the few survivors (Rudolf Reder) once witnessed how the victims, who had already been packed into the gas chambers, were kept waiting for their death for hours because of failure in the diesel engine that delivered the gas – and presumably this frequently happened.[47] After the camp was cleared a Jewish special squad was employed, as on other occasions, to remove all traces of the operation.

A smaller extermination camp – where operations did not begin until October 1943 (because the labour squads mutinied) – was opened in May 1942 at Sobibor am Bug, also in the Lublin district. The number of its victims – who came from east Poland, the occupied Soviet Russian territories, Czechoslovakia, Austria, Holland and France – is estimated at over 250,000. The camp at Treblinka, near Malkinia am Bug (again in the Lublin district) – which was opened on 23 July 1942 and continued in operation until the autumn of 1943 when it was closed following a revolt staged by the prisoners in August – proved an even more efficient instrument of destruction. Polish estimates put the figures of those murdered here also by exhaust gas at between 700,000 and 800,000 Jews from central Poland (Warsaw) and the districts round Bialystok, and from Germany, Austria, Czechoslovakia, Holland, Belgium and Greece. In Treblinka – in pursuance of the policy of concealing the true nature of the operations – a carefully constructed model of a railway station complete with waiting rooms and other amenities was built.

The inmates of Majdanek – a large (and eventually 'official')* concentration camp in the neighbourhood of Lublin – were not condemned to instant execution; it appears that gas chambers were not installed there until the autumn of 1942. Like the camp at Plaszow in the Cracow district, which was officially designated a concentration camp in 1944, Majdanek was, in the main, a forced labour settlement, based on the mass exploitation of Jewish prisoners in imitation of the 'Osti' [Ostindustrie GmbH]† Centre of the SS industrial undertakings, initiated by Globocnik (see p. 88). Most of the prisoners came from Poland (especially from the Warsaw and Lublin ghettos), Soviet Russia, Czechoslovakia, France, Greece and Germany. Apart from those who were literally worked to death – a favourite method of extermination which accounted for the majority of Jews (well over 200,000 of them) who had been forcibly removed to Majdanek – tens of thousands were gassed or shot both inside and outside the camp, including some who were never even registered or were never admitted to the camp at all. Since none of the camps I have mentioned, except Majdanek, had crematoria, the mass

*Until 9 April 1943 it was officially known as a 'Prisoner-of-war Labour Camp'.
†Eastern Territories Industries Inc.

graves were subsequently opened and the corpses burnt in incinerators made out of railway lines.

In the meantime operations had started at the extermination centre attached to the camp at Birkenau. Until November 1943 and again from the end of November 1944, this formed part of the Auschwitz concentration camp; even by itself it represented the largest of all the National Socialist concentration camps. It served at one and the same time as an extermination centre and as a centre for the industrial exploitation of the (mainly Jewish) prisoners, as long as these were fit for work. Jews from Poland, Slovakia, the Protectorate (Theresienstadt!), France, Belgium, Holland, Germany, Croatia, Greece, and eventually Hungary in particular, were deported to Auschwitz-Birkenau. The camp was an outstanding example of the 'European' character of the extermination programme – which for their own good reasons the authorities preferred to put into effect outside the countries of origin of the victims, except as far as the eastern territories and Serbia were concerned.

When the transports arrived at Birkenau, the infamous 'selection' procedure was set in train to separate those to be transferred to the camp as 'fit for work' from those destined for the gas chambers – most of whom were not even registered.* Himmler did not order gassing to stop until 2 November 1944. Its victims included gypsies, Poles and Soviet Russian prisoners-of-war as well as Jews.

The special function of Auschwitz within the framework of the 'final solution' has been described by its first and best-known commandant, Rudolf Höss, in his autobiographical notes:

In the summer of 1941 – it is difficult to be more precise after all this time – I suddenly heard that the *Reichsführer-SS* wished to see me; the message was brought by his adjutant in person. Contrary to his usual practice he dismissed his adjutant before confiding in me as follows: the Führer has ordered the solution of the Jewish problem. We – the SS – are to be responsible for carrying out this order. The extermination stations in the east are inadequate for the task on the vast scale envisaged. I have therefore decided that Auschwitz is to be used for the purpose, first because it is favourably placed as regards technical communications, and secondly because it will be easy to close

*It was decided that prisoners from Theresienstadt, who were allocated to the gas chambers, but not immediately, should be allowed to write postcards to Theresienstadt, in order to counter any rumours that might have been spread.

off and camouflage the area. .... *Sturmbannführer* Eichmann of the RSHA, who will shortly be coming to see you, will give you further details.[48]

Höss, to whom Eichmann explained that 'the use of carbon monoxide gas for despatching the mass transports expected' was 'quite out of the question', as he had seen for himself during his inspection of 'the whole process' at Treblinka, searched round for a new method of destruction. After 'successful' experiments carried out in his absence by his *Schutzhaftlager-führer*, Fritzch, 'on his own initiative', and after Höss himself had tested it on camp prisoners and Russian prisoners-of-war, he reported that he had decided, with Eichmann's agreement, to use Zyklon B – a prussic acid, 'that we are now using to destroy vermin in the camp and is thus in plentiful supply'.* From thenceforth it was used to destroy men – at first (after the 'experiments' in the detention cells of Block 11 at the base camp at Auschwitz) in the mortuary cellars of the first crematorium in the base camp, then in hutments in the neighbourhood of the camp at Birkenau, and finally in the gas compartments of the new crematoria that were erected there.†

A letter of 29 January 1943 from the director of the central works department of the *Waffen-SS* and Police at Auschwitz to the Head of *Amtsgruppe* C (Building) of the SS WVHA, *SS-Brigadeführer* Dr Kammler, describes the construction of one of these new extermination buildings (which, incidentally, was not completed by the expected date):

By making use of all available labour, work on Crematorium II has been completed, save for a few constructional details – and this in spite of every sort of difficulty, and temperatures below freezing day and night. The ovens were fired by the chief engineer of the firm that did the work – Topf & Sons of Erfurt – during his tour of inspection, and they functioned perfectly. Due to the frost it has not been possible to complete the reinforced concrete roof of the mortuary cellars, but this is of minor importance as we can use the gas cellars instead.

Topf & Sons have not been able to deliver the ventilation plant on the date specified by the central works department. As soon as it is delivered, it will, of course, be installed, and we anticipate that

*Höss also wrote: 'It is true that none of us thought of questioning the Führer's orders. ... But we were all prey to secret doubts.'

†In addition thousands of sick prisoners, those who had become 'unfit for work' or were suspected of being 'carriers of disease' were murdered by injections of Phenol; others were shot; others again lost their lives as a result of being used for 'medical' experiments.

everything will be in full working order by 20. 2. 43.*

As the murder campaign in Poland gathered momentum Himmler became ever more firmly convinced that speed was essential 'if the true nature of the proceedings were not to become known'; Globocnik shared this opinion, 'so that we don't get stuck in the middle of it one day'.[49] Himmler betrayed his anxiety on this point by his continual insistence on the need to accelerate the programme and to maintain absolute secrecy – an insistence which involved him in a bitter struggle to overcome obstacles such as those represented by transport shortages and the need for Jewish labour in the war economy. By early 1942 'resettlement' (as extermination was called) was in full swing. Under the code name 'Operation' or 'Mission Reinhard', it was directed in the Government General and the Bialystok region by Globocnik, the Lublin *SS und Polizeiführer*, who appointed *Polizeihauptmann* Wirth 'inspector' for the three extermination camps.[50]

The object of the operation, as specified by Globocnik, was four-fold: (*a*) the resettlement programme itself, (*b*) the acquisition of manpower for the labour force, (*c*) the acquisition of resources, and (*d*) the confiscation of hidden valuables and real estate.† What it was achieving must have been quite clear

*Nuremberg Document NO 4473. (Photocopy in the Institut für Zeitgeschichte, Munich.) A further letter from the director of the central works department of the *Waffen-SS* and Police at Auschwitz on 31 March 1943 to the German Armaments Works Inc. [SS industrial undertakings] Auschwitz, stated: 'This is to let you know that we are still awaiting delivery of the three gasproof towers ordered on 18 January 1943 for Bw 30b and 30c; these should be exactly the same size and shape as those already delivered.' The note also mentioned an order placed on 6 March for a gasproof door, 100/192, for mortuary I of Crematorium III 'which should be exactly the same size and shape as that installed in Crematorium II, with a similar "spy-hole" made of double 8 mm. glass with rubber surround and metal fittings. This order must be regarded as urgent.' Nuremberg Document NO 4465. (Photocopy in the Institut für Zeitgeschichte, Munich.)

†Minute to Himmler on 5 January 1944, with an appendix. Nuremberg Document NO 064 and 057. (Photocopy in the Institut für Zeitgeschichte, Munich.) In a previous situation report from the headquarters of Operation Reinhard, 15 December 1943, Globocnik had estimated that 'cash and valuables, including textiles (a total of 1,901 truck-loads)' accruing to the Reich from this operation amounted to approximately 178,745,960,59 RM. A minute from Himmler to the Head of the SS Economics and Administrative Department of the previous January had posed the significant question: 'What is the total amount of textiles we have delivered to the Reich Ministry of Economics as a result of the resettlement of the Jews?'

to those in the know from a suggestion put forward by the President of the Board of Food and Agriculture [*Hauptabteilung Ernährung und Landwirtschaft*] at a meeting of Heads of Departments in the Government General on 24 August 1942:

Supplies for the existing populace, whose numbers have been swelled by the arrival of 1.5 million Jews, should cease. The 300,000 Jews who are working as labourers or in some other capacity in the German interest should be issued with the rations specified for Jews, augmented as may be necessary from time to time to maintain their working capacity. The rest of the Jews, who number some 1.2 million, should no longer be issued with foodstuffs of any kind.

To this Governor-General Frank, who liked to pose in public as a 'strong' man, added the following vague, but pertinent comment: 'It is purely incidental if we condemn 1.2 million Jews to starve to death. We naturally hope that this can be avoided by speeding up the anti-Jewish measures.'

The measures themselves were the subject of an entry in Goebbels' diary on 27 March 1942:

Starting with Lublin, the deportation of the Jews from the Government General to the east has been set in train. It is a pretty barbarous business – one would not wish to go into details – and there are not many Jews left. I should think one could reckon that about 60 per cent of them have been liquidated and about 40 per cent taken for forced labour. The former *Gauleiter* of Vienna [Globocnik], who is in charge of the operation, is carrying it out with a good deal of circumspection, and his methods do not seem to be attracting much publicity. . . . One simply cannot be sentimental about these things. . . . The Führer is the moving spirit of this radical solution both in word and deed. . . .[51]

The deportations began again, on an ever-increasing scale,[52] in July 1942, after a number of difficulties connected with transport shortages due to military requirements had been ironed out in June, and essential repair work on the line to Sobibor had been completed in July. As Ganzenmüller, the State Secretary in the Reich Ministry of Transport, informed the head of Himmler's personal staff, *SS-Obergruppenführer* Wolff, in his notorious letter: 'a train containing 5,000 Jews has been leaving Warsaw for Treblinka every day since 22. 7; in addition a train containing 5,000 Jews has been leaving Przemysl for Belzec twice a week.'

The clearance of the Warsaw ghetto actually began on the same day – an order having been issued to the Jewish Council that it was to see to it that 'as from 22. 7. 42, 6,000 Jews are assembled at the collection point every day not later than 16 hours'. In spite of the fact that all who were fit for work and had 'not yet been conscripted for labour service' were at first exempted from resettlement [instead they were herded with their families into Jewish 'neighbourhoods'], the number of men, women and children deported (as the operation got into its stride) reached a final total of 310,322.[53]

On the previous 17 July, Krüger, the HSSPF *Ost*, had informed General Schindler, the Inspector of Armaments [*Rüstungsinspekteur*] in the Government General, that the ghettos were to be cleared. Hitler, in accordance with the National Socialist practice of granting special powers to the police, had appointed Krüger State Secretary for Security in the Government General in the May of that year. Whereupon on 3 June 1942, Governor-General Frank, who had by this time given up all attempts to unify the administration, handed over all 'matters appertaining to the Jews' to Krüger (who, for all practical purposes was now in charge of the 'final solution' in the area) as being 'within the jurisdiction of the security police'. The affair reached its logical conclusion on 25 June 1942 when the head of the Administration Department in the Government General issued a ruling to the effect that 'Jews are not be to drafted for forced labour without the previous consent of the competent [*SS und*] *Polizeiführer* in the area'. A long-drawn-out battle over who was the competent authority – a question of considerable importance in view of the 'security' precautions surrounding the decision to include all the Jews in the extermination programme – thus ended in a resounding victory for the security police. The uncontrolled employment of Jews by private German firms and ordnance factories had long been a thorn in the flesh of the police and no doubt accounted for the general ruling that the 'whole question of Jewish labour' was to be withdrawn from the administration (which had shown itself to be too easy-going) and taken over by the *SS und Polizeiführer*.

Katzmann, the local *SS und Polizeiführer*, observed indignantly 'the military authorities are the worst ... they have actually abetted the Jewish parasites by issuing special passes without any sort of check', adding that now that all passes had to be examined 'most employers felt obliged as to intervene on behalf of the (arrested) Jews'.[54] On 17 July Krüger told General

Schindler that the ordnance factories could keep their Jewish workers 'for the time being', on condition that control of these workers was transferred to the SS and that the workers themselves were 'interned' either within the factory precincts or in adjacent barracks erected for the purpose.[55] The next step would be the transfer of all ordnance factories employing Jewish workers to the SS. How much Himmler disliked these compromises and with what reservations he accepted them is clear from the instructions that he sent to Krüger from Lublin on 19 July 1942 – two days after he had been a 'speechless' spectator in Auschwitz-Birkenau at 'the whole extermination process as it affected a transport of Jews which had just arrived', and had roundly declared that the 'security precautions' he had ordered 'were not to be brought to a halt for any reason whatsoever'.*

I hereby decree that the resettlement of the whole Jewish population of the General Government is to be completed by 31 December 1942. After 31 December no one of Jewish origin will be allowed to live in the Government General. They will have to live in collecting camps [*Sammellager*] in Warsaw, Cracow, Tschenstochau, Radom and Lublin. By the same date, any undertaking employing Jewish labour must be wound up or, if this proves impossible, transferred to a collecting camp.

These measures are essential if the ethnical division of races and peoples contemplated in the new order in Europe is to be accomplished, and the safety and racial purity of the Reich and its satellites assured. Any relaxation of this ruling would constitute a threat to law and order in the territories under German sovereignty, would provide a rallying point for the forces of resistance, and would serve as a centre of contagion, both morally and physically.

Total purification is necessary on all these grounds and must therefore be achieved. If it is anticipated that for any reason the date line cannot be met, I must be informed at once so that I can arrange to send additional assistance in good time. All attempts by other departments to make changes in the programme, or to approve exceptions, will be reported to me personally.'[56]

*'If for no other reason, because I have no means of housing the people sent to me, Eichmann's programme is to go ahead and to be speeded up month by month. You must make every effort to see that progress is made with building at Birkenau. The gypsies must be exterminated. Likewise all Jews unfit for work – and without further delay. The first large contingent of Jews fit for work will shortly be sent to the ordnance factories, which will give you more room. An ordnance factory is to be built in Auschwitz itself, so you should make all due preparations.' A conversation with Himmler from *Commandant at Auschwitz. Autobiographical Notes of Rudolf Höss*, edited by M. Broszat (Stuttgart, 1958), pp. 177 and 179.

The greater the efforts of the *Gauleiter* of Thuringia, *Gauleiter* Sauckel [the Commissioner General for the Employment of Labour – *Generalbevollmächtiger für den Arbeitseinsatz* – responsible for the conscription of foreign labour for the war industries of the Reich] to draft Poles from the Government General, the more the war industries in that territory were obliged to rely on their Jewish employees. The labour shortage was aggravated by the fact that Himmler interpreted any agreements that had been drawn up in the narrowest possible sense. It is true that Jews employed by the military authorities or under the direct orders of the OKW Armaments Inspectorate [*Rüstungsinspektion*] in 'ordnance factories certified as such,'[57] were usually spared for the time being; but all others, even if they were employed by the military authorities in the Reich or the Government General on work of equal importance to the war effort or in private firms (for instance, in clothing or repair workshops, in roofing-felt factories, and so forth), were forcibly removed for resettlement in increasing numbers – more often than not without any advance notice to the military authorities concerned. Protests by the *Rüstungsinspektion* were useless. In a discussion on the subject between officials of the inspectorate and Krüger's representatives on 14 August 1942 in Cracow, the latter went so far as to quote Göring:*

The Reich Marshal's view is that the Jews must not be considered indispensable. Neither the *Rüstungsinspektion* nor any other department would be able to keep their Jewish employees until the end of the war. The orders issued were quite definite and clear-cut, and were valid not only for the Government General, but also for all the other occupied countries. The reasons for them must be of a quite exceptional nature. In these circumstances it would not be worth while to train Jews as skilled workers. Where the employment of Jews was absolutely essential, the case must be submitted for decision through the HSSPF to the *Reichsführer-SS* and Head of the German Police.

It is true that the SS agreed at this conference to certain

*Hilberg, *op. cit.* p. 236 quotes a report from the liaison officer of the Economics and Armaments Department of the OKW attached to the Reich Marshal as stating that, on 14 August 1941, Göring had declared that 'the Jews in the countries occupied by Germany are finished'; in so far as they might be needed for work, they would be 'formed into labour battalions and interned in some sort of a labour prison camp'. On 12 September Keitel forbade the 'employment of individual Jews by the *Wehrmacht* in any sort of privileged auxiliary service of any kind', decreeing that they might be employed 'only' in 'labour camps established for the purpose'.

compromises. Thus Jews in the Warsaw ghetto, 'employed in *Rüstungsinspektion* enterprises were rounded up in a special "war industry" ghetto', apart from 'other Jews'. The 'same regulation' was brought into force for Warsaw ghetto undertakings working for the Military Commander* in the Government General, which were 'to be amalgamated for this purpose'. In addition, General von Gienanth, the *Wehrkreis* Commander, could, in individual cases, obtain Krüger's agreement to the continued employment of Jews working in particular war industries. In a number of towns, including Galizia, according to a report of the L. of C. Commander, Lemberg, Jews working for the *Wehrmacht* had already been interned. In general, however, resettlement went ahead without advance notice and without taking military interests into account, despite renewed protests on the part of the authorities. On 5 September 1942 Keitel issued a categorical order that substitutes were to be found for all Jewish workers in Poland.

Faced with this situation, General Gienanth, conscious of the 'practical arguments' he could bring to his defence, made up his mind to act. His L. of C. Commanders (and the competent civilian authorities) had told him that it would be impossible to carry out Keitel's order because no Polish substitutes were available; they had also told him that the police measures had led to a sharp falling-off in production and were indirectly threatening supplies to the front. On 18 September 1942, therefore, he sent the following minute to OKW Operations Staff:[58]

1 The following orders for the Government General have been issued to date
  i Polish and Ukrainian workers will be replaced by Jews, so that the former can be released for work in the Reich; the undertakings affected will create camps for Jewish workers.
  ii Undertakings employing Jews wholly or in part will be established, so that Jewish labour may be fully utilized in the war effort.
The removal of the Jews, in the majority of cases without advance notice to the *Wehrmacht*, has caused serious redeployment problems and delays in current production. Work for the SS, urgently required before the onset of winter, is unlikely to be completed by due date.

*On 15 July 1942 the official title of the Military Commander had been reduced in respect of his powers to that of Commander of the Military District (*Wehrkreisbefehlshaber*) Government General.

2 It may prove possible to replace a certain number of unskilled workers, if the Commissioner General for the Employment of Labour is willing to release the 140,000 Poles designated for work in the Reich, and if we are successful in getting police cooperation. Previous experience leads us to doubt this.

The employment of trainees at present in government technical colleges as skilled workers would be possible only on a very limited scale. Skilled workers must first be trained and training – taking agriculture as one of the main examples – may last from several months to a year, and even longer in the case of highly qualified workers and craftsmen.

Whether the solution of this peculiarly complex problem –upon which the maintenance of the efficiency of the Government General in the war economy depends absolutely – can be hastened by the release of skilled workers from the Reich, is beyond my competence to judge.

3 According to the figures provided by the Central Labour Office [*Hauptabteilung Arbeit*], manpower in industry now totals over a million, of which 300,000 are Jews – 100,000 of them skilled workers. In those undertakings working exclusively for the *Wehrmacht*, the number of Jewish skilled workers varies between 25 and 100 per cent of the total labour force; in the textile factories producing winter clothing, it amounts to 100 per cent. In other undertakings, as, for example, the important motor manufacturing works which produces the '*Furhman*' and the '*Pleskau*' models, the majority of platers and wheelwrights are Jewish. The harness-makers, with few exceptions, are all Jews.

A total of 27,000 are at present employed by private firms engaged in re-conditioning uniforms – of which 22,000 (97 per cent) are Jews. Some 16,000 of them are textile and leather-work craftsmen. One wholly Jewish enterprise, with 168 employees, is engaged in processing spare parts. All the factories producing equipment in the Government General, the Ukraine, and, to some extent, in the Reich itself, are dependent on this enterprise.

4 The immediate removal of the Jews would cause a considerable reduction in Germany's war potential and supplies to the front and to the troops in the Government General would at least be held up for the time being.

  i A serious drop in production in the armaments industry of between 25 and 100 per cent would occur.

  ii There would be an average decrease in efficiency of some 25 per cent in the M.T. vehicle repair workshops – that is to say, a drop of some 2,500 in the number of M.T. vehicles repaired each month.

  iii Replacement units are likely to be required for supply purposes.

5 Unless important work is to suffer, Jews should not be removed until substitutes have been trained and can be drafted to take their place. This could only be done locally – but it should be directed

from a single office in conjunction with the *Höhere SS und Polizeiführer*.

6 As has now been established, orders of the first importance for the conduct of the war – particularly orders for winter requirements – are being placed in the Government General by various *Wehrmacht* departments direct, without the knowledge of the *Rüstungsinspektion* or of the *Wehrkreisbefehlshaber*, General Government. The removal of the Jews is making it impossible to fulfil these orders by due date.

It is likely to take some time to amalgamate all these undertakings systematically.

Please exempt Jews working in industry until this has been done

In the light of the views expressed on the 'Jewish Operations' in several military reports that were forwarded to him, it would seem that there was some justification for Himmler's suspicions that the arguments contained in them were not based solely on expediency – a practice had grown up in the National Socialist totalitarian régime of criticizing not the order itself but the way in which it was put into effect. Be that as it may, Gienanth was relieved of his command on 30 September 1942. On 9 October Himmler sent a circular minute to Pohl, Krüger, Globocnik, the RSHA and *SS-Obergruppenführer* Wolff (with copies to Quartermaster General Wagner and Lieutenant Colonel von Tippelskirch of OKW Operations Staff), in which he dealt with Gienanth's minute in angry, even insulting terms:

1 I have issued instructions that all so-called armament workers employed merely in boot and shoe factories, timber yards and clothing workshops in Warsaw and Lublin will be removed under the direction of *SS-Obergruppenführer* Krüger and *SS-Obergruppenführer* Pohl to concentration camps. The *Wehrmacht* should transfer any orders outstanding to us and we will guarantee delivery of the clothing required. I have also ordered that steps be ruthlessly taken against all those who think they can use the interests of the war industry to cloak their real intention to protect the Jews and their own business affairs.

2 Jews who are directly employed in the war industry – that is to say, in armament or vehicle workshops and so forth – are to be released gradually. As a first step they are to be assembled on one floor of the factory. Subsequently all the hands on this floor are to be transferred – on an exchange basis if possible – to a 'secure' undertaking, so that all we shall have in the Government General will be a number of 'secure' concentration camp undertakings.

3 Our next endeavour will be to replace this Jewish labour force with Poles and to amalgamate the great majority of the Jewish concentration camp enterprises with one or two large, not wholly Jewish,

concentration camp undertakings – if possible in the eastern part of the Government General. In due course these will also be cleared of Jews in accordance with the wishes of the Führer.[59]

The next day – 10 October 1942 – OKW Operations Staff (QII) sent a teletype message to the new *Wehrkreisbefehlshaber* in the Government General, General Hänicke, with copies to the OKW Economics and Armaments Department, the Commander of the Replacement Army, the Quartermaster General, and the *Wehrmacht* commanders in Ostland and the Ukraine. Its first sentence read as follows: 'The High Command of the *Wehrmacht* is in entire agreement with the principle laid down by the *Reichsführer-SS* that all Jews employed by the armed forces in military auxiliary services and in the war industries are to be replaced immediately by Aryan workers.' The message went on to quote the instructions that Himmler had issued on 9 October as to how 'these measures' were to be 'carried out'. It ended: 'The military authorities responsible for the undertakings are charged with carrying out these instructions in cooperation with the competent *SS und Polizeiführer*.'[60]

This was a fateful decision in that it gave Himmler a free hand to speed up the extermination process and maintain the security which surrounded it, while at the same time exploiting the Jews (in detention and, increasingly, in SS enterprises) in the interests of the war economy – albeit for a limited period. On 13 October 1942, *Oberst* Forster, the Chief Supply Officer of the *Wehrkreisbefehlshaber*, met Krüger in Spala and agreed with him on how the order was to be carried out. Under this agreement Jews employed individually by the military authorities were to be dismissed at once, 'regardless of whether or not a substitute could be found'. If the scope of a service which depended on the technical skill of individual Jews (dental technicians, for instance) was going to suffer unduly or if the total number of Jews employed in the various army services in the district was less than 100 after the 'combing-out' process had been completed, then the service departments could apply to the *Wehrkreisbefehlshaber* [Military District Commander] for a relaxation of this rule. The essence of the agreement was that all Jews retained in the war industries should become 'labour detainees of the *Höhere SS und Polizeiführer* – or at any rate, according to instructions issued by the *SS und Polizeiführer* in Lemberg, 'officially classified as such'.[61] Further agreements between Forster and Krüger stipulated that all the 'Jewish camps' that had been established by the *Wehrmacht* were to be handed over to the SS which would then supply the military authorities with Jewish workers from the 'new concentration camps'. The Jewish hands employed in the manufacture of equipment, vehicles, barracks and clothing, etc. – henceforth to be known as 'the armaments industries of the *Wehrkreisbefelshaber*' as distinct from the *Rüstungsinspektion* industries – were at first to be interned within the precincts of the factories so that, where practicable, these could later be turned into 'exclusively Jewish undertakings'. The result of all this was that the SS from now on had its own Jewish slave labour which it could offer to the military authorities who, on their side, were required to pay the SS a daily hiring fee of 5 zlotys for a man and 4 zlotys for a woman.* Meanwhile Krüger was solemnly assuring the army that the 'most important consideration in all these measures' was that there should be no 'interference with production'.†

The Krüger-Forster agreement [which I have described in some detail], together with the strong bias shown by Hitler and Himmler in favour of completing the extermination of the Jews, subject only to any special war production demands specified by their area officials, had far-reaching and typical results. For Jewish workers in industries not covered by the agreement the final hour had struck. Those employed by the *Wehrmacht* [in fact employment of this nature continued for some months] were gradually handed over to the SS, after which some were hired out to the war industries, while others were taken into the SS's own camps or disposed of in some other way. Operations against the inhabitants of any ghettos and ghetto-towns still in

*'If subsistence is provided by the army . . . the daily fee is to be reduced to 1.60 zloty. Employment tax and insurance contributions will not be paid.'

†Nuremberg Document(s) NOKW 134. Also *IMT*, vol. xxxvii, pp. 398 *et seq.* on a similar regulation which, according to a minute sent by Katzmann to the Armaments HQ [*Rüstungskommando*] in Lemberg, applied in the Galizia district by agreement with the *Wehrmacht*. Under this regulation, Jewish workers, but 'in no circumstances their next of kin' were to be housed in tenements in any ghetto still available, unless they could, 'provisionally', be interned in barracks provided by the management of the undertakings, or rounded up in separate police camps. 'The *SS und Polizeiführer*, Galizia, and the armaments unit hereby agree that the working capacity of the labour force must be maintained and that that will require suitable accommodation, clothing and medical attention.'

existence proceeded simultaneously. Krüger's orders of 28 October and 10 November 1942 for the establishment of 55 'Jewish residential districts' in the Government General as a unique concession did not mean that new ghettos were going to be created. All it meant was that the Jewish settlements (which at one time had numbered about 1,000) were to be further reduced to 55 more or less strongly guarded ghettos (some of which had been in existence for a long time, while others had already been 'cleared' once) into which Jews from the labour camps that had been closed down and from other ghettos were to be transferred. The orders could have had a secondary motive: to trick (or frighten) Jews who had escaped into returning to the only places open to them.

Apart, however, from these 'residential districts' there remained numerous Jewish labour camps; furthermore about 35,000 registered Jews (in reality double that number) remained in the Warsaw ghetto. Although two-thirds of all the Polish Jews[62] would have been 'removed' by the end of the year, the chances of being able to complete the transference of all the Jews in the Government General to five collecting camps by 31 December 1942 – the date specified by Himmler on 19 July – looked increasingly remote. By the middle of October Krüger himself was voicing his doubts: the commanders of the Security and the ordinary uniformed police had told him that the immediate dismissal of all their Jewish employees would involve the undertakings affected in 'serious difficulties' and he had had to grant them 'limited postponement'. After all, Himmler's main concern had been that the 'Jews should no longer be allowed to run around as they pleased. If they were kept in closed camps and driven to work under guard, the *Reichsführer*'s main objective would have been achieved.' It went without saying that the 'SS and the police must set a good example and must speed up the removal of the Jews in so far as it lay in their power'.

The intervening delay, particularly in Warsaw, and the transport shortages that followed the Stalingrad crisis, recalled the plan to Himmler's attention. In spite of the perilous situation at the front, he pleaded with the State Secretary in the Reich Ministry of Transport, Dr Ganzenmüller (in his letter of 20 January 1943, see p. 83) for 'more trains', basing his insistence on the removal of the Jews on the threat offered by 'partisans' –

grounds that had nothing to do with the policy of the 'final solution' even if one accepts that a very small number of Jews may have been goaded into joining the partisans and offering desperate resistance.

Somewhat earlier – on 9 January – Himmler had paid an unexpected visit to Warsaw, and had sent for Colonel Freter, the officer commanding the armaments unit.[63] He had told Freter that he wanted to find out for himself 'if it were true that the order issued direct from the Führer that the Warsaw ghetto was to be cleared by the end of 1942, had not, in fact, been complied with'.* And he 'commissioned' Freter to convey to the armaments inspector, General Schindler, his, Himmler's, astonishment at finding that 'his instructions regarding the Jews had not been obeyed'. In vain the colonel tried to explain that 'the regulations applying to the continued employment of Jews in Warsaw' had been drawn up in consultation with Krüger. Himmler gave the then *SS und Polizeiführer* in Warsaw 'until 15 February 1943' to close down all private firms, to clear the Warsaw ghetto, and to transfer all the Jews and the undertakings in which they were employed together with their machinery and equipment to Lublin, and sent a message to Schindler to the effect that 'the approval of Field Marshal Keitel to the transfer had been obtained'. Any orders outstanding with the firms that were closed down would be taken over and completed by the SS, so that although the *Wehrmacht* 'must expect delivery dates to be slightly behind schedule

*That such an order had been issued can be assumed from the fact that on 4 December, Pohl, the head of the SS Economics and Administrative Department, had directed (in accordance with Himmler's instructions of 1 December) that 'three senior engineering experts' should be sent from the department to Warsaw 'to go through the ghetto with a toothcomb and assemble all the machinery at a given locality' and then 'to examine it' to see 'whether any of it could be used in the SS's own undertakings'. Throughout all this Himmler had maintained that it would be 'necessary to get the Reich Minister of Economics' approval in writing before we transfer this machinery to our own concerns'. – Further, Himmler, in his capacity as Reich Commissioner for the Strengthening of Germanism, had issued a 'general order' on 15 December 1942 that the 'exceptional profits' represented by the 'total immovable assets of the Jews in the Government General' should be handed over to the *Höhere und SS Polizeiführer* 'for purposes connected with strengthening Germanism', rather than to the civilian authorities. A similar order regarding 'movable assets' had preceded this ministerial order. – Governor General Frank described Himmler's order as 'legally unenforceable'. *IMT*, vol. XXIX, p. 660.

during the period of transfer' any delay, would 'subsequently be made good through an increased tempo of work in the concentration camps'. Himmler then reiterated his intention of having 'all the Jews concentrated in two camps, Auschwitz and Lublin' for 'reasons of security'.

SS und Polizeiführer von Sammern then set to work. He was hoping to make a start with resettling a first contingent of 8,000 Jews and with transferring some 20,000 Jewish workers and eight undertakings to Lublin,* in compliance with Himmler's wishes, on 3 February, but in this he was disappointed. Believing, understandably, that they were about to be forcibly removed to one of the extermination camps – as rumour had had it for months past – the victims organized armed resistance. On 16 February – the day after his date-line – Himmler issued an order that, as a first step, a concentration camp was to be established *within the Warsaw ghetto*,† into which all the Jews still living in Warsaw and all the firms previously in private hands and now taken over by the Reich were to be transferred. 'As soon as possible the whole concentration camp, together with its industries and inmates' would be moved 'to Lublin and its surroundings'. As soon as this had been done the ghetto would be razed to the ground in order to remove every trace of the living quarters of 500,000 'sub-humans', which could 'never be used for the German people'.‡ But it was not all plain sailing. Before the three-day 'large-scale operation', (which von Sammern and his assistant, Stroop, had planned for 1 April 1943) could be set in motion, the heroic – and now famous – Warsaw ghetto rebellion had broken out – a rebellion which lasted 28 days, but which, in view of the disparity in the strength of the forces engaged, could have only one end. On 16 May Stroop was able to report that the 'operation' had been completed: the synagogue had been blown up and a total of 56,065 Jews apprehended or definitely destroyed.[64] It would appear that some of the prisoners were shot, others sent to Treblinka, about 15,000 forcibly removed to Lublin and the remainder to other forced labour camps.[65] On 11 June Himmler

*Stroops' testimony (*IMT*, vol. xxvi, p. 635). It had only been possible to apprehend 6,500 Jews in the resettlement operation of January 1943.
†My italics.
‡Himmler's orders to Pohl and Krüger of 16 February 1943. (Photocopy in the Institut für Zeitgeschichte, Munich.)

gave instructions that the Dzielna prison in the former Warsaw ghetto was to be turned into a concentration camp, the inmates of which were to be set to work to level the whole ghetto area to the ground (after salvaging any materials worth saving) and to transform it into a 'large park':[66] an enterprise that had to be abandoned on the approach of the Red Army in June 1944.

In the meantime Himmler had also begun to tackle the clearing of the great ghettos that still existed in other parts of Poland. Besides settling the Warsaw question, solving the transport problem (with Ganzenmüller's help), and seizing 'asocial' elements in the Government General (on the flimsy pretext of needing to take preventive measures against the partisans)* he set about eliminating the ghetto at Bialystok. It had occurred to Gestapo Müller 'in the course of stepping up the rate of transfer of labour forces into concentration camps as from 30 January 1943 in accordance with orders received' (as he wrote in his teletype message) that he might seize the opportunity to move 30,000 Jews from Bialystok – and subsequently 5,000 working Jews from Theresienstadt. Müller at all events asked Himmler for 'special permission' to transport 5,000 prisoners unfit for work and all Jews over 60 from Theresienstadt 'in order to reduce to some extent the present excessive number of camp inmates – some 48,000'. ['We shall, of course, see to it,' he added soothingly, 'that the present practice of removing only those Jews without special connexions and of no particular note is adhered to.'] By applying a 'suitable standard of . . . selection, it should be possible to increase the strength of the labour force in Auschwitz by (at least) between 10,000 and 15,000' out of the 45,000 deportees (who included 3,000 Jews from Holland and 2,000 from Berlin).†

*Himmler's minute to Gestapo Müller of 11 January 1943. In the event, this 'press-gang' action, whereby people were picked up 'indiscriminately in the street, in the cinemas, in the churches and in their homes' was criticized by the authorities in the Government General because of its deleterious effect on 'the position as regards partisans'. Frank's Diary. *IMT*, vol. XXIX, pp. 638, 647 and 670.

†Müller's teletype message to Himmler of 16 December 1942 (PS 1472). *IMT*, vol. XXVII, p. 252. It would appear (and the 'turn-round' plans of the Eastern Region of the German Reich Railways would seem to confirm) that only 7,001 of the anticipated 10,000 Jews, almost all of whom were *under* 60 years old, were actually deported from Theresienstadt to Auschwitz between 20 January and 1 February 1943. Surprisingly enough the Economics and Administrative Department made inquiries about the result of

Reports sent in by the head of the Labour Investment Office in Auschwitz – *SS-Obersturmführer* Schwartz – to the Economics and Administrative Department show how the selection procedure was manipulated in order to achieve the target. It appears from these reports (some of which have been preserved) that Jews employed in the armaments industries in Berlin were arrested 'without warning' at their places of work and deported at once (with their families).* Sauckel, acting on Hitler's direct orders,† had informed the Presidents of the Regional Labour Departments (*Landesarbeitsämter*) on 26 November 1942 that 'in agreement with Kaltenbrunner, the CSSD', 'even those Jews still in employment are now to be deported from the Reich'. They were to be replaced 'as soon as possible' by Poles from the Government General: Kaltenbrunner had, in fact, told Sauckel that 'it is hoped to make an early start with moving Poles from the Lublin district to make room for German settlers'. To avoid or minimize a drop in production[67] Jews who belonged to 'the so-called "qualified" category of the Jewish workers' – but only those – could be given a brief reprieve while their Polish replacements were being trained. On 26 March 1943 Sauckel had written another minute to the effect that 'the *Reichsführer-SS*' had issued instructions on security grounds (!) that 'any Jews who are still working as free agents outside the labour camps at the end of February are to be removed at once from their place of work and either re-employed in closed conditions or collectively disposed of.‡ Earlier – on 8 March – Schwartz had reported from Auschwitz as follows:

Transport from Berlin: Arrived 5. 3. 43. Total load – 1,128 Jews. Registered for work – 389 men and 96 women. Special treatment

the selection procedure only in so far as it concerned the 5,000 who had been deported by 26 January. A further proposal – by Kaltenbrunner himself this time – to deport 5,000 Jews of over 60 years old from Theresienstadt was turned down by Himmler, presumably to avoid endangering the cover story. Three transports went from Bialystok to Auschwitz and five to Treblinka between 5 and 13 February 1943.
* Mostly to Auschwitz – relatively few to Theresienstadt.
† In September or October 1942 – according to Speer's evidence.
‡ Nuremberg Document L 156. (Photocopy in the Institut für Zeitgeschichte, Munich.) 'In order to preserve the element of surprise essential to the success of this measure', Sauckel had added, he had 'avoided giving earlier [more detailed] instructions', and had 'only put those regional labour offices in the picture in areas where there were a great many Jews working as free agents'.

[that is to say, sent to the gas chambers] – 151 men and 492 women and children. Transport from Breslau: Arrived 5. 3. 43. Total load – 1,405 Jews. Registered for work – 406 men and 190 women. Special treatment – 125 men and 684 women and children.

Transport from Berlin: Arrived 7. 3. 43. Total load – including 25 preventive detainees – 690. Registered for work – 153 men, 25 preventive detainees and 65 women. Special treatment – 30 men and 417 women and children.*

The ghetto in Cracow was also closed during March, most of its inmates being transferred to the Plaszow labour camp. Meanwhile Katzmann had been pursuing the deportation programme in the Galizia district 'with so much energy' that he believed he would be able 'to clear the whole of the Jewish residential area by 23 June 1943'. When revolt finally flared up during the second half of June he instituted 'the harshest measures . . . simultaneously in all parts of the district'; the clearing of the Lemberg ghetto, in particular, was carried out 'brutally from start to finish'. According to Katzmann's evidence the number of Jews deported from Galizia between 10 November 1942 and 27 June 1943 rose from 254,989 to 434,329. Nevertheless there were still twenty-one labour camps containing 21,156 Jews in the district; however, as Katzmann added, this number 'would be steadily reduced'.[68]

All this was exactly what Himmler wanted; he had been consistently pressing for the 'expulsion' of the 300,000 to 400,000 Jews still in the Government General, urging that they be sent to join the Jews in the east as speedily as was 'humanly possible'.[69] In August 1943 the ghettos in the two important industrial centres – Sosnowiec and Bedzin – were cleared. The lack of forethought shown in carrying out the operation (which affected Upper Silesia and the adjoining areas) meant among other things that 500 of the 2,000 dwellings planned for German settlers had to be 'erected there and then', because – as the competent National Socialist official reported – the Jews had made up 'a third of the total available labour force'.† Two factories

*On 20 February 1943 Schwartz reported that from a January intake of 5,012 Jews from Theresienstadt, 920 had been 'registered for work' and 4,092 'specially accommodated'; on 15 March he reported that of 964 Jews sent from Berlin as workers 365 had been 'registered for work' and 599 'specially accommodated'.

†'Between 500 and 600 Jews are urgently needed – which leads me to believe that it might be advisable to reinstate those already used to the work – for

engaged in the Adolf Hitler tank production programme actually lost all their 700 Jewish workers overnight.[70] By now – as Krüger observed during a conference with Frank, Kaltenbrunner and General Hänicke at the end of May – the 'measures' were affecting even those Jews employed in the most vital war industries, who, because of this, should have been left where they were. Himmler was desperately anxious that even the practice of hiring out Jews in the SS camps by the day to the armaments factories should cease, but Krüger himself had had to admit that 'in the final analysis this simply could not be done' since 'it was impossible to replace skilled Jewish workers with Poles, just like that!' With this in mind, Krüger had been to see General Schindler and had told him that the armament factories could keep 'their strongest and best workers' ['the Maccabees, they call them' was how he put it] for the time being; at the same time he had asked Kaltenbrunner, who was present, to urge Himmler to waive his orders in so far as the removal of these particular workers was concerned.[71] In spite of this, on 30 August 1943, the *SS und Polizeiführer* in the Cracow district issued 'firm' instructions that 'by arrangement with the *Rüstungsinspektion* Jewish workers were in future to be employed only in the SS central labour camp [ZAL – *Zentral-Arbeitslager*].

The second half of August saw the clearance of the Bialystok ghetto – the last of the great ghettos in Poland (except for Lodz). [This marked the beginning of the end for all the ghettos in Ostland: Minsk and Vilna disappeared in September and Riga in October; the last to go was the ghetto at Kowno, which, though decimated like all the others, remained in existence until July 1944.][72] The fate of the ghetto at Lodz [which had been annexed to the Reich] hung longer in the balance. Himmler had intended to turn it into a concentration camp in June 1943, as the ghetto undertakings wanted to move to Lublin. But in the end he had acceded to the request of State Governor Greiser and had abandoned the project, leaving 'Litzmannstadt' for the time being as the *Gau* ghetto for Reich *Gau* Wartheland (that is to say, under civil administration). Its population was to be kept to an

the sake of efficiency. . . . The Jews are kept in the camps in such a way that no one ever sees them in public.' Teletype message from *SS-Obersturmbannführer* Brehn to the Senior SS and Police Commander, South East, Kattowitz, on 21 August 1943. Nuremberg Document NO 3083. (Photocopy in the Institut für Zeitgeschichte, Munich.)

absolute minimum,* and, in fact, at Greiser's suggestion, the 'experienced' *Sonderkommando* Bothmann started limited operations in Chelmno in 1944. Eventually (in August 1944) the great majority of the inmates of the ghetto – most of them more dead than alive – were transferred to Auschwitz.

The idea of moving the undertakings dependent on Jewish labour together with their plant and equipment to the Lublin area had arisen, as is well known, in connexion with Himmler's earlier orders as well as in the negotiations over the fate of Lodz. While Operation Reinhard was being carried out under Globocnik's direction during 1943, the SS's own industries *seemed* to be expanding rapidly with Himmler's approval. These industries depended in the main on the Jewish camps run by the Lublin *SS und Polizeiführer* and were operated by the organized exploitation of all those Jews who were still fit for work and whose extermination had therefore been deferred. On 12 March 1943 the SS founded their own company – '*Osti*' (see p. 116) – with Pohl as chairman of the board of directors and Globocnik as managing director – to take over some of the factories that had been built or were under construction in the Lublin district. On 21 June 1943 Globocnik was able to claim with pride that '45,000 people' (*sic!*)† were already employed in the SS labour camps (that is to say, in the '*Osti*' works, in the undertakings developed from the former privately-owned firms in Warsaw, and in those enterprises that had surrendered their prison labour to the *Rüstungsinspektion*). 'In all probability this number will be substantially increased during the next few months', he added. What he was actually suggesting was that 'skilled workers and plant' from Litzmannstadt as well as the Bialystok undertakings should be transferred to Lublin (to the labour camp, Poniatowa) where production could continue, and that Litzmannstadt could

*Nuremberg Document(s) NO 519. (Photocopy in the Institut für Zeitgeschichte, Munich.) In return for Himmler's concession Greiser told him in June 1944 that Reich Minister Speer, at the instigation of the Armaments Inspectorate, had asked for the number of persons employed in individual factories in the ghetto in order to bring to Hitler's notice the 'wire crossing' which prevailed as a result of his (Himmler's) orders (for the evacuation of the ghettos).

†Nuremberg Document NO 485. (Photocopy in the Institut für Zeitgeschichte, Munich.) In his letter to Brandt about 'building up the labour camps in accordance with the *Reichsführer*'s wish to see the Jewish labour potential fully exploited', Globocnik had written '45,000 Jews'.

then be 'liquidated' since 'only some of the 78,000 Jews now living there are employed in war production'. At the same time Globocnik was obliged to admit that the 'labour capacity' of his camps was not being fully utilized. 'The *Wehrmacht* headquarters,' he complained, 'and some industrial federations in the Reich, either out of hostility towards the SS' or because they were hoping to make a private 'profit', were holding up orders on the flimsiest of grounds – whereas Litzmannstadt had recently been 'inundated with orders', presumably 'to prevent deportations'. In the event nothing came of Globocnik's proposals. To begin with, the ten labour camps run by the *SS und Polizeiführer* in the Lublin district were taken over as branch camps of the main Lublin concentration camp by the SS Economics and Administrative Department[73] on 7 September 1943 – a procedure which was to be repeated in the case of 'all the labour camps remaining in the Government General' with the idea of 'dismantling the sparsely populated camps and those not engaged in work of importance to the war effort'. On 3 November 1943 a far more radical step was taken, which, according to the report of the deputy managing director of Osti 'has rendered quite useless all the building and construction work that has been done'. The Jews employed in war industries, not only by the former private firms of Schultz & Co., and Többens but also by the SS enterprises and those belonging to the German Armament Works [*Deutsche Ausrüstungswerke* – DAW], were withdrawn suddenly, and without prior notice to the camp leaders. (Some of these were engaged in the production of shell fuses.) On 3 November and the following days at least 17,000 Jews [in some evidence the figure was put as high as over 40,000] were herded into previously dug graves and slaughtered by machine gun fire. Operation Reinhard, which had been officially completed in October 1943 with the dismantling of the three extermination camps,[74] had a successor in 'Operation Erntefest' (Harvest Feast) – of which the outstanding feature was the mass shootings.

Even after this some small and some large SS and *Rüstungsinspektion* labour camps for Jewish workers* were still to be

*Directly before the mass shootings General Schindler had managed to get Krüger's consent to release Jews in the SS labour camps to armaments firms. Some were, in fact, released for this purpose – but only 4,000 out of the 10,000 promised. Hilberg *op. cit.* p. 341.

found in the Government General. In the spring of 1943 some tens of thousands of Jews were engaged in war work in East Prussia and Upper Silesia, while a Krupps factory in Lower Silesia was still employing thousands of Jews in 1944.[75] It would even appear that some Jews were actually brought out of Auschwitz 'to work in armament industries in the Reich'.* And when the Red Army finally crossed the Vistula, tens of thousands of Jews were forcibly removed from the Polish camps to Germany, where most of those who had not fallen victim to the orders of the Commander of the Security Police and the SD in the Government General – to liquidate the prison population and the Jews and get rid of their corpses 'in view of the unexpected turn of events'[76] – were sucked under in the whirlpool of catastrophe that drowned the Third Reich.

The plan to concentrate all the Jews left alive in a few 'collecting camps' was thus never fully realized. Himmler had nevertheless gone a long way towards achieving his dreadful target. On 6 October 1943, in Posen, he had told the Reich and *Gauleiters* quite openly (and he was exaggerating only in point of time):

I have emptied the large Jewish ghettos in the L. of C. area. .... By the end of the year the Jewish question will have been settled in all the occupied countries. Only a few individual Jews who have managed to slip through the net will be left. Then we shall set about tackling the problem of the non-Jewish partner in mixed marriages and the problem of the half-Jew, systematically and sensibly, and we shall find a solution and put it into effect.

And with the same stubborn inner conviction, he believed he could allay the heavy burden which lay, inevitably, on the consciences of those who put the murder orders into effect:

I am talking to you within these four walls and you must listen to what I have to say and let it go no further. All of us have asked ourselves: What about the women and children? I have decided that this too requires a clear answer. I did not consider that I should be justified in getting rid of the men – in having them put to death, in other words – only to allow their children to grow up to avenge themselves on our sons and grandsons. We have to make up our minds, hard though it may be, that this race must be wiped off the face of the earth.

*Minute of the head of Department D II of the SS Economics and Administrative Department to the Commandant of Auschwitz, 7 September 1943. The successful summer offensive east of the line Pionki-Radom-Kielce led to further transfers (and to liquidation) of the Jews. Hilberg, *op. cit.* p. 344.

Himmler's own hand-written record of his 'discussions with Hitler on 19 June 1943 at Obersalzburg' is proof enough of the fearful results that Hitler himself desired from the programme of the extermination of the Jews: 'The Führer talked to me about the Jewish problem and said that the deportation of the Jews must go on regardless of any unrest it might cause during the next three or four months, and that it must be carried out in an all-embracing way.'

In public speeches Hitler had triumphantly and repeatedly referred to the 'fulfilment' of his prophecy of 30 January 1939 about the fate of the Jews if they (!) succeeded in unleashing a second world war: 'People always laughed at me for my prophecies. Countless numbers of those who laughed in the old days laugh no longer, and one day, maybe, those who are still laughing will laugh no more.' [8 November 1942.]

'This struggle will not end, as people suppose, with the destruction of the Aryan peoples, but with the extirpation of Judaism in Europe.' [24 February 1943.]

Since the summer of 1942 Auschwitz had increasingly become the principal reception area for the deported European Jews. A proposal put forward on 15 August 1944 by an official of the SS Economics and Administrative Department – on the subject of reimbursement in respect of future 'requirements of prisoners' clothing' – is a sinister reminder of what happened in that camp. 'In this connexion,' he wrote, 'the attention of the Reich Ministry of Economics might be drawn to the *vast quantities of rags* from unserviceable civilian clothing that have accumulated as a result of the various *actions taken in Auschwitz* and other camps.[77] These are being put at the disposal of the Reich Ministry of Economics, and further deliveries will follow.' Operations in Auschwitz were rounded off by the liquidation of hundreds of thousands of Hungarian Jews in the most systematic and comprehensive 'action' that had hitherto been taken – since when the name of the camp has become a symbol of the greatest massacre known to history.

2 The Concentration Camps 1933-45

Translated by Marian Jackson

Martin Broszat

Introductory Note

Since the appearance of Eugen Kogan's masterly book *Der SS-Staat* (1946)* the National Socialist concentration camps have not been the subject of a systematic historical portrayal. Documentary sources and the results of individual research available to the historian have meanwhile increased considerably. Yet a strange contradiction remains: although the National Socialist concentration camps have become a familiar concept to those seeking to shape historical and political opinion, little reliable information on them exists.

The following account, produced as expert evidence for the Auschwitz trial in Frankfurt, is not itself a fully comprehensive history of the National Socialist concentration camps, but it perhaps provides the framework for one. Its primary aim is to describe the chronological development of the concentration camps, the structure of their organization and leadership, and their function, importance and effects which underwent a considerable change during the twelve years of National Socialist rule. There was no planned system of concentration camps from the start. It was only gradually that the camps grew into a permanent, expanding institution of the Hitler State. Their development was neither compulsive nor unopposed in the transitional years 1933/6 which succeeded the improvised state of emergency in the spring of 1933 with its rivalries and internal question marks.

Even the last catastrophic phase of the concentration camps (1942–5) leaves, apart from the picture of systematized ideological and bureaucratic terror, the impression of 'wild' improvisation. An 'anatomy' of National Socialist tyranny should not neglect this symptom of an 'entrepreneur-like' accumulation of power.

Compared with the dimensions to which the concentration camps grew in the second half of the war their importance before 1939 may seem small and almost inoffensive. Yet particular emphasis is placed in this account on pre-war developments

*Translated into English as *The Theory and Practice of Hell* (London, 1950).

because it was then that vital preliminary decisions were taken. The concentration camps were an important criterion as to whether Nazi absolutism, once it was firmly entrenched, would content itself with the authoritarian transformation of the State, or whether it would strive further to absorb and dissolve its legal and constitutional framework.

The fact that the concentration camps were retained after 1933/4 without objective necessity signified an intentional prolongation of the state of emergency, and it was not accidental that after the outbreak of the war they assumed gigantic dimensions. For even in internal affairs war was the element most characteristic of the National Socialist leadership: it was the great state of emergency which enabled it to carry through totalitarian control. The protective custody camps for enemies of the State became centres of forced labour, biological and medical experiments and the physical extermination of Jewish and other unwanted life.

Martin Broszat

Munich, summer 1964

The Phase of Revolutionary Take-over 1933-4

1 Protective custody – concept and institution

The term *Schutzhaft* (protective custody), which was to become the embodiment of the political fight against the opposition in the Third Reich, was applied immediately after the proclamation of the emergency decree of 28 February 1933 to the arrests which principally involved communist officials.* Relevant Prussian orders of the year 1933 refer varyingly to 'political protective

*Neither the emergency decree of 28 February 1933 nor the circular of the Prussian Minister of the Interior (Göring) of 3 March 1933 instructing the Prussian police on how to implement the emergency decree contains the concept of protective custody. Although arrests made by the police under the decree in the Reich were referred to in reports of the Prussian Police President as *Schutzhaft* as early as March 1933, similar arrests made on the order of the Bavarian authorities were described as transfer into *Polizeihaft* (police custody). In April 1933 the term 'protective custody' gained official acceptance also in Bavaria.

custody', 'police custody for political reasons' and 'political custody'.* The linking of 'protective custody' with the concept of 'police custody'† refers to police jurisdiction. Before 1914 the term 'protective custody' referred in Prussia and other German *Länder* exclusively to short-term police detention for the protection, and in the interest, of the person concerned (if, for example, he was in danger of being mobbed). During the First World War, however, it became customary to describe as protective custody the detention of persons arrested as being politically suspect because of the state of military emergency. Preventive military protective custody in this sense was also applied by *Reichswehr* commanders, in agreement with the *Reichswehr* minister, in 1919/20 during temporary, locally restricted states of emergency in order to suppress communist or separatist outbreaks, particularly in Berlin, in Bavaria (during the suppression of the *Räterepublik*)‡ and in the Ruhr. In the end the term protective custody was applied also to police detention for the protection of law and order under the Prussian law on the administrative jurisdiction of the police of 1 July 1931 (para. 15), although provision was made for the arrested person to be brought before a judge within 24 hours.

Soon after Hitler's appointment as Chancellor, the possibility of considerably prolonged periods of police detention (up to three months) was given under the emergency decree for the protection of the German people, issued by the President on 4 February 1933. It was, however, stated explicitly that prolonged police detention was permissible only if criminal activities (high treason, armed disturbance of public safety) were suspected; in addition the prisoner was given the right to appeal to a judge who in case of doubt decided whether the accused should remain in custody.

Only the emergency decree for the protection of people and State, issued after the *Reichstag* fire, abolished among other basic

*For example the circular of the Prussian Minister of the Interior of 14 October 1933 on the application of protective custody.

†Later a distinction was made between persons taken into protective custody for political reasons and criminals and antisocials, classified as 'prisoners detained by the police as a precautionary measure' [*Polizeiliche Vorbeugungs-häftlinge*]; the latter were sent to concentration camps by the Criminal Police during the so-called 'prevention campaign'. This distinction still appeared in the last count of inmates of Dachau concentration camp, on 26 April 1945.

‡The German equivalent of a Soviet. [*Translator's footnote.*]

rights of the Weimar Constitution the inviolability of personal freedom (Article 114), thus creating the basis for a form of police arrest of political enemies (in the widest sense) which differed fundamentally from imprisonment based on a judicial verdict and from police detention, admissible for short periods only.* Official definitions of National Socialist origin confirm explicitly that protective custody based on the emergency decree of 28 February 1933 was not intended as an instrument for dealing with punishable offences but as a 'preventive' police measure aimed at eliminating 'threats from subversive elements'. Hans Tesmer, *Regierungsrat* in the *Geheime Staatspolizeiamt* (Gestapa) described in retrospect in 1936 the basic change resulting from the decree of 28 February 1933:

Whereas hitherto the police, under Para. 112 *et seq.* of the Code of Criminal Procedure, could only make arrests as auxiliaries of the Public Prosecutor when he was instituting criminal proceedings, or could under certain conditions ... take people briefly into police custody, they were now entitled, when combating subversive activities, to use the most effective means against enemies of the State – deprivation of freedom in the form of protective custody.

2 The wave of arrests of March/April 1933 and the first concentration camps

As its introductory paragraph shows, the decree of 28 February 1933 was directed primarily against the Communist Party, its organizations, press, meetings and officials. To the Cabinet assembled on 28 February 1933, the morning after the *Reichstag* fire, to discuss the proposed decree, Hitler declared, according to the minutes, 'that a ruthless settlement with the KPD [German Communist Party] was imperative. The psychologically correct moment for this settlement had come' and it should 'not be made dependent on legalistic considerations'. Hitler also had his eye on the *Reichstag* elections fixed for 5 March, expecting from a rapid annihilation of the Communist Party an even surer victory for the national Right (NSDAP and *Deutschnationale*)

*In a later circular, dated 26 February 1937, the Chief of the Security Police explicitly requested the subordinate *Stapo(leit)stelle* 'in future to make no use of the possibility of police detention under Para. 22, sub-para. 4 of the decree of 4 February 1933, in order to avoid judicial investigation of police measures'. Such action was anyway 'superfluous as in all these cases it is possible to order "protective custody".'

which supported his government. At the Cabinet meeting of 28 February he remarked that 'As a result of the *Reichstag* fire he no longer doubted that the Reich Government would gain 51 per cent in the elections.'

It is impossible to say whether the *Reichstag* fire really led Hitler to suspect the existence of a communist threat and conspiracy or whether he seized the occasion consciously and hastily to destroy the communist organizations and to put their leaders out of action. His resolve – in the last resort ideologically motivated – brutally to suppress the communists had long existed. Seven years earlier Hitler had said in the course of a private speech in Hamburg:

A movement which wants to fight Marxism must be just as intolerant as Marxism itself. It must have no doubts that ... if we are victorious Marxism will be destroyed, and completely destroyed; we too know no tolerance. We shall not rest until the last newspaper has been destroyed, the last organization liquidated, the last centre of education wiped out and the last Marxist converted or exterminated. There is no half-way house.

On the implementation of the *Reichstag* fire decree the Prussian Minister of the Interior, Göring, instructed the Prussian police authorities in a circular dated 3 March 1933 as follows:

It is the aim and object of this decree that the wider powers which it gives should primarily be used against the communists, but also against those who work with the communists and who support or further their criminal objectives, even if indirectly. In order to avoid blunders I must point out that actions taken against members or institutions belonging to parties or organizations other than communist, anarchist or Social Democrat, can only be upheld under the decree for the Protection of People and State of 28. 2. 1933 if they represent a defence against communist activity in the widest sense.

The *Reichstag* fire decree not only abolished the fundamental right to freedom but it also authorized the Reich government to take direct control of all measures against communist organizations and other opponents by doing away with the sovereignty of the *Länder*. Dr Frick, the Reich Minister of the Interior, was thus able in the course of time to appoint Reich Commissars with police powers in those *Länder* where it was not certain anyway that the police would act in the National Socialist interest. Within a few weeks the police in the Reich – a vital sector in domestic politics – was almost universally controlled by SA or

SS leaders, political leaders of the NSDAP and other 'reliable' Party supporters. Following the example set by Göring as acting Prussian Minister of the Interior in mid-February 1933, most of the new National Socialist Chiefs of Police in the other *Länder* also gave the SA and SS auxiliary police powers. The *Reichsführer-SS*, Heinrich Himmler, appointed *Kommissarischer Polizeipräsident* [Provisional Police President] on 9 March 1933 (with Reinhard Heydrich in charge of the Political Department of *Abteilung* VI of the Munich Criminal Police), was named *Politischer Polizeikommandeur* [Political Police Commander] of Bavaria on 1 April 1933. As a result the Political Police in Bavaria became independent; instead of forming part of the Munich police administration it was reorganized as a special ministerial authority within the Bavarian Ministry of the Interior. From the beginning Himmler tried to place leading positions in the Political Police into the hands of the SS.

In these circumstances the operation to destroy communist organizations, authorized by the emergency decree of 28 February 1933, was very radically interpreted and carried out in most of the Reich. In Berlin Göring gave instructions on the night of 28 February to arrest all communist *Reichstag* and *Landtag* deputies together with a few thousand other communist officials.

In Bavaria the Held Government, which was still in office, apart from banning communist meetings and newspapers, at first confined itself on 1 March to the instruction 'to take communist instigators into police custody'. After the appointment on 9 March of Adolf Wagner, the *Gauleiter* of Upper Bavaria, as *Staatskommissar* [State Commissioner] at the Bavarian Ministry of the Interior the number of those marked out for arrest rose considerably and included non-communist political opponents of the régime. There is reference to this in a letter of Wagner's of 13 March 1933 to Dr Hans Frank, also newly appointed as National Socialist *Staatskommissar* at the Bavarian Ministry of Justice:

May I draw your attention to the fact that the order for the arrest of all communist officials and *Reichsbannerführer** has not so far been carried out as thoroughly as necessary for the preservation of peace and security. In view of yesterday's discussion with the *Regierungs-*

*Socialist Democrat strong arm squad leaders. [*Translator's footnote.*]

präsidenten it may be assumed that the authorities concerned will now carry out the order with greater thoroughness.

It is likely therefore that still more persons will be taken into police custody.

Should the prisons at the disposal of the judicial authorities be insufficient I suggest the use of methods formerly employed in dealing with mass arrests of members of the National Socialist German Workers' Party. As is well known they were shut up in any empty ruin and nobody worried whether or not they suffered the inclemency of the weather.

At the same time Wagner recommended the setting up of special protective custody quarters separate from the police prisons and those of the Ministry of Justice. On 20 March 1933 Himmler, in his capacity of *Kommissarischer Polizeipräsident* of Munich, arranged for the first concentration camp to be set up in the grounds and stone huts of a former gunpowder factory in the vicinity of Dachau, near Munich. The *Völkische Beobachter* reported on 21 March 1933:

... This is where all communist and, where necessary, *Reichsbanner* and Social Democrat officials are concentrated; because to house these officials in ordinary prisons is impossible in the long run and imposes too great a burden on the machinery of the State. It has become apparent that these people cannot be allowed to remain free as they continue to agitate and to cause unrest. ...

The judicature itself was anxious to get rid of the prisoners held in protective custody in its gaols. Most of them were still in local Bavarian prisons at the end of April. The Minister of Justice, Frank, wrote to the Bavarian Minister of the Interior on 21 April 1933:

According to reports received from the Prosecutors General, prisons continue to be crowded as a result of being filled with prisoners in protective custody. I am therefore compelled once more to draw your attention to troubles caused by over-crowding. Keeping too many prisoners in insufficient space seriously affects their physical health and leads to major imprisonment psychoses, particularly in the absence of any possibility of work. Moreover, with the existing staff it is impossible to supervise the prisoners effectively. In addition, the crowding caused by accommodating protective custody prisoners has resulted in serious delays in carrying out sentences. As I said in my letter of 11 April 1933 No. IV 11302*a*, in many instances prison sentences would not be served. For the same reason suspects who ought to have been remanded in custody for the unhampered investigation of their case could not and cannot be remanded. Present conditions therefore prevent the orderly administration of justice and endanger vital interests of State and people. They are unbearable for the Law and cannot be tolerated any longer. I must therefore urge you to see that prisons are immediately relieved of all persons in protective custody. . . .

A copy of this letter has been sent to the *Politische Polizeikommandeur* of Bavaria.

A number of fortnightly reports of the Prussian *Regierungspräsidenten,* or Police Presidents, used for statistical purposes by the police section of the Prussian Ministry of the Interior, provide information on the number of persons detained in protective custody on the basis of the decree of 28 February 1933. This information shows that the first wave of arrests by the Prussian police, primarily of communist officials, reached its peak in March and April 1933. For many of the thirty-four *Regierungsbezirke* [administrative districts] of Prussia exact information exists in the form of fortnightly reports on the number of persons taken into protective custody during these two months. They permit the drawing up of the following partial balance sheet for March and April 1933:

Period	Prussian *Regierungsbezirke* making returns (out of a total of 34)	Persons taken into protective custody in these *Regierungsbezirke*
1–15 March	24	7,784
16–31 March	16	2,860
1–15 April	20	3,017
16–30 April	19	2,693
March/April	(=60 per cent) on average 20 out of 34	16,354

These partial figures referring to roughly 60 per cent of Prussia's *Regierungsbezirke* show that very probably the total of persons taken into protective custody by the police in Prussia in March/April 1933 was at least 25,000 (probably it was somewhat higher still), as the many arrests in the Reich capital, Berlin, are not included in these figures.

This approximate number of 25,000 arrests in Prussia refers exclusively to cases of protective custody reported by the police. It does not include the 'wild' arrests of political opponents made by the SA and the SS, particularly in the big cities. On the other hand it must be borne in mind that of those arrested many were

kept and released after only a few days or weeks in custody.*
There is a striking difference in the number of those taken into
protective custody by the police in the individual Prussian
Regierungsbezirke which reflects not only the difference between
town and country, between the social, denominational and political
structure of the various districts but also between the more
moderate or the more extreme police authorities. In the first half
of March for instance only 421 persons were taken into protective custody in the whole of East Prussia (*Regierungsbezirke*
Königsberg, Gumbinnen and Allenstein), whereas in Silesia
(*Regierungsbezirke* Liegnitz, Breslau and Oppeln) the number
was 1,142. For the same period the rural *Regierungsbezirk* of
Schleswig reported 382 cases, whereas another rural *Regierungsbezirk,* Hildesheim, reported only 77. The differences between
the Prussian areas of the Rhineland and of Westphalia are particularly pronounced. Absolutely the highest number of reported
arrests comes from *Regierungsbezirk* Düsseldorf where *SS-
Gruppenführer* Weitzel was Police President. In March/April
1933 a total of 3,818 persons was taken into protective custody
there, whereas the comparable figure for the *Regierungsbezirk* of
Trier was a mere 78.

The state of emergency created by the decree of 28 February
1933 and the intention, clearly stated by Hitler, Göring, Röhm,
Himmler and others, of having a violent 'settlement' with the
communists and other enemies of the so-called national movement, encouraged the armed formations of the SA and SS,
hitherto kept reasonably in check, to proceed to arbitrary action.
In the big cities in particular there were violent incidents which
not infrequently involved bloodshed. The then head of the
Political *Abteilung* (IA) of the Berlin Police *Präsidium*
[Presidency],†Rudolf Diels, later reported on these operations:

From all parts of the capital we in the IA received rumours, police
information, complaints and victory reports of SA operations. Unlike
the Party, the SA was all prepared to seize power. It had no need of
homogeneous leadership; the *Gruppenstab* set the example but gave no
orders. The SA *Stürme,* however, had firm plans for operations in the

*The draft of a letter from the Prussian Minister of the Interior to the Reich
Minister of the Interior of June 1933 says: 'According to the information so
far at my disposal there were in protective custody in Prussia in March 1933
on average 15,000 persons and in April 1933 13,000 persons.'
†Which after 26 April 1934 became the *Geheime Staatspolizeiamt* (Gestapa).

communist quarters of the city. In those March days every SA man was 'on the heels of the enemy', each knew what he had to do. The *Stürme* cleaned up the districts. They knew not only where their enemies lived, they had also long ago discovered their hideouts and meeting places. . . . Not only the communists but anybody who had ever expressed himself against Hitler's movement was in danger. . . .

SA men broke up the contents of the home of Reich President Ebert's son. They forced their way into the homes of the owners of the publishing houses of Ullstein and Mosse. They took off any of the members of the *Weltbühne* and the *Tagebuch* on whom they could lay hands. . . . SA leaders no longer went anywhere on foot. The gay victors roared along the *Kurfürstendamm* and the *Linden* in elegant automobiles. Manufacturers or shopkeepers had presented them with these cars or put them at their disposal in order to assure themselves protection. The cars of Jews and democrats were simply confiscated. . . . In those March days the concentration camps around Berlin were set up. News was received of camps near Oranienburg, Konigswusterhausen and Bornim. . . . 'Private prisons' were set up in various parts of the city. The 'bunkers' in the Hedemann and Vossstrasse became hellish torture chambers. The SS Columbia prison, the worst of these torture chambers, was established. . . .

The uprising of the Berlin SA electrified the most distant parts of the country. Revolutionary conditions prevailed in many big cities where the powers of the police had been transferred to local SA leaders. . . . In Lower Silesia *SA-Gruppenführer* Heins of Breslau established a reign of terror. In the northern Rhineland it was *SS-Gruppenführer* Weitzel who as Police President of Düsseldorf together with *SA-Führer* Lobek displayed fanatical radicalism. The Ruhr towns were dominated by Terboven's SA. East Prussia, where *Gauleiter* Koch had allowed neither the SA nor the SS to come to the fore, was ruled by the political leaders. The fight was directed against 'reaction'. It was as though the country was in a state of war in which the aristocracy as the imaginary enemy was subjected to duress. In Stettin the example of *SA-Gruppenführer* von Heydebreck encouraged the Pomeranian SA to terrorize the country. From Rostock, Stargard and Greifswald came reports of cases of maltreatment. Some victims had died under torture.[1]

3 New wave of arrests in the summer of 1933 and official efforts to return to normality

The forcible elimination of the communists, who could no longer take their seats in the *Reichstag* elected on 5 March, freed Hitler from his most hated enemies, and created the necessary conditions for the adoption by a two-thirds majority of the Enabling Law (on 23 March 1933) which brought Hitler substantially closer to absolute power. From his new position he was able to eliminate a number of other enemies: on 2 May steps were taken to destroy the Free Trade Unions: on 9 May the assets of the *Reichsbanner* and the SPD [German Socialist Party] were confiscated: on 22 June the Social Democratic Party was officially banned and on 7 July its representatives in the Reichstag, the provincial parliaments and local government were deprived of their seats.

In the weeks that followed, the bourgeois parties dissolved themselves under public pressure. This elimination of the non-communist political groups and organizations produced another wave of arrests. In the summer and autumn of 1933 Social Democrats, Democrats, the leaders of the Centre Party, of the Bavarian People's Party, *Deutschnationale*, Royalists, bourgeois and above all Jewish journalists and writers, lawyers, occasionally also unpopular industrialists, officials, etc., were sent to camps – some set up by the SA, some by the SS or the police; they were sent to Dachau, Oranienburg, Papenburg, Esterwegen, Dürrgoy near Breslau, Kemna near Wuppertal, Sonnenburg, Sachsenburg and to other camps as well as to prisons and detention centres. An order issued on 26 June 1933 by the Bavarian Political Police of which Himmler was in charge shows that in Bavaria, for example, instructions had gone out that, of former members of the Bavarian People's Party, 'in addition to *Reichstag* and *Landtag* deputies', there should be taken 'into protective custody those persons who have been particularly active in party politics'.

In Prussia the number of persons in protective custody, after a slight fall, rose again to 14,000 in May and June. Up to June 1933 the Prussian Ministry of the Interior had officially recognized six camps as State concentration camps (and financed them out of public funds): 'training camp Quednau', Sonnenburg (a camp housed in a former penitentiary), the camps Hammerstein and Lichtenburg and the prisons of Werden and Brauweiler near Cologne. These camps, it was noted at the Prussian Ministry of the Interior in June 1933, 'without exception' provided only a 'provisional' form of custody, 'shortly to be abandoned in favour of productive employment of the Prisoners in newly established concentration camps in the marshy regions of *Regierungsbezirk* Osnabrück'. The plan was to concentrate Prussian protective custody prisoners in the marshy regions of the

Emsland, while using them productively. By extending the existing concentration camps of Esterwegen and Börgermoor, room for 10,000 prisoners would be created, 'as during the next few years a permanent figure of 10,000 prisoners can be expected'. Except for these concentration camps in the marshy regions of *Regierungsbezirk* Osnabrück, only 'the Sonnenburg penitentiary, already used as a concentration camp' (in the *Regierungsbezirk* of Frankfurt/Oder) and 'possibly the camp under construction at Lichtenburg, *Regierungsbezirk* Merseburg' should be retained.

According to an internal calculation of the Reich Ministry of the Interior there was on 31 July 1933 a total of 26,789 persons in protective custody in the Reich, distributed as follows between the individual Länder:

Prussia	14,906	Braunschweig	248
Bavaria	4,152	Oldenburg	170
Saxony	4,500	Anhalt	112
Württemberg	971	Bremen	229
Baden	539	Lippe-Detmold	17
Thuringia	16	Lübeck	27
Hesse	145	Mecklenburg-Strelitz	16
Hamburg	682	Schaumburg-Lippe	24
Mecklenburg-Schwerin	35		

The wave of arrests in the summer of 1933 had emphasized anew the arbitrary and brutal methods of the SA and SS who did not act only as auxiliary police but fought 'Marxists, Jews and reactionaries' on their own, and thus came increasingly into conflict with the police and the administrative organs of the State. Göring, the Prussian Prime Minister and Minister of the Interior, Dr Frick, the National Socialist Reich Minister of the Interior, and Dr Gürtner, the *Deutschnationale* Reich Minister of Justice, began to worry about the high-handedness of the SA, and even Hitler himself could not entirely ignore their arguments. The new Chancellor needed to consider not only the conservative Army and the Reich President. He realized that in the last resort the authority of his régime depended on his handling of the economic depression and unemployment. But this demanded a certain degree of legal stability. In addition, Hitler saw clearly that his own position might be threatened if a stop was not put to the revolutionary conduct of the SA under *Stabschef* Ernst Röhm.

Hitler clearly expressed his disapproval of further 'senseless revolutionary activity' to the *Reichsstatthalter,* the SA leaders, at the beginning of July 1933. The economy in particular demanded a transition to evolution. Dr Frick, Reich Minister of the Interior, declared on 10 July 1933 in a circular to the *Reichsstatthalter* and *Land* governments that the national revolution was 'concluded' with the dissolution of the remaining bourgeois parties. The NSDAP as the pillar of the State must henceforth support the process of 'lawful construction'. The stabilization of the economy in particular was 'seriously threatened if there is further talk of continuing the revolution or of a second revolution'. Unauthorized intervention in the economy and disregard of orders of the authorities meant opposition 'to the Führer himself' and would in future be 'most severely punished'. On 2 August the SA auxiliary police was disbanded in Prussia. Thereafter the police gradually succeeded in stopping the worst SA and SS outrages in Berlin and the provinces and in closing down the SA torture centres and a number of lawless SA camps.

On 25 July 1933 the Prussian Minister of Justice directed Public Prosecutor's Offices, 'on the occasion of the end of the National Socialist revolution', to pardon those sentenced or to stop taking criminal proceedings in the majority of cases awaiting trial in which members of the SA and SS had rendered themselves liable to prosecution during the pursuit of opponents. In order to deal more effectively with similar occurrences in the future, a central Public Prosecutor's Office was established at the beginning of August under the supervision of the Prussian Ministry of Justice. Efforts were made to deal energetically with recurring cases of maltreatment and murder of protective custody prisoners in unauthorized camps and to take legal action against those responsible. In spite of strong opposition from the Düsseldorf Police President and SS leader, the SS guards in the moor camps of Papenburg-Esterwegen were even temporarily replaced by members of the Berlin police force.

In a circular addressed to the Prussian *Regierungspräsidenten,* dated 14 October 1933, the Prussian Minister of the Interior directed that persons detained for political reasons should 'in principle be detained in State concentration camps' or – in so far as this was impossible or when only a very short period of detention was envisaged – 'in State or local police prisons'. Any 'other form of detention' was 'not permitted in future'. Only the camps at Papenburg, Sonnenburg, Lichtenburg and Brandenburg, the provincial prison of Brauweiler near Cologne and the provincial workhouse of Mohringen near Hannover were officially recognized and approved concentration camps. 'All other establishments for the accommodation of political prisoners in protective custody' must be 'dissolved not later than the end of this year'. Therefore 'the transfer of new prisoners to such institutions' was 'not permitted'. In another circular dated 10 November 1933, the Prussian Minister of the Interior complained to the *Oberpräsidenten* and the *Regierungspräsidenten* and also to the *Land* police authorities that on several occasions civil servants had been put into concentration camps without consultation with the Ministry of the Interior. The circular further asked the *Regierungspräsident* of Düsseldorf for 'an immediate report' on the reasons for which a number of civil servants had been taken to camp Kemna near Wuppertal and continued:

As regards camp Kemna itself, it is true that some time ago Police President Veller, during a visit to my Ministry, informed the Chief of the political division of the establishment of this camp; but in view of the unsuitable nature of the factory buildings used, of the lack of washing facilities and other sanitary defects I have not approved the establishment of this camp nor of its continued existence. Indeed I cannot see the need to keep this camp. If prisoners cannot for the moment be transferred to the State concentration camps in the Emsland because further interrogation might be necessary, they must be kept in police prisons of which there is no shortage in Wuppertal ... it is my intention to disband this camp completely by the end of the month and to have the prisoners taken to State concentration camps.

On 15 December 1933 the Prussian Minister of Justice reported that it had 'happened repeatedly' that lawyers had been taken into protective custody without consultation with the Ministry of Justice and that as a result 'serious inconvenience' had been suffered by the litigating parties and by the accused and that 'the standing of the Law and thus of the State itself (were) threatened'.

The first Prussian instructions on the implementation of the emergency decree of 28 February 1933 laid down that only the *Kreis* police authorities were entitled to take people into protective custody and that at the start of the period of detention the prisoner must be handed a written protective custody warrant. It seems that this was frequently ignored in the course of 1933, so that the Prussian Gestapo Chief, Diels, thought it necessary on 16 January 1934 to enjoin the *Oberpräsidenten* and *Regierungspräsidenten* to obey these instructions:

Whereas in the early days of the take-over it was possible to overlook this because the protection of the State against the plots and machinations of its enemies required quick measures, unhampered by formal instructions, today the instructions issued must be strictly observed. . . . Anyone failing to do so will be called to account for misuse of authority and restriction of liberty.

A circular of the Reich Minister of the Interior to the *Land* governments of 9 January 1934 had the same end in view. It referred to complaints from which it appeared 'that in some cases protective custody is used for purposes irreconcilable with those for which it was intended'. It was the duty of the authorities 'to examine carefully in each instance whether there is justified cause for ordering protective custody'. In particular denunciations (by the NSDAP) needed 'to be investigated before protective custody is ordered'. 'Public law and order needed to be seriously threatened', and protective custody must 'continue only while this threat really exists'.

Protective custody must not be used as a 'punishment', i.e. as a substitute for a sentence passed by a court of law or by the police, and its duration must not be fixed at the outset. In principle it is therefore not permissible to order a person to be taken into protective custody instead of starting criminal proceedings against him. Recently there have been several cases when lawyers were taken into protective custody. In so far as the lawyer merely represents his client's interests in suitable form he may not be taken into protective custody even if the claim or application of his client is directed against an organ of the State. . . .

Frick's circular was aimed not least at Bavaria where SA and SS and local NSDAP *Hoheitsträger* [functionaries] were exerting strong pressure on the police executive, some of them continuing to issue protective custody orders on their own initiative. The fusion of State and Party functions was particularly striking in the leadership of the Bavarian political police. As Political Police Commander, Himmler and his deputy Heydrich were subordinate to the Bavarian Minister of the Interior, Adolf Wagner, who was also *Gauleiter* of the NSDAP of Upper Bavaria. But as

Reichsführer-SS Himmler had his own instrument of power and from the outset tried to fill the leading positions in the political police in Munich with SS men. Although as *Stabschef* of the SA Ernst Röhm was officially the superior of the *Reichsführer-SS*, the latter was independent of Röhm as regards police matters, i.e. as commander of the State apparatus of the political police, and could even, in agreement with the Minister of the Interior, use the police executive against the SA. But in the case of a conflict between the SS and the State organs he often formed a united front with the *Stabschef* of the SA.

Characteristic of this situation was the case of the three prisoners, Handschuch, Frantz and Dr Katz, who in the autumn of 1933 had died under torture while in protective custody in the SS-controlled concentration camp of Dachau. As the Public Prosecutor's Office had not been allowed to investigate the cases on the spot, the Bavarian Council of Ministers, at the request of Hans Frank, the Bavarian Minister of Justice, considered the case on 5 December 1933 and decided 'to pursue with determination the criminal proceedings arising from the happenings in Dachau concentration camp' and 'to oppose ... possible covering-up attempts'. If need be 'the *Land* police (should) be asked for assistance'. Himmler, on learning of the decision, announced that 'the matter was primarily the concern of the *Stabschef* of the SA, *Reichsminister* Röhm. He would have to consult him first.' Röhm then said in Himmler's presence to the representative of the Bavarian Minister of Justice, that the events in question were of a 'political nature', that they must 'at all events first be dealt with by the political authorities' and that he, Röhm, thought that 'for the time being they could not satisfactorily be handled by the judicial authorities'. That was his 'view as *Stabschef* and also as *Reichsminister*' who wanted to ensure that the Reich was 'not damaged' by legal proceedings of this kind. The argument that any damage to the standing of the National Socialist movement must be avoided was advanced by the Party then and later in almost every case of this kind with varying degrees of success. But as chiefs of the political police in Bavaria Himmler and Heydrich in 1933 and 1934, like the Prussian Gestapo under the leadership of Diels, occasionally clashed also with local SA bigwigs who either chased political opponents themselves or put the local police authorities on their tracks. In numerous Bavarian localities, for example, Catholic priests who were regarded as opponents of National Socialism had been arrested although – probably primarily in deference to the Vatican – Himmler had ordered as early as 2 July 1933 that the arrest of priests required his special approval. In a circular to the Bavarian police stations of 18 March 1934 Heydrich, who was effectively the Bavarian Political Police Commander, again pointed out that several diocesan authorities had 'complained to the Ministry of Education because the arrest of priests had seriously disrupted the work of the Church in a number of parishes'. Protective custody should therefore in future be restricted to particularly 'serious cases'.

During the endeavours to unify and consolidate the political police in the various *Länder* two conflicting trends were discernible in the spring of 1934: (*a*) the efforts of the Reich Minister of the Interior to establish through the *Reichsstatthalter* certain rules and to limit the use of protective custody on a nation-wide scale; and (*b*) Himmler's successful bid to assume control of the political police in the whole of the Reich. The position of the Reich Minister of the Interior seemed at first to be strengthened because under the law on the reconstruction of the Reich of 30 January 1934 the sovereignty of *Land* governments was extinguished and was transferred to the Reich. The *Land* governments thus came directly under the authority of the Reich government, and under the new centralist constitution the Reich Minister of the Interior – through the *Reichsstatthalter* – was given direct authority over the *Land* governments, including control of their police forces.

At the same time, however, Himmler initiated another amalgamation. As he appeared to Hitler, in his role of RfSS and head of the SD, to be obviously well placed to reorganize and unify the work of the political police, he succeeded between November 1933 and January 1934 in being appointed commander of the political police, or of the State police, in all *Länder* except Prussia. At the end of January 1934 Himmler controlled the State police of Bavaria, Württemberg, Baden, Hessen, Saxony, Anhalt, Thuringia, Brunswick, Oldenburg and the Hanseatic towns of Hamburg, Bremen and Lübeck. This was a position of considerable power and the *Reichsführer-SS* had no intention of surrendering it to the Reich Ministry of the Interior.

In Bavaria, Himmler's and Heydrich's strongest bastion, there were violent clashes in the spring with the *Reichsstatthalter*, von Epp; in a memorandum dated 20 March 1934, addressed to the Bavarian Minister of the Interior, von Epp had drawn attention to numerous instances of 'improper use of protective custody' in Bavaria and expressed anxiety that as a result 'confidence in the law' which formed 'the foundation of every State' might be 'shaken'. Whereas in Prussia the release of prisoners since the summer of 1933 had led to a sharp decline in the number of protective custody prisoners little had changed in Bavaria, so that *Reichsstatthalter* von Epp was forced to request an 'examinination of pending protective custody cases' because of the 'disproportionately high number of prisoners in protective custody' in Bavaria.

When the Ministry of Justice in Bavaria also raised strong objections to the uses to which protective custody was put, the Bavarian Minister of the Interior found it necessary at the end of March 1934 to order that the 'use of protective custody should henceforth be restricted'. Presumably at the instigation of Himmler and Heydrich he replied, on 14 April 1934, to the complaint of the *Reichsstatthalter* with a report in which – in the opinion of the *Reichsstatthalter* – 'every sentence [was] questionable and refutable', which contained numerous 'inaccuracies, distortions, misrepresentations and falsifications' and because of its form prevented 'factual study'. The relevant department of the Bavarian Ministry of the Interior (the political police) had rejected as presumptuous the request that the *Reichsstatthalter* should examine protective custody issues; it indicated a 'complete misunderstanding of the position of the *Reichsstatthalter*', as well as indirectly constituting a slight on the Reich Minister of the Interior.

The influence of the *Reichsminister* of the Interior on the actual issuing of protective custody orders was small from the start. But his authority to draw up uniform guide lines for the handling of protective custody in the entire Reich was as yet unchallenged. It was with this end in view that on 12 April 1934 he issued the fundamental protective custody regulation which was rounded off with some additions on 26 April 1934. What was remarkable about the regulation was that the Reich Minister of the Interior stated by way of introduction that the emergency decree of 28 February 1933 had only 'temporarily abrogated' the right of freedom of the individual and that it was merely that the 'time [was] not yet ripe for the complete abolition of protective custody'. But the misuse of protective custody, of which there had been many instances in the past, must be avoided at all costs. In expressing the view that the decree of 28 February 1933 had merely created a temporary state of emergency which must at some time come to an end, the Reich Ministry of the Interior was agreeing with the interpretations of the Reichstag fire decree given by several courts, including the Supreme Court of the Reich, which, however, failed to find acceptance.

The regulation of 12/26 April 1934 laid down that in Prussia only the *Geheime Staatspolizeiamt*, the *Oberpräsidenten* and *Regierungspräsidenten* or the Police President of Berlin and the *Staatspolizeistellen* in the *Regierungsbezirke*, and similar authorities in the other *Länder* (no longer therefore the *Kreis* authorities) were entitled to make protective custody orders. The regulation explicitly laid down that 'Officials of the NSDAP and the SA (*Kreisleiter, Gauleiter,* SA leaders) are not authorized to make protective custody orders'. They could, however, 'suggest to the competent authorities that a protective custody order should be made'. But these authorities 'must examine the reasons for these measures and bear the sole responsibility for taking them'. The circular continued: 'Anyone who without being authorized to do so arrests a person or deprives him in any other way of the use of his personal freedom is guilty of wrongful arrest (paragraphs 239, 341, 358 of the Penal Code). In such an event criminal proceedings must ruthlessly be taken.'

The regulation went on (paragraphs 2–5) to give the following guide lines on the procedure for making protective custody orders, laying down when it was permissible to issue such orders, where the protective custody should be spent and how long it should continue or when the order should be re-examined. These guide lines remained in force until the beginning of 1938:

2 *Protective Custody Order*
    i Upon arrest or not later than 24 hours after having been taken into protective custody the prisoner shall be handed a written and signed protective custody order.
    ii The order must state the reasons for the arrest.
    iii The next of kin (wife, parents, children, brothers or sisters) shall, unless there are special objections, be told upon inquiry why the

prisoner has been taken into protective custody and where he is.

iv If members of the NSDAP are taken into protective custody the responsible *Gau* or *Kreis* authorities and also the appropriate authorities of the Party (*Gau* or *Kreis* Court) shall be informed, with a statement why protective custody was ordered.

3 *Scope*

i The use of protective custody shall be permissible only
  a for the protection of the prisoner,
  b if the prisoner by his behaviour *directly* endangers law and order, particularly by subversive activities.

ii No protective custody order shall therefore be made unless the conditions of paragraph 1 also apply in particular:
  a in the case of persons who merely avail themselves of one of the rights (e.g. laying information, bringing an action, lodging an objection) which are theirs under civil and public law,
  b in the case of lawyers acting on behalf of clients,
  c for personal reasons, e.g. slander,
  d for economic reasons (wages questions, dismissals of employees, etc.).

iii Protective custody shall not be used as punishment for criminal offences or offences which although not criminal are reprehensible. Criminal offences shall be dealt with by the courts. The arrest of the accused shall be subject to the provisions of the code of criminal procedure (paragraphs 112 *et seq.*). Temporary arrest under paragraph 127, sub-paragraph 2, of the code of criminal procedure (police detention) shall be permissible even without a judicial warrant of arrest. Only in exceptional circumstances can the subsequent use of protective custody appear to be justified in the case of a criminal offence. In such cases a judicial warrant of arrest shall be obtained as quickly as possible.

4 *Enforcement*

Protective custody shall be served only in State prisons or concentration camps.

5 *Duration*

i Protective custody shall continue only as long as its purpose (paragraph 3 i) requires.

ii The use of protective custody as a punishment substitute for a definite period is not permissible.

iii Immediately upon arrest the prisoner shall be informed of the reasons for the protective custody order. If protective custody is prolonged the supreme *Land* authority shall be immediately informed, unless it has itself made the order. If the supreme *Land* authority has not itself made the protective custody order the prisoner shall be released on the eighth day after arrest, unless by this time the supreme *Land* authority has *explicitly* confirmed the protective custody order. The prisoner shall be informed in writing of the confirmation.

iv If the protective custody order has been made or confirmed by the supreme *Land* authority this authority shall *officially* examine *three months* after the date of arrest whether the prisoner can be released. If the protective custody is prolonged this revision shall be repeated every three months. . . .

The protective custody regulation of the Reich Minister of the Interior of 12/26 April 1934 expressed the desire of the administration to restore normal conditions and if possible to do away completely with the exceptional institution of protective custody and concentration camps, a desire which was actively supported by the judicial authorities. In Prussia most of the 'wild' concentration camps were disbanded in the spring of 1934. Of the SA and SS camps only Oranienburg, the Emsland camps, Lichtenburg and Columbia House in Berlin remained. In February 1934 the Secret State Police and the Prussian Central Prosecutor's Office had managed to disband the illegal concentration camp set up in the Vulkan dockyard in Stettin where numerous cases of maltreatment of prisoners had occurred. In April 1934 the main culprits (*SS-Obersturmführer* Dr Hoffmann, Pleins, Fink and others) were sentenced to several years' hard labour or imprisonment.[2] The SA and SS terror, which in the spring and summer of 1933 had dominated the scene, seemed broken.

That stable normalization was still a long way off, however, is highlighted by a memorandum by the head of the police section of the Reich Ministry of the Interior written in the spring of 1935 which states:[3]

Recently there has been a serious increase in protective custody orders. I believe there is an urgent need for a definitive clarification of the guide lines applicable to the reasons for, and the duration and execution of, protective custody. The protective custody regulation of the Reich Ministry of the Interior has long been nullified in practice by the activities of the political police. It is almost impossible to receive an adequate report on a protective custody case. The petitions which we receive in this connexion invariably stress one point which seems significant also to me: those concerned and their relatives come to terms with the fact of protective custody but not with the complete uncertainty of the grounds on which protective custody may or may not be ordered. This undoubted *lack of legal security* creates unrest and bitterness. It is indeed . . . intolerable that different principles should be applied in different parts of the country. . . . For reasons of official policy I must also raise fundamental objections to the renewed detention in protective custody of civil servants without the prior knowledge of their superiors, as well as to the State police practice, which sometimes has even worse effects, of making investigations about civil servants. I shall only mention the case of the *Kreisleiter* of Esterwegen who spent eight days in protective custody because, as emerged retrospectively, he had sent an accurate report about instances of maltreatment by the SS to his *Landrat*.

The memorandum concludes with the observation:

Either this is the responsibility of the Reich Minister of the Interior: in that case he must to a far greater degree than hitherto be put in a position to give orders where issues concerning the political police are involved,
or this responsibility is henceforth taken over with all that this implies by the *Reichsführer-SS,* who in practice already claims control of the political police in the Reich. . . .

In fact the camps and the instrument of protective custody did not disappear. On the contrary, while the camps and the number of prisoners in protective custody were reduced, the establishment of concentration camps was standardized under the direction of the SS in such a way as finally to remove completely protective custody issues from the control of the legal and administrative authorities and to make them the exclusive sphere of the unified SS and police in which the public had no say. At the same time that Frick issued his protective custody regulation, in April 1934, Diels was replaced in Prussia as Inspector of the Gestapo by Himmler or, in fact, by Heydrich. Himmler had achieved his aim of controlling the whole of the political police of the *Länder*. Göring, however, remained Chief of the Prussian Secret State Police which by the law of 30 November 1933 became an independent branch of the internal administration (with the State police office as the supreme *Land* authority) and was thus removed from the authority of the Prussian Ministry of the Interior and placed directly under the Prussian Minister President.

As his deputy, with the title of 'Inspector of the Secret State Police', Himmler continued in practice to supervise the Gestapo while Heydrich, appointed Chief of the Prussian Secret Police Office on 22 April 1934, moved into the Prinz-Albrecht-Strasse as the real master. An essential pre-condition was thus created which ensured that as regards protective custody and the concentration camps, matters would develop in accordance with the wishes of Himmler and the SS.

The Structure of the SS Concentration Camp System 1934-7

1 Outline of developments

The protective custody regulation of the Reich Ministry of the Interior of 12/26 April 1934 remained in force as a guide line until January 1938.* But what in fact happened was that the attempt to make the concentration camps a firm and permanent institution triumphed over the move towards ending the state of emergency.

In his memoirs the Gestapa Chief superseded by Himmler and Heydrich [i.e. Diels] recalls that in December 1933, during a discussion in Göring's presence, Hitler was not altogether hostile to the arguments for reducing the number of prisoners in protective custody. But he firmly rejected the idea of surrendering the opportunity – introduced with protective custody – of employing the police to remove from the scene persons who were politically or otherwise undesirable, or who were regarded as dangerous. The special courts in existence since March 1933 and the many new legal provisions for punishing undesirable political activity or any other form of activity directed against the government might have been thought to provide ample facilities for dealing with enemies or rivals of the NSDAP; evidently Hitler, who on principle distrusted the law, was not going to be satisfied with criminal prosecutions by the judicial authorities.

The attempts, not altogether hopeless, of the administrative and judicial authorities to restore a state of law during the spring and early summer of 1934, suffered a severe setback on 30 June when on Hitler's personal orders Röhm and the SA leaders closest to him were shot out of hand. At the same time Hitler ordered the murder of other public figures (Gregor Strasser,

*In Bavaria it was applied in accordance with a special order of the Bavarian Minister of the Interior of 2 May 1934 which in part reproduced verbatim the provisions of the special regulation of the Reich Ministry of the Interior of 12/26 April 1934 and in part adapted them to the special Bavarian conditions. For example it laid down that only if 'a longer period of detention [seemed] imperative [should] the prisoner be sent on the orders of the Bavarian political police of Dachau concentration camp with the next mass transport' and that 'the release of prisoners in protective custody detained in Dachau concentration camp ... [was] exclusively the responsibility of the Bavarian political police'.

Schleicher and others) who had become a nuisance to him and in retrospect proclaimed the operation to have been 'legal'. The dramatic loss of power suffered by the SA directly benefited the SS and Himmler who ceased to be subordinate to the SA leadership. In the concentration camp sphere also the powerful rival of the SS was now eliminated. As a consequence of the Röhm affair armed SS units replaced, partly under the threat of force (as in Oranienburg), the former SA guards of various camps.

In the weeks that followed, Hitler tried at first to let bygones be bygones. Upon Hindenburg's death on 2 August 1934 he took over the office and powers of Reich President, thus strengthening his position still further. On 7 August 1934 he issued a general amnesty order under which certain prisoners in protective custody, primarily members of the SA, were released. In the amnesty order Hitler declared:

Furthermore it is my wish, now that the operation of 30 June 1934 has been concluded, that the regulation of the Reich Minister of the Interior of 12/26 April 1934 on the use and enforcement of protective custody shall in future be carefully observed by all the authorities.

However, this manifestation of the Führer's wishes amounted to little more than an attempt to pacify the anxiety aroused among top civil servants by the Röhm affair. Indirectly at any rate, Hitler continued to protect a number of crass offenders against the protective custody regulations, and by quashing verdicts and granting pardons clearly expressed his view of investigations by the Public Prosecutor's Office into SA and SS activities in the camps.

A case in point was the Saxon concentration camp Hohnstein where in 1934 several instances of serious ill-treatment of prisoners had been discovered. Charges were brought against twenty-three SA leaders and camp guards, including the Commandant, *SA-Standartenführer* Jähnichen and *Oberregierungsrat* Erich Vogel, the Gestapo official responsible for receiving and interrogating prisoners who in the course of his duties had taken a hand in torturing them. In a letter of 19 December 1934 to the Reich Minister of Justice, Dr Gürtner, the Saxon *Gauleiter*, Mutschmann, recommended that the case should be dropped on the grounds that it would adversely affect the standing of the National Socialist Movement. But Gürtner replied on 8 January

1935 that he had 'severe reservations' about quashing the proceedings which the Führer and Chancellor alone could order:

The form of ill-treatment [in Hohnstein] reveals a brutality and cruelty in the perpetrators which are totally alien to German sentiment and feeling. Such cruelty, reminiscent of oriental sadism, cannot be explained or excused by militant bitterness however great.[1]

The case came before the Dresden *Landgericht* [provincial court] but it was severely criticized by the Party. Mutschmann himself intervened in the proceedings by interceding with the Director of the *Landgericht*. Nevertheless on 15 May 1935 prison sentences, although relatively mild, were passed on the twenty-three accused SA members. The Party sought to revenge itself in its own fashion. Two members of the NSDAP who had belonged to the jury which found the accused guilty were expelled from the Party. The Public Prosecutor, who had conducted the case for the prosecution and who himself belonged to the SA, was asked by his SA superior to resign. Gürtner came to hear of the sequel and in a letter dated 5 June 1935 asked the Führer's deputy for redress because otherwise 'the independence of the judiciary which is the basis of an orderly administration of justice [will] disappear'.[2]

In a letter to Hitler of 18 June 1935 Gürtner further recommended the rejection of Mutschmann's request that the pending separate proceedings against *Oberregierungsrat* Vogel should be quashed. But at the end of November 1935 it became known at the Reich Ministry of Justice that Hitler had pardoned all those sentenced in the Hohnstein trial and had ordered the proceedings against the Gestapo official Vogel to be quashed after Mutschmann had personally interceded with Hitler.[3]

Also symptomatic are several other documented cases of the year 1935 which concerned concentration camps. On 30 January 1935 the Reich Minister of the Interior in an order to the Bavarian *Staatskanzlei* [State Chancellery] pointed out as he had done several times previously that there was a 'disproportionately large number of prisoners in protective custody' in Bavaria and that 'on the part of the Bavarian political police' nothing had so far been done to reduce it or to provide an 'adequate explanation'. 'The latest figures still' showed 'the number of prisoners in protective custody in Bavaria as being several hundred more than the total of prisoners in protective custody in all the other *Länder*, including Prussia'. He, Frick, was therefore ordering an immediate investigation by the Bavarian Minister of the Interior and requesting by 1 March the preparation of 'a list of all prisoners who have spent more than six months in protective custody with full particulars of the reasons'. Himmler, in his capacity as Commander of the Bavarian Political Police, saw a copy of this letter and discussed it with Hitler. A hand-written note on his copy reveals in laconic fashion the result of this interview. It reads: 'Submitted to the Führer on 20. 2. 1935. The prisoners will remain. H[einrich] H[immler].' Irregularities and high-handedness in the issuing of protective custody orders and in their enforcement in the concentration camps in 1935 led the Reich Minister of Justice to make repeated representations to the *Reichsführer-SS*. He drew attention to the high rate of deaths in the camps and recommended measures to reduce it. In addition the Reich Minister of Justice urged that lawyers should in future be allowed to be present when a person was taken into protective custody and that the prisoners should be given the opportunity of legal assistance. Himmler replied with two terse notes, dated 6 November 1935:

a On the occasion of my interview of 1 November 1935 I submitted to the Führer personally your letter of 16. 10., together with the statement of deaths in the concentration camps. In view of the conscientious direction of the camps special measures are not considered necessary. (Signed) H. Himmler.

b On 1. 11. 1935 I transmitted to the Führer and Chancellor the request submitted to us that lawyers should be permitted to intervene in protective custody cases.

The Führer has prohibited the consultation of lawyers and has asked me to inform you accordingly. (Signed) H. Himmler.

In 1935 there was a new wave of arrests of persons suspected of 'inflammatory' Marxist activity. Internal Gestapa figures for the six months from October 1935 to March 1936 show that a considerable number of people were arrested for 'activity on behalf of the KPD and SPD'. It may be assumed that a substantial number of the prisoners were, at any rate temporarily, transferred to concentration camps.

In the majority of cases, the arrests made by the State police for political reasons during this period seem to have been for trifling offences. An interesting insight is provided by the reports of the Bavarian political police for the period of 30 March to 2 November 1936 (i.e. roughly seven months). They not only give the number of arrests made in Bavaria in this period – altogether 1,791 persons* – but also give detailed reasons, as required by the regulations, for the arrest. What is striking is that the formulation is frequently very vague. In no less than 237 cases (approximately 13 per cent) the reason for the arrest is given as 'behaviour harmful to the State' or 'hostile to the State', while in a number of cases there is even vaguer reference to 'political activities' or 'seditious behaviour' and similar remarks.

Persons arrested by the State Police for KPD and SPD activity (October 1935–March 1936)

month	in the Reich as a whole	in Prussia alone
October 1935	1,510	952
November 1935	1,098	564
December 1935	832	594
January 1936	1,238	758
February 1936	1,195	879
March 1936	1,393	881

Reasonably concrete information is given for the arrest of the following groups of persons:

a for preparation or suspicion of preparation of *high treason*: 252 persons (14 per cent)
b for activity on behalf of, or propaganda for, the *KPD or SPD*: 156 persons (8 per cent)
c for prohibited activity on behalf of the *Ernste Bibelforscher* [Jehovah's Witnesses]: 137 (7 per cent)
d for disturbance of or threat to public safety or anti-social behaviour: 137 persons (7 per cent)
e for offences or suspicion of offences against Paragraph 175: 83 persons (4.2 per cent)

Relatively the largest number of arrests seems to have been of persons denounced to the police for so-called subversive remarks. In 340 cases (almost 20 per cent) the reasons for the arrest are given as 'subversive remarks', 'spreading atrocity stories', 'insulting the Führer', 'insulting leading personalities', 'defamation of the swastika', 'vilification of *Gauleiter* Streicher', etc. It

*In the same period 1,047 persons in Bavaria were released from protective custody.

may be assumed that there were similar complaints behind a substantial number of other vague charges (such as 'behaviour prejudicial to the State').

The intention apparently was to use protective custody as a means to nip in the bud any criticism of the National Socialist leadership. In the transitional period 1935/6 this was an important function of the concentration camps.

During 1935 it became increasingly obvious that Hitler had no intention of giving up the concentration camps or the instrument of protective custody, or to subject them to judicial control. There was no further mention of the temporary character of the emergency decree of 28 February 1933. The courts, too, adapted themselves to the wishes of the Führer: judges increasingly accepted the view that coercive measures based on this emergency decree were justified not only in dealing with the communist threat against the State in the narrower sense but also in defending the State and the National Socialist community against opposition as a whole. The Prussian Court of Appeal, as the highest Prussian legal instance, in its decision of 8 December 1935 concerning the sentences passed on some juveniles for activities in a Catholic youth movement, put forward the thesis of the indirect communist threat and argued that it was the aim of National Socialism to create an indivisible national community. Organizational activities in which undue emphasis was laid on religious beliefs represented obstacles in the way of this aim, acted as a factor of disintegration and thus indirectly assisted communist aims for sedition.

In the spring of the same year the Prussian *Oberverwaltungsgericht* [Supreme Administrative Tribunal] in a judgment of 2 May 1935 had advanced the view that actions for the annulment of an administrative act [*Verwaltungsklage*] were permissible only in a limited number of complaints against coercive measures of the Secret State Police as an independent authority of the internal administration with special political and police responsibilities. The Prussian law on the Secret State Police of 10 February 1936 said explicitly in paragraph 7: 'The orders and affairs of the Secret State Police are not liable to investigation by administrative tribunals.' After the enactment of this highly important law the only way of opposing Gestapo measures, in particular the use of protective custody, was to make a disciplinary complaint [*Dienstaufsichtsbeschwerde*], an illusory means of redress because in the last instance the complaint was dealt with by the Gestapa. Police detention of political opponents was thus finally removed from judicial control and challenge. After the enactment of the law Dr Werner Best, Heydrich's deputy in the Secret State Police Office, wrote:

With the establishment of the National Socialist Führer State, Germany for the first time has a system of government which derives from a living idea its legitimate right to resist, with all the coercive means at the disposal of the State, any attack on the present form of the State and its leadership. National Socialism's political principle of totalitarianism, which corresponds to the ideological principle of the organically indivisible national community, does not tolerate within its sphere the development of any political ideas at variance with the will of the majority. Any attempt to gain recognition for or even to uphold different political ideas will be ruthlessly dealt with, as the symptom of an illness which threatens the healthy unity of the indivisible national organism, regardless of the subjective wishes of its supporters.

Proceeding from these principles the National Socialist Führer State has created for the first time in Germany a political police which we regard as modern, i.e. as meeting our present-day needs; an institution which carefully supervises the political health of the German body politic, which is quick to recognize all symptoms of disease and germs of destruction – be they the result of disintegration from within or purposeful poisoning from without – and to remove them by every suitable means.

To discover the enemies of the State, to watch them and to render them harmless at the right moment is the preventive police duty of a political police. In order to fulfil this duty the political police must be free to use every means suited to achieve the required end. It is correct to say that in the National Socialist Führer State the institutions called upon to protect State and people and to carry out the will of the State possess as of right the authority required to fulfil their task, an authority which is derived solely from the new conception of the State and one which requires no special legal legitimization. ... It is no more possible to lay down legal norms for the means to be used by a political police than it is possible to anticipate for all time to come every form of subversive attack or every other threat to the State. ... From these inescapable facts there has developed the concept of the political police as a new and unique body for the protection of the State whose members, in addition to their official duties, regard themselves as belonging to a fighting formation. ...

In a simultaneous article on 'Fighting Subversion' Heydrich said that a successful struggle against the enemies of State and people in the shape of Jews, communists, Freemasons and 'politically active' representatives of the churches was possible only 'if the opponent is put out of action once and for all' and if he 'is recognized intellectually by his methods and means'. The prerequisite for police action against the opponent of the régime was 'the ideological struggle against the opponent's basic principles' which could 'be conducted only by the National Socialist Movement'. Therefore the 'State Police [must work] in close collaboration with the Security Service of the *Reichsführer-SS*' which as 'a branch of the whole of the SS is entrusted by the Reich leadership of the NSDAP with investigating and supervising the ideological opponents of National Socialism'.

The required close collaboration between the Security Service of the Movement and the State Police of the government is ensured by the fact that the *Reichsführer-SS* is by virtue of his position supreme chief of the Security Service and at the same time deputy chief of the Secret State Police and that the head of the Secret State Police Office under him is also chief of the *Sicherheitshauptamt* [Central Security Office].

The absorption of the functions of the State Police by the Party organization of the SS and the process of taking these functions away from the internal administration was largely achieved as regards the political police by April 1934 and was definitely assured by the Prussian law on the Gestapo of 10 February 1936. With the appointment on 17 June 1936 of Himmler as Chief of the German Police the process was finally extended to the entire police. The fact that one man was in charge of both the SS and the police ensured that henceforth SS and police worked hand in hand also in institutional matters.

In the special sphere of the concentration camps this process had begun in Dachau as early as 1933. The years 1933/7 represent a transitional phase in the history of the National Socialist concentration camps for two reasons: during this period most of the receiving centres founded largely by the SA during the revolutionary phase of the National Socialist seizure of power and the more or less 'wild' camps for political prisoners were closed, the overall number of prisoners in protective custody was considerably reduced and the worst abuses were halted. At the same time and beginning with Dachau, the SS, buttressed by the position of strength already created by Himmler and

Heydrich in Bavaria, secured a monopoly of the few remaining camps which they standardized. Dachau became the model for camp discipline and for general regulations governing the division of duties, guard personnel, etc., and also for the widening of detention to include non-political categories of persons.

2 The Dachau model: punishment and treatment of prisoners and guard regulations

In the first month of its existence Dachau concentration camp, established in March 1933, resembled most of the so-called 'wild KZs'. The prisoners sent there were largely at the mercy of the guards who in Dachau from the start consisted mainly of armed members of the *Allgemeine SS*. Such service regulations as there were for the guards were very general; consequently arbitrariness, violence and a tendency, demonstrably encouraged by the camp leadership, to show helpless political enemies or Jewish prisoners who was the master, became widespread. The first Commandant of Dachau was *SS-Oberführer* Wäckerle under whose leadership many instances of maltreatment as well as a number of brutal murders occurred. The Public Prosecutor's Office of the *Landgericht* Munich II, investigating in 1933 the cases of four prisoners murdered in Dachau in the second half of May 1933, noted among other things that Commandant Wäckerle had laid down in writing a set of rules of draconic 'special regulations' for the prisoners. These contained no instructions for the guards but were a first attempt, obviously inspired by Himmler, to press the treatment of prisoners in the camp into a system of punishments and classifications. Interrogated by the Public Prosecutor, Wäckerle said that 'he had drawn up these regulations himself on the order of his superiors' and that they had been 'approved by the Commander of the Political Police (Himmler)'.[4] According to the special regulations 'martial law' was in force in the camp and prisoners attempting to escape would be shot without warning. In addition the regulations contained a long list of actions punishable principally by confinement, varying from open to close arrest, for up to three months. Close arrest meant solitary confinement in a 'completely dark room' with bread and water. Arrest was intended primarily as a punishment for insubordination, unpunctuality or rudeness and to discourage prisoners from making complaints.

Under paragraph 8 of the 'special regulations' certain offences, such as assault, incitement to disobedience or the attempt to do so were subject to the death penalty. Finally, provisions were made to divide the prisoners into three grades distinguished by accommodation and food. To begin with, all prisoners were put into grade II and then, depending on their 'behaviour', transferred either to the higher grade or to the punishment grade (III) in which prisoners slept on boards instead of mattresses and received short rations. Grade III was also intended for prisoners 'whose past [demanded] particularly strict supervision'.

The regulations laid down that 'jurisdiction [was] without exception exercised by the camp Commander'. For cases subject to the death penalty (paragraph 8) the following procedure was laid down:

In all cases under paragraph 8 sentence will be passed by a camp court consisting of the camp Commander [*Lagerkommandeur*], one or two officers appointed by the camp Commandant [*Lagerkommandant*] and an SS man who is a member of the guard unit. The case for the prosecution will be presented by an SS-man, on the staff of the camp headquarters and appointed by the camp Commander. If the number of votes cast is equal the president of the camp court will have the casting vote. The president will be the Commander of the camp for the time being.

It is doubtful to what extent the 'special regulations' were actually enforced in Dachau, and in particular it is not known whether the procedure for sentencing prisoners to death in the camp as provided for in these regulations was used; but there emerged here – in contrast to most of the existing SA camps – the tendency to develop a systematized terror and to lay down certain principles for the treatment of prisoners, for example the division into individual groups with different conditions of imprisonment. What also became very clear was Himmler's attempt to organize the camps as legally independent administrative units outside the penal code and the ordinary processes of law. The Public Prosecutor's Office in Munich, which was handed the 'special regulations' at the end of May 1933, asked the Bavarian Minister of Justice to investigate whether the arbitrary imposition of martial law and of the death penalty by the camp Commandant or the political police was legally admissible. But Himmler and the subordinate Commandants continued to employ the threat of similar punishments. The Commandant of Dachau, Wäckerle, had, however, become a liability. On 1 June 1933 the Public Prosecutor's Office charged him, together with the camp doctor, Nuernbergk, and *Kanzleiobersekretär* Mutzbauer of the camp headquarters with aiding and abetting in the murder of the prisoner Sebastian Nefzer,[5] and Himmler was compelled to dismiss Wäckerle.

Under the direction of the new Dachau Commandant, *SS-Oberführer* Theodor Eicke, appointed at the end of June 1933, the treatment and punishment of prisoners was further systematized. A division of authority was established and detailed service regulations were provided for the guard formations. Under Eicke, Dachau became the model for the other camps and after Eicke's appointment as Inspector of Concentration Camps in mid-1934, his personal influence on the future organization and 'spirit' of the SS guard formations was second only to Himmler's.

Theodor Eicke, born in 1892 in Hampont (Alsace-Lorraine) had given up a career as pay-master in the Imperial Army in 1919 to join the police administration in Thuringia. After qualifying as an Inspector in 1920 he was briefly employed by the security police and the criminal police and finally by the police administration in Ludwigshafen on the Rhine, but he quickly lost his various jobs because of anti-republican political activities and was at times unemployed. From 1923 to 1932 he worked for I.G.-Farbwerke Ludwigshafen as an executive and looked after their works anti-espionage service; early in 1928 he became a member of the NSDAP and the SA, but shortly afterwards transferred to the SS where he was quickly promoted. At the end of 1930 he was appointed leader of the *SS-Sturm Ludwigshafen*, and a year later as *SS-Standartenführer* he was put in charge of the *SS-Standarte* of Rhine-Palatinate. Sentenced to two years' penal servitude in March 1932 for preparing political bomb attacks, Eicke fled to Italy in the summer of 1932 on Himmler's instructions and as *SS-Oberführer* took charge of the SS refugee camp which the Italian Fascist authorities had set up in Malcesine on Lake Garda. In mid-February 1933 Eicke returned to Germany. But because he tried to settle by force an old quarrel with Bürckel, the *Gauleiter* of the Palatine NSDAP, he was taken into protective custody on 21 March on Himmler's orders and transferred for observation to the psychiatric university clinic of Würzburg where he was under the care of *Privatdozent* Dr Heyde.

In June, when it became necessary to replace the Dachau Commandant, Himmler remembered Eicke who from the clinic in Würzburg had sent lengthy letters to the *Reichsführer-SS* clamouring for release. At the end of June 1933 Eicke was appointed as the new Commandant of Dachau. When Himmler was put in charge of the Prussian Secret State Police in April 1934 he entrusted Eicke in May 1934 with the reorganization and unification of all concentration camps. He was officially appointed 'Inspector of Concentration Camps and SS guard formations' (SS-Death's Head formations) [*Inspekteur der Konzentrationslager und SS-Wachverbände (SS-Totenkopfverbände)*] on 4 July 1934. On 11 July 1934 he was promoted to *SS-Gruppenführer* and thus acquired the same rank as that of Himmler's other collaborators (Heydrich, Pohl) who contributed substantially to the development of the SS.

The innovations introduced under Eicke's leadership in Dachau found expression among other things in the 'disciplinary camp regulations'[6] issued on 1 October 1933 'for the maintenance of discipline and order' and particularly in the 'service regulations for escorts and guards'.[7] The new disciplinary regulations of which only fragmentary evidence survives, embodied most of Wäckerle's earlier 'special regulations', in particular that of the right of the camp Commandant to authorize punishment and to be responsible for its execution 'to the Political Police Commander personally'. Eicke's regulations also provided for a graded system of arrest (eight days, fourteen days, twenty-one days and forty-two days close arrest). Solitary confinement with bread and water, which drove many prisoners to despair and suicide, was retained. Corporal punishment was added as a new form of punishment to be introduced in all concentration camps. The regulations provided for 'twenty-five strokes of the cane' which could be ordered in addition to arrest. Eicke also seems to have been responsible for the special order that caning must be carried out by several SS personnel (and later also by prisoners) in the presence of the SS guards, the prisoners and of the Commandant or the *Schutzhaftlagerführer* [Commandant in charge of the camp for prisoners in protective custody]. The object of this regulation was to lay down in writing and to stress that caning could not be carried out arbitrarily by individual guards and that it was a regular form of punishment. Because the caning was carried out by several SS men the ill-treatment became impersonal and anonymous and every member of the guard formations was accustomed from the beginning to this act which he might at any time be ordered to perform.

In common with the previous 'special regulations', Eicke's disciplinary regulations stipulated the death penalty for certain offences. Paragraphs 11 and 12 said that a prisoner who talked politics 'for the purpose of incitement' or gathered with others, passed on 'atrocity propaganda' and similar things, 'shall be hanged as an agitator according to revolutionary law'; a prisoner who 'assaults a guard', 'refuses to . . . obey' or indulged in any form of mutiny 'will be shot on the spot as a mutineer or subsequently hanged'. Deliberate sabotage was also punishable by death (paragraph 13).

Milder forms of punishment included 'hard or particularly dirty labour . . . under special supervision' and as secondary forms of punishment 'punishment drill, beatings, withholding of mail, deprivation of food, hard quarters, tying to a post, reprimands and warnings'. The disciplinary regulations further provided:

All punishments will be recorded. Arrest and hard labour will prolong protective custody by not less than eight weeks; secondary punishment will prolong protective custody by not less than four weeks. Prisoners in solitary confinement will not be released within a foreseeable period.

The principle that prisoners should be treated with the maximum, though impersonal and disciplined, severity and should be shown no lenience was stressed at the outset of the penal regulations and was repeated in stereotype fashion by Eicke during the training and instruction of the SS guards. Remembering the training in Dachau where he was posted in 1934 the later Commandant of Auschwitz, Rudolf Höss, recollected what Eicke's sermons amounted to:

Any trace of pity revealed to the 'enemies of the State' a weakness which they would immediately exploit. Any pity whatsoever for 'enemies of the State' was unworthy of an SS-man. There was no place in the ranks of the SS for men with soft hearts and any such would do well to retire quickly to a monastery. He [Eicke] could only use hard, determined men who ruthlessly obeyed every order. It was not for nothing that their emblem was the Death's Head and that they carried a loaded gun. They were the only soldiers who even in peace time faced the enemy day and night, the enemy behind the wire. . . .

Eicke had drummed the concept of 'dangerous enemies of the State' so forcefully and convincingly into his SS-men that anyone who knew no better was firmly convinced by it. . . .

The purpose of Eicke's everlasting lectures and orders to the same effect was . . . to turn his SS-men completely against the prisoners, to stir up their feelings against the prisoners. . . .

Further evidence of the effort to standardize the treatment and supervision of prisoners is found in the service regulations for escorting and guarding prisoners, introduced together with the disciplinary regulations on 1 October 1933 by Eicke in Dachau. They laid down to the last detail the procedure of the roll-call of prisoners, of the march off to work in military style, the duties of sentries and escorts, the controls and even the wording of individual commands, the distance which guards should keep from prisoners, the form of salute which the prisoners should give, how to load rifles and release safety catches, etc. The service regulations said specifically:

The only duty of the escort is to guard the prisoners. They will watch the prisoners' behaviour at work. Lazy prisoners will be urged to work. But any form of maltreatment and chicanery is strictly prohibited.

If a prisoner is openly careless and lazy at work or gives impudent answers the guard will take his name. After work he will make a report. Self-help indicates a lack of discipline. If the prisoners are to respect the SS guards the SS-man on guard duty cannot be permitted to lounge about, to lean against something, to push his rifle on to his back or to place his hand over the muzzle.

A guard who shelters from the rain becomes a figure of fun and does not behave like a soldier. . . . The SS-man must show pride and dignity. . . . The use of the familiar *Du* [thou] amounts to fraternization. It is humiliating for a man who wears the Death's Head to allow himself to become an errand boy for bolsheviks and bosses. . . . The SS escort will not engage in private conversation with the prisoners. . . .

The regulations for the immediate use of firearms in the case of suspected escape or mutiny by the prisoners were particularly strict:

Anyone who allows a prisoner to escape will be arrested and handed over to the Bavarian Political Police for negligently releasing a prisoner. A prisoner who tries to escape will be shot without warning. Guards who in the execution of their duties shoot a prisoner will not be punished.

If a guard is assaulted by a prisoner the attack will be countered not by physical violence but by the use of firearms. A guard who fails to observe this regulation may expect to be dismissed immediately. . . .

In case of mutiny or revolt by a detachment of prisoners all guards on duty will open fire. Warning shots are not permitted on principle.

There is evidence that these guard regulations were introduced also in the other concentration camps which Eicke took over as Inspector of Concentration Camps after 1934. When in March/April 1935 two prisoners were shot in Columbia-Haus concentration camp in Berlin allegedly for resisting, the culprits justified themselves to the investigating Public Prosecutor by referring explicitly to the service regulations, the observance of which 'up to the present' had been made 'obligatory [for them] by their superiors'.

At the same time the camp Commandant, Dr Reiner, in a report of 8 May 1935 to Himmler, stated that he had 'passed on clearly the instructions given by the Inspector' regarding the treatment of prisoners and had forbidden anyone to lay hands on a prisoner, to insult prisoners or to have private conversation with them. Reports of refractory behaviour or disobedience on the part of prisoners, he had passed on with the request that they should receive a beating; in cases where his request had been granted by the Inspector the accused had been punished in front of the assembled prisoners. He himself had always been present.

In cases where reports of concentration camp prisoners being shot while trying to escape or offering resistance were made to sound plausible, the Public Prosecutor's Offices even at that time as a rule stopped their investigations and brought no charges, although legally these were clear cases of murder or manslaughter. Large sections of the legal profession at any rate were fully aware of the illegality of these happenings. In the above-mentioned case of the concentration camp Columbia-Haus, the Berlin Chief Public Prosecutor declared: 'The service regulations cannot exonerate the accused. As they do not represent a legislative enactment they cannot set aside the illegality of the accused's action. This is a case of a regrettable gap between service instructions and legally permissible action.'

The general guard regulations evolved in Dachau in October 1933 remained in force in spirit until the end of the war. A subsequent circular, dated 27 July 1943, from the Inspector of Concentration Camps to camp Commandants contained seven pages of 'instruction in the duties and obligations of guards' which in content and tone agreed largely with Eicke's old directions.

The same was not the case with the penal regulations. It seems that only veiled use, if any, was ever made of the capital punishment by shooting or hanging provided for in the Dachau penal system of 1933. The execution of so-called death sentences, if it could not be plausibly presented as an instance of a prisoner being shot while trying to escape or resist, was likely in the first years after 1933 to result in an indictment by the Public Prosecutor's Office. The SS found that it was holding a double-edged sword. The records of the Reich Minister of Justice show that Eicke himself had stated in April 1935 that at that time a 'secret counter order' had gone out 'to the effect that these severe penal regulations are not really used' but merely intended for purposes of 'intimidation'. In order to prevent the growing doubts of the legal profession over the numerous cases of unnatural death in the concentration camps from coming to a head, the Gestapo in October 1935 also issued special guide-lines for concentration camps which obliged the Commandants to report immediately on their own initiative to the Public Prosecutor's Office cases in which there was no clear medical evidence that death was due to natural causes. Limits were thus set to the high-handedness of the Commandants.

From the report of the Commandant of Columbia-Haus concentration camp quoted above, it appears that even at that period (1935) camp leaders were not entitled to impose the heaviest penalties on their own authority. Beatings also required the approval of the Inspector of Concentration Camps. In the years of the relatively orderly implementation of protective custody orders, from 1935-6 to 1939, arbitrary killings became rarer. The main forms of punishment in all concentration camps were regular beatings, close arrest, hard labour, making detention conditions worse by prohibiting prisoners from writing or receiving letters, as well as tying prisoners to trees, etc., a form of punishment originally introduced by Eicke in Dachau. Although even in this period there were instances of prisoners being mal-treated and killed by SS guards, particularly as hatred of the prisoners was consciously cultivated, between 1935 and 1939 such instances were relatively few in number.

3 The Inspector of concentration camps and Leader of the Death's Head Formations (direction and administration; development of the concentration camps and Death's Head Formations until 1939)

The period of Eicke's activity in Dachau saw not only the crystallization of what later became the standard principles for the treatment of prisoners but also the development of the basic organization, of the division of authority in the direction and administration of the camps. Eicke, writing to Himmler on 10 August 1936, said, looking back, that when he took over in Dachau he had found 'a corrupt guard detachment of barely 120 men'.

We were generally regarded as a necessary evil which merely cost money; insignificant guards behind barbed wire. At times I was forced literally to beg the treasuries for the meagre wages of my officers and men. As *Oberführer* in Dachau I myself received a monthly salary of RM. 230. . . . At the beginning there were no cartridges or rifles, let alone machine guns. Of the entire staff only three men could handle a machine gun. My men were billeted in draughty factories. Everywhere there was poverty and misery. At that time these guards were under the command of the *Oberabschnitt Süd* which left the worries and anxieties to me but, unasked, sent me people of whom for some reason or other it wanted to be rid in Munich; in consequence they contaminated my men and their spirit. I encountered disloyalty, graft and corrup-tion. For these reasons I was forced to dismiss about sixty men in four weeks. No progress could be made because the unit was under the command and influence of the *Oberabschnitt Süd* and was used as a depository for so-called *Versorgungsanwärter* [ex-soldiers entitled to ex-servicemen's welfare benefits]. When I found it impossible to continue like this the *Reichsführer-SS* granted my request and placed the small guard unit under my exclusive command. From then on there was uninterrupted progress. . . .

The guard unit in Dachau became independent and ceased to be part of the *Allgemeine SS* in the autumn of 1934, after Eicke had been appointed Inspector of Concentration Camps but was still continuing for a time as Commander of Dachau (Eicke's successors as Commandant in Dachau were: 1935 *SS-Oberführer* Heinrich Deubel, 1936–9 *SS-Oberführer* Hans Loritz, formerly Commandant of camp Esterwegen).

Until the autumn of 1934 the guard unit of the concentration camp belonged 'for SS purposes' to the *Oberabschnitt Süd* of the *Allgemeine SS*, and the Commandant was responsible only for their use in the camp and for their training as guards. In Dachau the special '*SS-Sturmbann* Dachau'[8] or *Wachtruppe Oberbayern der Allgemeinen SS* [Guard unit Upper Bavaria of the General SS] formed in 1933 for guard duties was housed as early as 1933/4 in special SS huts or barracks alongside the actual camp. The SS-men of the guard unit were paid like normal members of the *Allgemeine SS* and were equipped with arms and trained in their use. The leader of the *SS-Sturmbann* Dachau did not take his orders from the camp Commandant. The latter controlled only those members of the guard unit whose turn it was to do guard and escort duty in the camp. Supervising the guards was the responsibility of the so-called 'barrack duty service' [*Kasernentagesdienst*], later called 'duty officer' [*Führer vom Dienst*]. It was to him, whose office was outside the camp in the SS barracks, or to the leader of the *SS Sturmbann* Dachau that, according to the guard regulations of 1 October 1933, instances of violation of duty by the guards were reported.

Distinct from the changing staff of the guard and escort services there was the permanent SS personnel in the camp itself. Even in Eicke's day in Dachau this staff was divided into various sections. As early as 1933 there existed in addition to the Commandant's headquarters a political section of the camp as an outpost of the political police in the camp, a special office of the camp doctor and probably also a special *Verwaltungsführer* [official in charge of administration] who was responsible for the camp finances, so-called prisoners' effects, the camp workshops, and food and clothing. In the protective custody camp proper, which in Dachau in 1935 consisted of ten companies or blocks each with approximately 250 prisoners (eight of them being companies of political prisoners), the company or block leaders [*Kompanie-bzw. Blockführer*] generally held the rank of *SS-Scharführer* (the equivalent of a lance-sergeant), the *Rapportführer* the rank of a *Hauptscharführer* (the equivalent of a senior NCO) and the *Schutzhaftlagerführer* the rank of an *SS-Führer* (the equivalent of an officer). As the camps grew in size a first and a second *Schutzhaftlagerführer* were usually appointed who were 'on duty' alternately for 24 hours. The *Blockführer* and the *Rapportführer* had no other SS personnel at their disposal and used so-called prisoner officials (block and room seniors) who were chosen not by them but by the *Schutzhaftlagerführer*.

From 1935/6 onwards there was a firm separation of duties, the camp being divided into five different sections. Rudolf Höss, the future Commandant of Auschwitz, said after the war while on remand in prison in Cracow, that in 1936 the Inspectorate of Concentration Camps had issued a camp order which served as a model for all camps. The sections and their spheres of duty were the following:

   i *Commandant's Headquarters* [*Kommandantur*]
     (Camp Commandant, Adjutant, postal censorship)
   ii *Political Section*
     (Chief of the political section, records department)
  iii *Schutzhaftlager*
     Schutzhaftlagerführer, Rapportführer, Blockführer, Arbeits-dienstführer [labour service officer], *Kommandoführer* [detachment leader]
  iv *Administration*
     (Chief of administration, administration of prisoners' property, camp engineer)
   v *Camp doctor*

The 'duty officer' of the guard unit did not form part of the internal camp organization but was regarded as being merely seconded to the camp.

This scheme is confirmed by an undated note in the files of the Inspector of Concentration Camps on the 'purpose and structure of the concentration camps', which was written sometime in 1938, at any rate before the start of the war, and which lists the same sections as mentioned by Höss. The available evidence clearly shows the very important role of the political section. Höss describes it as follows:

The chief of the political section is always an official of the Gestapo or the Criminal Police. He is at the disposal of the camp Commandant for the work of the political section. In the execution of his duties as an official of the Gestapo or *Kripo* he is responsible to the Gestapo or *Kripo* authorities in charge of the concentration camp concerned.

He is assisted by suitable members of the staff of the Commandant's headquarters.

The chief of the political section interrogates prisoners on behalf of the police authorities, the judges and the camp Commandant. He is responsible for the card index of prisoners and the correct upkeep of the files on the prisoners as well as for taking down particulars of new arrivals. He asks for missing information in protective custody cases. He is responsible for ensuring that prisoners are transferred at the correct time to the police and the judicial authorities. He ensures that the *Schutzhaftlagerführer* receives the necessary files so that he can prepare reports on the behaviour of prisoners.

He is responsible for informing the police authorities concerned when orders for the release of prisoners are issued and for carrying out the release. In the case of accidents involving prisoners he informs the Public Prosecutor's Office and demands a post-mortem by the legal medical officer. In all cases of death it is his duty to inform the close relatives of the deceased. He is responsible for the transfer of the bodies of prisoners to the nearest crematorium and, if this is desired by the relatives, for sending the urn with the ashes to the cemetery authorities of the place of residence of the late prisoner.

In the case of an escape he ensures that the police authorities concerned institute a search.

He informs the authorities responsible for sending the prisoner to the camp of any change resulting from release, transfer, death or escape.

Attached to the political section there is the records department which registers the details of each prisoner. Photographs, fingerprints and precise personal descriptions are kept of every prisoner and added to his files.

In a special paragraph of his notes, not so far published in the original, Höss describes the way in which the political sections carried out their duties as these later (1940/3) evolved in Auschwitz under the direction of *SS-Untersturmführer* and *Kriminalsekretär* Maximilian Grabner who originated from Vienna:

For the establishment of Auschwitz concentration camp, Grabner was made available by his office, *Stapoleitstelle* Kattowitz, as chief of the political section. Grabner had no idea about concentration camps. . . . *Standartenführer* Dr Schäfer [*Stapoleitstelle* Kattowitz] was, however, unable to put anyone better at my disposal. . . . Grabner's biggest fault was his tolerance towards his comrades. From a mistaken sense of loyalty he failed to report countless, often terrible incidents and excesses on the part of SS officers and men in order to protect those concerned from punishment . . . [and] contributed substantially to the rapid spread of these outrages. In fact it was his very duty ruthlessly to report to the camp Commandant any infringement of the camp regulations. This he only did if he knew that I was about to discover some irregularity. Being a member of the criminal police he was clever enough not to let himself be caught. . . .

Grabner knew many things and was probably informed about everything that went on in the protective custody camp, but he could not bring himself to denounce comrades unless it was essential to do so. . . . Because he owed loyalty to two superiors – the *Stapoleitstelle* and the Commandant's Headquarters – his powers and duties were not clearly definable and could not therefore be closely controlled. He could always retire to one sphere or the other. On principle I never interfered in *Stapo* matters, particularly not in investigations or interrogations carried out by the political section at the request of the *Stapo* or the investigation commissions of various *Stapo* authorities, that is to say of the BdS [*Befehlshaber der Sicherheitspolizei*] Cracow, which were always working in Auschwitz. When Grabner was charged with special duties by his *Stapoleitstelle* he always informed me. . . . These were so varied and numerous that Grabner really worked more for the *Stapo* than for the camp. . . . With the rapid increase in the number of prisoners the camp duties of the political section increased. But Grabner had only a few able colleagues. . . . Most of them were unsuited to this type of work. They readily left the work to the prisoners who were used . . . in ever-growing numbers. Although Grabner always assured me that they dealt only with unimportant things, the leading prisoners in the camp were in fact exactly informed about all important happenings in the political section. . . .

For Grabner the political section had become too complex. . . . The programme for the extermination of Jews alone would have needed a *Stapo* official. For Auschwitz-Birkenau at least a Commissar and three secretaries would have been needed. . . . Grabner was responsible also for the crematoria and the strict observation of orders issued to them. . . . He was also responsible for the execution of those sentenced to death by courts martial. . . . In the summer of 1943 Grabner was 'dead beat' although he was not prepared to admit it until sickness and an SS court forced him to give up.

After this glance ahead at later practice within the sphere of activity of the political section in Auschwitz we shall now return to the general development of the direction of the concentration camps.

When Eicke in 1934 was entrusted by Himmler with the take-over of the concentration camps by the SS and with their reorganization, one of his major tasks was to consolidate the various small local protective custody camps dotted all over the Reich into a few bigger camps and to introduce in them uniform direction and supervision by SS leaders and units. By March 1935 this process had reached the stage where there were seven camps (Dachau, Esterwegen, Lichtenburg, Sachsenburg, Columbia-Haus, Oranienburg and Fuhlsbüttel near Hamburg) with a total of 7,000 to 9,000 prisoners.* Militarized SS guard formations were stationed at all these camps. After the end of 1934 they were no longer part of the *Allgemeine SS* but were described as *SS-Wachverbände* or – after the Death's Head insignia on their collar patch introduced in Dachau as early as 1933 – as *SS-Totenkopfverbände* and as such, together with the SS general service troops [*Verfügungstruppen*], formed a special branch of the armed SS. The Dachau *Wachtruppe Oberbayern der Allgemeinen SS* became the *SS-Totenkopfstandarte Oberbayern* and similarly the *SS-Wachstürme* (later *Sturmbanne* and *Standarten*) in the other concentration camps were given corresponding regional descriptions which were worn on the uniform sleeve. In March 1935 there were the following Death's Head units of varying strength:

SS Death's Head (or guard) formations:
'Oberbayern' (concentration camp Dachau)
'Ostfriesland' (concentration camp Esterwegen)
'Elbe' (concentration camp Lichtenburg)
'Saxony' (concentration camp Sachsenburg)
'Brandenburg' (concentration camp Oranienburg and
Columbia-Haus)
'Hansa' (Hamburg-Fuhlsbüttel)

A directive of the chief of the *SS-Hauptamt* dated 9 March 1936 laid down that members of the SS who belonged to the staff of the camp itself (though only up to the rank of *Obersturmbannführer*) should wear a 'K' on the collar patch of their uniform and be thus distinguished from the SS other ranks and officers of the *Wachstürme* stationed in barracks outside the concentration camps. In addition there were the following regulations covering the use of uniform:

For drill and guard duty members of the *SS-Wachverbände* will wear the *earth-brown uniform* with the Party brassard [*Kampfbinde*] and collar patches but without the national emblem on the sleeveband or armbands [*Armelstreifen*]. For field service the Party armlet need not

*With 2,500 prisoners Dachau was the biggest of the camps at that time (probably even bigger than Esterwegen). The records of Sachsenburg concentration camp show that at the end of 1935 there were approximately 1,180 prisoners in Sachsenburg. The number of prisoners in Columbia-Haus and Fuhlsbüttel was considerably smaller.

be worn. The staff of the Commandants' Headquarters may wear the earth-brown uniform on duty. Guards of honour in public places will always wear the black SS service dress. The wearing of the earth-brown uniform as off-duty dress is not permitted.

From the end of 1934 onwards *SS-Gruppenführer* Eicke was *Inspekteur der Konzentrationslager* as well as *Führer der SS-Wachverbände*. In 1938/9 the official description came to be: *Führer der SS-Totenkopfverbände und Konzentrationslager*. The new institution, with its own *Stab des Führers der KL und SS-TV*, set up its headquarters in Berlin (NW 7, Friedrichstrasse 129, Block F) in 1935 and *de jure* and for organizational purposes was under the control of the *SS-Hauptamt* in the charge of *SS-Gruppenführer* Heissmeyer, who was also in charge of the *SS Verfügungstruppe* and the General SS. On 2 August 1936 Eicke's staff moved to Oranienburg near Berlin (close to the new concentration camp of Sachsenhausen, established in 1936) where the central administration of the concentration camps remained until 1945.

From the existing documentary evidence it emerges that the *SS-Hauptamt* issued the guide-lines for the organization, division and dress of the SS Death's Head formations and dealt with the engagement of young volunteers.* The *Verwaltungsamt* of the SS [*SS-Brigadeführer* Pohl), affiliated to the *SS-Hauptamt*, was responsible for the supply and administration of the Death's Head formations and the concentration camps which after 1935 were paid for out of Reich funds. As administrative chief of the SS, Pohl submitted budget estimates for the SS Death's Head formations and the concentration camps and discussed with the responsible authorities of the Reich Ministry of Finance the size of the funds. The funds granted to the SS Death's Head formations and the concentration camps were charged to the budget of the Reich Ministry of the Interior.

*A letter of the Chief of the *Hauptamt*, *SS-Gruppenführer* Heissmeyer, of early March 1936 on recruitment into the SS guard formations shows that the *SS-Hauptamt* transmitted requests for replacement from the SS Death's Head formations to the leaders of the *SS-Oberabschnitte*, entrusting them with the recruitment of volunteers. The letter says: 'In order to speed up the setting-up of this unit the leaders of the *SS-Oberabschnitte* are asked each to provide the names of 80 volunteers by 25 March 1936 at the latest.' The letter then laid down various conditions: recruits must be born between 1914 and 1919, measure not less than 1.70 metres, be completely healthy and 'racially impeccable'.

It appears that as regards the actual direction of the camps and decisions concerning their development and that of the Death's Head formations Eicke, as leader of the SS-TV and KL, continued to have a free hand in spite of being formally subordinate to the *SS-Hauptamt*, and that he felt responsible only to Himmler personally. It is significant that in important questions he approached Himmler direct, with emphatic reference to the fact that the Death's Head formations and the concentration camps were under his 'personal' control and that when writing to Himmler he merely sent a copy of his letter to the Chief of the *SS-Hauptamt*.

In the shaping of the camps and the practical aspects of protective custody Eicke was compelled to consider not so much the not very influential chief of the *SS-Hauptamt*, Heissmeyer, but the Gestapo under Heydrich. As the Gestapo was responsible for issuing protective custody orders and orders for the release of prisoners and as it was informed about internal conditions in the camps through the political sections which were under its control, it was able to exert direct and indirect influence on the camps. As a result there was some tension between the Gestapo and the Inspector of Concentration Camps. On 10 August 1936 Eicke reported to Himmler that the Chief of the Bureau of the Secret State Police at the Reich Ministry of the Interior and Heydrich's deputy, *SS-Standartenführer* Dr Best, had 'said in certain quarters that disgusting things went on in the concentration camps' and that 'it was time that they were again placed under Gestapo control'. At the same time attempts were made to withdraw the SS Death's Head formations from Eicke's central control and to place them under the authority of the *SS-Oberabschnittsführer* of the *Allgemeine SS*. However, Eicke was able to ward off these attempts. Up to the start of the war he remained Inspector of the Concentration Camps and leader of the Death's Head formations.

The number of prisoners in protective custody in concentration camps reached its lowest total in the winter of 1936/7 with about 7,500 persons.* During this period of internal political

*In the negotiations for the 1937 concentration camp budget the estimates for the first half of the year were still based on a total of 7,500 prisoners whereas for the second half of the year a total of 10,000 prisoners was budgeted for.

consolidation of the régime the exceptional instrument of the concentration camps seemed largely superfluous. Even the State police had to take this into account. Indicative of this state of affairs is a circular of the Prussian Gestapa of 17 December 1936 to the *Stapo(leit)stellen* reminding them to make use of protective custody only in cases of emergency: 'Excessive use of protective custody must discredit this strongest weapon of the Secret State Police and give encouragement to the widespread efforts to abolish protective custody.'

While the number of camps continued to be reduced a start was made with the construction of 'modern' and large camps. After the closure in 1935 of the camps at Oranienburg and Fuhlsbüttel, which had originally been taken over by Eicke, Esterwegen concentration camp was closed down in 1936 and handed over to the judicial authorities which from the spring of 1934 onwards maintained several prisons (including some for prisoners convicted for political offences) in the moorland regions of the Emsland. At the same time the notorious SS camp Columbia-Haus in Berlin was dissolved. The Esterwegen prisoners and their guards were transferred to camp Sachsenhausen near Oranienburg, newly established in September 1936. A year later, in July 1937, camp Sachsenburg was also dissolved. Its place was taken, after August 1937, by the new big camp of Buchenwald, near Weimar.

Between August 1937 and July 1938 there were four concentration camps on Reich territory: Dachau, Sachsenhausen, Buchenwald and Lichtenburg (used from the summer of 1937 onwards exclusively as a concentration camp for women). The new camps of Sachsenhausen and Buchenwald had been set up on uniform principles based on the experiments made at Dachau and as regards 'capacity' also followed the Dachau model.

Together with the concentration of prisoners in three large camps went the reorganization, begun in August 1937, of the Death's Head formations. In August 1937 a Death's Head formation of 1,000–1,500 men was stationed at each of the three camps. The SS personnel (not counting the guards) employed in the three camps themselves numbered at that time:

in Dachau	121 persons (SS members)
in Buchenwald	120 persons (SS members)
in Sachsenhausen	111 persons (SS members)

The staff of the Inspector of Concentration Camps and SS Death's Head formations consisted at that time of 43 persons.

At the end of 1937 the SS Death's Head formations had a total strength of 4,833 persons, of whom 216 were *Führer* and 976 *Unterführer*. Of the 216 SS leaders of the Death's Head formations 33 were employed as Commandants, *Schutzhaftlagerführer*, *Rapportführer*, *Verwaltungsführer* or in similar positions. Most of the rank and file consisted of very young SS members, aged between 16 and 20. Statistics for the end of 1938 show that 93·5 per cent of the members of the Death's Head formations were single, and that 69 per cent had left the Church (at the same time the percentage of so-called 'believers' was 21·9 per cent among the *Allgemeine SS* and 53·6 per cent among the *Verfügungstruppen*). The percentage of those who had left the unit at their own request or at the suggestion of their officers was relatively high among the Death's Head formations, amounting to 2·5 per cent.*

4 Extension of concentration camp detention: new categories of prisoners

During the transitional period 1934-9, there was a change also in the type of case committed to concentration camps, that is to say there was an extension of motivation. Not only political opponents of the government were sent to the camps but also other elements whose activities were, as the saying went, detrimental to the interest of the nation [*volksschädigend*]. In 1937/8 the overwhelming majority of the inmates of Dachau were political prisoners while in Sachsenhausen there was even in those days an equally large number of so-called anti-social elements, homosexuals, Jehovah's Witnesses and habitual criminals. Contrary to the principle expressed in the protective custody regulation of the Reich Minister of the Interior of 12/26 April 1934 that protective custody was not a substitute punishment, the custom had grown up to use it in this sense, that is to say to send to concentration camps persons regarded as harmful although they could not be punished under existing law.

This function of the concentration camps as filling a gap in the

*In 1937 81 members of the SS Death's Head formations were discharged at their own request and 65 for official, medical, ideological or other reasons.

ordinary judicial processes or providing additional preventive detention was also extended to the sphere of political prosecutions. As early as 1933 formal agreements were occasionally made between the judicial authorities and the police to transfer persons accused of or sentenced for treason or high treason to concentration camps upon completion of their sentence.* On 5 September 1935, for example, the Bavarian political police ordered that henceforth early note should be taken of the probable date of release from prison of 'all persons sentenced by the People's Court' in order to arrange for their immediate transfer to a concentration camp. During the same period the Bavarian political police ordered that: 'Communist officials, due for release after serving a sentence, shall on principle be taken into protective custody if they are dangerous enemies of the State or if it is likely that they will put themselves again at the disposal of the illegal KPD.'

It also frequently happened that if the judiciary abandoned its prosecution of persons accused of political offences or if proceedings ended with an acquittal, the Gestapo ordered persons released by the judicial authorities to be taken into protective custody. Such incidents were clearly meant as criticism of the judges and intended to correct the verdicts of the courts by police action. Hitler, particularly after the start of the war, on several occasions personally ordered prisoners in the charge of the judicial authorities to be transferred to the Gestapo, even in cases of non-political offences.

The tendency to use so-called 'preventive detention' in addition to a fixed term of imprisonment in the sphere of non-political offences found expression in the law of 24 November 1933 'against dangerous habitual criminals'. The law laid down that persons convicted twice of criminal misdemeanours or felonies should be regarded as 'dangerous habitual criminals' and sentenced by the courts not only to a limited term of imprisonment but also to a period of unlimited *protective detention*. The law further laid down that for less serious cases of so-called habitual crimes, in addition to the penalty certain 'corrective measures'

*Cf. the letter of the Prussian Gestapa of 24 November 1933 to the Prussian Minister of Justice which states that arrangements must be made to 'ensure that after completion of their prison sentence traitors are taken into protective custody', a procedure which will 'almost always recommend itself in view of the recidivist character of most traitors'.

should be taken, such as ordering the criminal to stay in a house of correction, an institution for alcoholics or some other appropriate place. According to this law the legal authorities did, however, remain responsible for ordering prisoners to be kept in detention or to be transferred to special institutions. Yet as early as the beginning of 1935 the police itself began to take so-called habitual criminals into preventive police custody and to transfer them to Dachau or other camps. This practice grew up mainly as part of Criminal Police supervision of so-called previously convicted habitual criminals, some of whom were taken into 'preventive police detention' for ignoring the police conditions to which they were subject (restrictions in the choice of domicile, withdrawal of driving licences, etc.).

The transfer of so-called habitual criminals to concentration camps began on a large scale only when in 1936 Himmler as Chief of the German Police gained control of the Criminal Police of the *Länder*, and when the establishment in 1937 of the *Reichskriminalpolizeiamt* provided the complete organizational prerequisites for a uniform intensification of Criminal Police activities. On 27 January 1937 the Prussian Criminal Police Office under *SS-Gruppenführer* Nebe asked the regional offices of the Criminal Police for

speedy transmission of a list of all the criminals in your district who in the opinion of the Criminal Police must be regarded as professional and habitual criminals or as habitual offenders against morality and who are at liberty. . . . As it is intended at a certain moment unexpectedly to take into preventive police custody a large number of professional criminals, the lists must be kept accurately and list numbers must not be altered. When the time comes only the list number of the professional criminals concerned will be telegraphically transmitted.

On 23 February 1937 Himmler himself ordered the Criminal Police to 'take into protective police custody about 2,000 professional and habitual criminals or criminals who are a threat to public morality'. Himmler's order and an instruction of the Criminal Police Office of 27 February 1937 laid down that these 2,000 persons should be selected from the lists and 'arrested with lightning speed everywhere in the Reich' on 9 March 1937 and 'transferred to the concentration camps of Sachsenhausen, Sachsenburg, Lichtenburg and Dachau'.

In contrast to the objective of the preventive detention provided for by the law of 24 November 1933 this operation was not concerned with persons with criminal records who had again committed an offence. Nor was there any clear definition of who should be regarded as a previously convicted 'habitual criminal'. It was left to the judgement of the Criminal Police to decide on the basis of its records who should fall within this category, the capriciousness of selection naturally being enhanced by the order that a certain number of persons should be arrested. As there was no other legal foundation for these arrests, Himmler explicitly based his order of 23 February 1937 on the emergency decree of 28 February 1933 for the protection of people and State. This decree, originally aimed only against the communists but in later years applied to all sorts of other groups of political opponents of the régime, was thus given an interpretation which clearly went beyond the sphere of combating political enemies and thus also beyond the competence of the political police. The arrests of March 1937 represented an unlimited extension of the accepted principles of after-prison supervision and crime prevention on the part of the police. They also represented a clear repudiation of justice, particularly of the law against habitual criminals introduced by the National Socialist government in 1933, and of the handling of protective detention by the legal authorities as provided for under this law. In addition the operation blurred the limits of protective custody and gave the police considerable latitude in making arrests and transferring prisoners to concentration camps without prosecuting them for political offences. The objections of the legal authorities were taken account of only to the extent that they moved the Reich Minister of the Interior at the end of 1937 to issue a basic order on 'preventive crime control by the police' which on principle admitted the new instrument of 'preventive police detention' and merely sought to restrict its application. Under this order of the Reich Minister of the Interior (of 14 December 1937) preventive detention was applicable, i.e. in the case of persons with not less than three previous sentences of imprisonment or hard labour of at least six months (professional or habitual criminals) 'and if they are likely to commit criminal acts in future'; in the case of persons with previous sentences in which the seriousness of the offence and the possibility of a repetition constituted 'so great a danger to the community' that it seemed inadvisable to leave them at liberty; further, in the case of persons with false names suspected of seeking to hide an offence; and finally also in the case of persons who, 'without being professional or habitual criminals' by their 'anti-social behaviour endanger the community'.

The order further laid down that, in contrast to protective custody which required quarterly revision, regular revision of the fate of prisoners detained in preventive police detention (and the possibility of their release) should be examined at the most once a year and not less than every two years.

Under this order it was also possible to take into preventive police detention so-called anti-social elements. Here too some preparatory work had been done in previous years in the individual *Länder*. In the general guide-lines issued by the Bavarian Political Police on 1 August 1936 on the making of protective custody orders, a distinction had been drawn between the arrest of political and non-political offenders. Listed as anti-social persons who could if necessary be taken into protective custody were: beggars, vagabonds, gypsies, vagrants, work-shy individuals, idlers, prostitutes, grumblers, habitual drunkards, hooligans, traffic offenders and so-called psychopaths and mental cases. Under regulations issued with the approval of the political police by the Bavarian Ministry of the Interior in 1935/6 it was possible to take into protective custody persons who were rigging the food market (if 'reprehensible egoism provides the motive power for this anti-social behaviour') or agricultural labourers who had broken their contracts.

In the years 1937/8 Himmler, openly supported by Hitler, progressively extended the range of persons who qualified for internment in concentration camps. Significant is Himmler's circular of 26 January 1938 announcing a 'single, comprehensive and surprise swoop' on so-called work-shy elements:

Work-shy elements within the meaning of this order are men who are old enough to work and who have recently been certified fit by an official doctor or who will be certified fit and who can be proved to have rejected offers of work on two occasions without just cause or have accepted work only to abandon it again shortly afterwards without adequate reason.

Local labour exchanges have been asked to ascertain the names of work-shy individuals who come to their notice during the period of 18. 2 to 4. 3. 1938 and to inform the State police authorities.

In addition the State police authorities will themselves investigate work-shy elements resident in their district. . . . Upon completion of these investigations the State police authorities will arrest the persons concerned during the period of 4. 3. to 9. 3. 1938. . . . Personal records of these individuals with detailed comments and proposals for action will be submitted not later than 15. 3. 1938 to the Gestapa (Ref. II D) which is alone responsible in every case for a decision regarding protective custody and transfer to a concentration camp. . . . At first protective custody will on principle last at least three months. The custody order will be revised by the Gestapa every three months. . . .

All protective custody prisoners will be sent to concentration camp Buchenwald near Weimar.

It is noteworthy that the direction of this operation against so-called work-shy elements was in the hands of the State police (the criminal police participating only in the investigations). Furthermore there was explicit reference to protective custody and not to preventive police detention, the reason for this being, as clearly emerges from Himmler's order, that the restricted concept of anti-social elements contained in the order of the Reich Minister of the Interior on preventive crime control did not fit the work-shy elements class and that Himmler therefore anticipated difficulties. Protective custody orders issued by the Gestapo, on the other hand, were protected from investigation by administrative tribunals under the Gestapo law. Himmler therefore entrusted the operation to the Gestapo and ordered the use of protective custody although it was not an operation clearly aimed at political opponents. Thus the operation against work-shy elements of March/April 1938 is a particularly striking example of the way in which Himmler himself disregarded the guide-lines for the use of protective custody and how concepts and institutions were exchanged in order to achieve the desired end.

A further category of protective custody prisoners who after 1935 formed a substantial group of concentration camp inmates came from the members of the *Internationale Vereinigung der Ernsten Bibelforscher* [Jehovah's Witnesses]. The organization had been dissolved in the Third Reich in 1933 and all recruiting or propaganda for Jehovah's Witnesses had been prohibited by law because the organization was primarily regarded as an instrument of pacifist activity. Numerous cases were indeed dealt with by the courts. But in the eyes of the Gestapo the attitude of the courts was too lenient, and as early as March 1935 it ordered a short period of protective custody and the issue of appropriate warnings in cases where the accused had been released from imprisonment on remand. In February 1936 the order went out that all former leaders of the *Internationale Bibelforscher-vereinigung* (IBV) should be taken into protective custody 'for up to two months'. In mid-May 1937 further measures were taken. The Gestapo ordered that:

Everybody who in any form furthers the aims of the illegal IBV or the unity of its followers will be taken into protective custody and immediately brought before the courts for a judicial warrant of arrest to be issued.

If no judicial warrant of arrest is issued the person who has been active for the IBV will be kept in protective custody if necessary for more than seven days or transferred to a concentration camp. ... Particularly strict standards will be applied regarding the duration of protective custody in the case of an official of the IBV or of someone who has already been in trouble over IBV activities. ... *

The various categories of prisoners in the camps carried special distinguishing marks. The uniform system of marking introduced before the war consisted in sewing a triangular piece of material on to each prisoner's uniform, the colour depending on his category:

for political prisoners	red
for Jehovah's Witnesses	purple
for anti-socials	black
for criminals	green
for homosexuals	pink
for emigrants	blue

In addition to the coloured triangle Jewish prisoners were made to wear a yellow triangle sewn on to the coloured triangle in such a way as to form the hexagonal Star of David. An addi-

*Cf. the circular of the Munich *Stapoleitstelle* of 27 August 1937 concerning the serving of protective custody orders on Jehovah's Witnesses released after completion of their sentence. The circular includes the statement that 'The Reich Minister of Justice has informed the Berlin Gestapo that he does not share the view sometimes expressed by subordinate officials that the detention in protective custody of Jehovah's Witnesses who have served their sentence endangers the authority of the courts. He fully understands the need for measures on the part of the State Police even after completion of a sentence. Nevertheless it is his wish that Jehovah's Witnesses shall not be taken into protective custody in circumstances which might be detrimental to the standing of the courts. ...'

tional mark in the form of a crossbar above the triangle was introduced for so-called recidivists who after their release had been sent back to the concentration camp on one or more occasions. Their situation was worse because on Himmler's instruction of 3 March 1936 they were assigned to special detachments (hard labour), their period of detention was revised only after three years and they were also subject to stricter conditions of detention (less mail, no parcels and no tobacco). Further distinguishing marks were introduced for prisoners of the punishment companies and for prisoners suspected of trying to escape. After the outbreak of war when the overwhelming majority of prisoners consisted of non-Germans, the nationality of the prisoner (P – Pole, F – French, etc.) was marked on his clothing with a large letter on the triangle.

New Developments in the Years 1938–9

1 The Protective Custody Order of 25 January 1938

Until January 1938 the regulation of the Reich Minister of the Interior of 12/26 April 1934 had provided the main guide-lines for the implementation of protective custody orders.

On 25 January 1938 a new fundamental order of the Reich Minister of the Interior partly condensed and partly altered the existing guide-lines. Its main innovations were:

a An extended definition of protective custody (covering not only political opponents in the narrow sense).
Paragraph 1, sub-paragraph 1 stated:
'Protective custody as a coercive measure of the Secret State Police for the protection of the State against anti-social activity may be applied in respect of persons whose behaviour endangers the existence and security of the people and the State.'
b The authority to issue protective custody orders was to be restricted to the Gestapa Berlin (hitherto *Land* governments or *Stapoleitstellen* and *Regierungspräsidenten* or *Stapostellen* could issue protective custody orders).
Paragraph 2 stated:
'i The *Geheime Staatspoliziamt* alone is competent to issue protective custody orders.
ii Applications for protective custody orders must be made

through the *Staatspolizeileitstellen* or *Staatspolizeistellen* to the *Geheime Staatspolizeiamt* . . .

c The concept of protective custody would apply exclusively to long-term detention in concentration camps:

Paragraph 6 stated:

'Protective custody will in principle be served in state concentration camps.'

Short-term protective custody on the other hand, which was as a rule served in police prisons, was now called 'provisional arrest' and revised, particularly by the regulation that it should end within ten days* unless there was an order for the prisoner to be taken into protective custody and transferred to a concentration camp.

Otherwise the new order took over the old regulations by which a copy of the protective custody warrant (now always issued by the Gestapa) had to be handed to the detained person in return for a receipt. The warrant was required to state the reasons for the arrest and the prisoner's relatives had to be informed. The rule of quarterly revision of protective custody orders was also retained. Responsibility for doing this and for ordering releases was now also transferred exclusively to the Gestapa.†

The protective custody order of the Reich Minister of the Interior of 25 January 1938 still reflected the desire to make protective custody subject to uniform rules, to direct it centrally, to control it and thus to ensure its orderly implementation. But the order already conflicted with tendencies which produced the opposite effect. As early as 1937 it had become obvious that Himmler was anxious to extend considerably the range of persons who could be sent to concentration camps. After the earlier decline in the number of camps and prisoners, the operation against so-called habitual criminals and anti-socials produced a new increase in the number of prisoners and brought about an extension of the camps' functions, a trend which was to become more marked in 1938. In the guide-lines which the Reich Criminal Police Office issued on 4 April 1938 in connexion with

*Extended after the beginning of the war to three weeks by the order of the Reich Minister of the Interior of 4 October 1939 because of the 'very greatly increased number of arrests by the *Stapo(leit)stellen*'.

†The new order came into force on 1 February 1938; the non-Prussian *Länder* were allowed until 30 August 1938 to deal with current protective custody matters through their own *Stapo(leit)stellen*.

the Fundamental Order of the Reich Minister of the Interior on the preventive crime control of 14 December 1937, the concentration camps were expressly given the character of 'State reformatories and labour camps'; in addition to fulfilling their former function of eliminating political opponents of the régime the camps were now also to house prisoners (criminals and anti-socials) detained by the police as a preventive measure.

2 Internment of 'Anti-Socials': 'the camps as 'educational and productive centres' of the SS

The continuation of the 1937 operations against so-called criminals and anti-socials, centrally directed and carried out 'with lightning speed' everywhere in the Reich, was not limited to the arrest of 'work-shy' individuals in March/April 1938 to which reference has already been made. A little later, after the annexation of Austria, a 'sudden swoop' was staged there also by the Criminal Police, prepared on the order of the Reich Criminal Police Office of 31 March 1938 for the purpose of preventive crime control. And on 1 June 1938 Heydrich gave instructions for a new comprehensive operation against anti-social elements everywhere in the Reich: between 13 and 18 June in each regional Criminal Police district 'at least 200 male able-bodied persons (anti-socials) as well as all male Jews with previous criminal records' were to be taken into 'preventive police detention' and ... 'immediately transferred to Buchenwald concentration camp ... in strict application of the order of 14 December 1937'.

The anti-socials to be arrested were described in the order as follows:

a Vagabonds at present moving from place to place without work;
b Beggars, even if they have a permanent domicile;
c Gypsies and persons travelling in gypsy fashion who have shown no desire for regular work or have violated the law;
d Pimps who have been involved in criminal proceedings – even if they were acquitted – and who still move in pimp and prostitute circles, or persons strongly suspected of being pimps;
e Persons with several convictions for creating disorders, doing bodily harm, causing brawls, breaking the peace, etc., who have thus demonstrated that they are not prepared to fit into the national community.

The introduction, setting out the reasons for the order, explains the purpose of the operation as on the one hand the elimination of persons who 'are a burden to the community and thereby do it harm', and on the other the need for labour: 'The strict implementation of the Four-Year Plan demands the employment of every able-bodied person and does not permit anti-social individuals to avoid work and thus to sabotage the Four-Year Plan.'

Here for the first time it was clearly stated that the employment of forced labour was one of the main purposes of the concentration camps. It may therefore be assumed that the main purpose of the police operations against so-called criminals and anti-socials, stepped up so noticeably in 1937/8, was not to protect the community but to supply forced labour for certain projects particularly dear to the National Socialist leaders and the SS. This assumption is confirmed by the fact that the orders stated expressly in various places that those arrested should be male and able-bodied persons. Above all, however, another factor should be noted: the period of intensified new arrests coincided with the construction of SS-owned enterprises for the production of building materials situated in and near the concentration camps. To put them into operation, large contingents of prisoners were required.

In the spring of 1938 the SS firm Deutsche Erd- und Steinwerke GmbH (DEST) had been founded, the main purpose of which was to set up brickworks and to exploit quarries. Its first task was to establish large brickworks at Sachsenhausen and near Buchenwald (at Berlstedt). In the summer it began to exploit and operate granite quarries at Flossenbürg (in the Upper Palatinate) and at Mauthausen near Linz. These operations caused the simultaneous establishment of new concentration camps at Flossenbürg and at Mauthausen.

The plan to use the concentration camps as a source of labour for the production of stone and brick under SS management was closely connected with the National Socialist building programmes – directed by Albert Speer – designed to 'transform the Reich capital' and other cities (Munich, Nuremberg, Weimar and Hamburg). Hitler, to whom the project of these *Führerbauten* (Führer works) was very dear, together with Speer and Himmler conceived the idea of exploiting concentration camp labour for these ends, at the same time providing the camps with a productive task. The *Reichsführer-SS* and his *Verwaltungschef*, Pohl, concentrated eagerly on the new task which also gave the SS a new function. Not only was it a question of using the prisoners more productively but the industrial interests of the SS, created by the establishment of SS enterprises, in turn demanded an increase in the number of camps and prisoners.

The choice of location of the newly established concentration camps of Gross-Rosen in Lower Silesia and Natzweiler in Alsace, established in 1940, was determined by the presence of workable granite. At both these camps SS-owned DEST works were set up which availed themselves of prison labour. Natzweiler had attracted Speer and Pohl because of the presence of very rare red granite.

3 Further arrest operations (Austria, Sudetenland, Anti-Jewish Operation) and the numerical development of the camps

The rise in the number of prisoners and camps in 1938 also had other reasons, for it was in this year that the first territorial expansion of the Third Reich took place, the year in which it became the Greater German Reich. The *Gleichschaltung* [unification] of the new territories (Austria and the Sudetenland) meant that the elimination of political opponents, largely completed in the Old Reich by 1933/4, must be carried out during the process of occupation and incorporation. Special commandos of the *Sicherheitspolizei* scoured Austria in March/April 1938 and the Sudetenland in October/November 1938 for so-called subversive elements. Thousands of new political prisoners were sent to Dachau, Buchenwald and Sachsenhausen. During a discussion in June 1938 on the productive function of the camps, *SS-Gruppenführer* Pohl, the *SS-Verwaltungschef*, pointed out that 'as a result of Austria's Anschluss [the] number of prisoners in the concentration camps [has] risen considerably'.

After the annexation of the Sudetenland even the Gestapa thought that the circle of persons arrested by the local organs of the Security Police, partly on the basis simply of denunciation, was drawn too wide. On 24 December 1938 Heydrich felt compelled to issue a directive to the *Stapo(leit)stellen* asking them to examine the reasons why people had been arrested:

From the available reports on arrests it appears that some of the prisoners who were detained at the time in the Sudeten German area are under arrest only because they are accused of having belonged to, officially or otherwise, a Marxist Party or of having in the past participated in anti-German activity. Sometimes the reason given was even more inadequate, for example 'Czech', and in certain cases no reason was given at all. Furthermore, arrests were frequently made on the basis of accusations which upon investigation proved to be false or much exaggerated. . . .

The reason for Heydrich's admonition of 24 December 1938 was above all found in the catastrophic congestion of the concentration camps. In addition to the newly arrested groups of prisoners in preventive detention and political protective custody after the so-called *Reichskristallnacht*, the pogrom of 9 November 1938, approximately 35,000 Jews had been picked up in the Reich and, on Hitler's special order, sent temporarily to the concentration camps. The operation, together with the wrecking of Jewish shops and the destruction of the synagogues, was designed to declare open war on the Jews in Germany and to show them in unmistakable form that they were not wanted. Sending the Jews to concentration camps was a conscious method of forcing the speed of Jewish emigration.

In November 1938 approximately 10,000 Jews were sent to Buchenwald, Dachau and Sachsenhausen where they were only very inadequately housed. In his application for further funds for the extension of the concentration camps, Dr Best, the representative of the *Reichsführer-SS*, pointed out on 26 November 1938 that 'the events of the last few days [have] increased the number of prisoners from 24,000 to roughly 60,000'.

Such statistical records for Buchenwald concentration camp as have been preserved give a picture of the general increase in the number of prisoners from spring 1938 onwards. Between September 1937 and May 1938 the total of prisoners in Buchenwald had risen only very gradually from 2,300 to 3,000. As a result of the Austrian political prisoners and the anti-social operation it more than doubled between June and August 1938, reaching 7,800. With the arrival of the prisoners from the Sudetenland and particularly with the anti-Jewish operation the number of prisoners rose in December 1938 to 17,000. A note on the files of the Reich Ministry of Finance records that Dr Grawitz, the Chief of the SS Health Department, called at the Ministry on 30 November 1938 to ask for means to improve sanitary conditions in the camps and said during the interview that as a result of 'the many recent arrests made on the Führer's instructions the concentration camps were so crowded that the situation verged on the intolerable. An epidemic might break out any time. . . .'

The Jews arrested after the *Kristallnacht,* most of them wealthy citizens, stayed in the camps only a few weeks and were released after promising to emigrate. On 31 January 1939 Heydrich informed the *Stapoleitstellen* and the *Führer der Totenkopfverbände und Konzentrationslager* that Himmler had 'decided that Jewish prisoners in protective custody may in principle . . . be released provided they are in possession of emigration papers'. However, the persons concerned should be 'threatened orally' that they would be put in concentration camps for life if after having been 'released for the purpose of emigration' they later returned.

In the spring and summer of 1939 the number of prisoners in each of the three big camps, Dachau, Sachsenhausen and Buchenwald, declined again to 5,000–6,000. Mauthausen and Flossenbürg at the time each contained at least 3,000 prisoners. The total number of prisoners at the beginning of the war was roughly 25,000. In addition to the five camps for men, a new and larger concentration camp for women was established in May 1939 at Ravensbrück near Fürstenberg in Mecklenburg, replacing the camp at Lichtenburg which had been dissolved.

After 1937 the number of Death's Head formations had also grown considerably. After the incorporation of Austria and the establishment of Mauthausen concentration camp a new *SS-Totenkopfstandarte* 'Ostmark' was formed, with quarters at Mauthausen, in addition to the three existing *Standarten* ('Oberbayern', 'Brandenburg', and 'Thüringen'). The budget of the *Totenkopfstandarten* in 1938 was about twice that of the concentration camps (including SS personnel). When a military conflict seemed likely during the Czech crisis in September 1938, Hitler ordered on 17 August 1938 that in case of mobilization the active *Totenkopfstandarten* should be used to strengthen the police within the framework of the Wehrmacht and that the duty of guarding the camps should be taken over by older members of the *Allgemeine SS*. Roughly 4,000 members of the *Allgemeine SS* aged 45 and over were accordingly called up in the autumn for military training with the Death's Head formations, as well as roughly 10,000 younger officers and men of the *Allgemeine SS* as police reinforcements.

These developments show that the Death's Head formations as well as the *SS-Verfügungstruppen* were in future to act as a military and police force of the SS. Guarding the camps, originally the only duty of the Death's Head formations (SS guard formations), had created new independent tasks. Discreetly Himmler continued to use the concentration camps in order to extend his sphere of authority and to strengthen his position.

The Concentration Camps during the first years of the War 1939–41/2

The beginning of the war was the real dividing line in the development of the concentration camps. This holds good quantitatively as well as qualitatively. Höss wrote in his memoirs: 'There came the war and with it the turning-point in the life of the concentration camps.' It was during the war that the number of camps and prisoners assumed gigantic proportions. The type of prisoner now also changed considerably. At the end of the war the camps on average contained only between 5 and 10 per cent of German prisoners. The overwhelming majority was made up of foreign nationals: Russians, Poles, Frenchmen, Dutchmen, Belgians, Czechs, Greeks, Serbs, Croats, etc. And among these the percentage of Jewish prisoners was particularly high.

During the war years the functions of the concentration camps were transformed in various ways: there was a change in the responsibility for and the direction of the camps and the method of issuing and enforcing protective custody orders was adapted to mass conditions.

During the war period as a whole, a distinction must be made between the years 1939–1941/2, when the growth of the concentration camps was still relatively slow, and their precipitate expansion during the last phase from 1942 onwards. The subordination of the camps to the *Wirtschaftsverwaltungshauptamt*

(WVHA) [SS Economic and Administrative Department] in March 1942 can be regarded as the turning-point.

1 Organizational changes after the start of the War

As proposed in Hitler's directive of August 1938 the active *Totenkopfstandarten* stationed in the concentration camps were replaced during the call-up preceding the Polish campaign by replacement formations (older age groups). After the autumn of 1938 these were transferred from the *Allgemeine SS* to the *Totenkopf* formations (on the basis of the emergency service decree) and prepared for their tasks.*

Shortly after the start of the war, Eicke left the Inspectorate of Concentration Camps and took over the organization and employment of the *SS-Totenkopfstandarten* used in action in Poland as well as raising the first *SS-Totenkopf* Division in Dachau after the end of the campaign. On 14 November 1939 he was appointed commander of the *SS-Totenkopf* Division. As General of the *Waffen-SS* he was killed in Russia on 16 February 1943 without having had any further connexion with the concentration camps during the war.

Eicke's successor as Inspector of Concentration Camps (but not as Führer of the *SS-Totenkopfverbände*) after an interlude during which *Hauptamtschef* Heissmeyer was in charge, was *SS-Brigadeführer* Richard Glücks who had been in charge of Eicke's staff at Oranienburg. His official title until March 1942 was: *Der Reichsführer-SS – Inspekteur der Konzentrationslager*.

Within the general layout of the central offices of the SS under the *Reichsführer*, the Inspector continued at first to belong to the *SS-Hauptamt*. When the two main departments of the *SS-Hauptamt* (the *Kommando* of the *Allgemeine SS* and the *Kommando* of the *Waffen-SS*) became the new *SS-Führungshauptamt* under *SS-Obergruppenführer* Jüttner in August 1940, the Inspectorate of Concentration Camps was incorporated in this office until March 1942. It seems, however, that, as under Eicke,

*Höss, who was adjutant in Sachsenhausen in 1939, wrote: 'On the day war broke out Eicke addressed the commanders of the replacement formations. ... He emphasized that the hard laws of war now demanded their rights. It was the duty of every SS man ... to identify himself body and soul with the cause. Every order must be sacred to him and he must carry out even the most difficult and hardest of them without hesitation.'

all important questions concerning the concentration camps were decided directly between the Inspector of Concentration Camps and the *Reichsführer-SS* and that the *Führungshauptamt* was on the whole merely informed of what went on or, for example over the appointment of new camp Commandants, merely carried out the arrangements made by the *Reichsführer-SS* with the agreement of the Inspector of Concentration Camps.*

It seems that even during the first years of the war the *Hauptamt Haushalt und Bauten* [Finance and Works and Buildings], under *SS-Gruppenführer* Pohl, intervened more in the camps than the *SS-Führungshauptamt*. In *Amt* I *Haushalt* [Finance], under *SS-Oberführer* Georg Lörner, there was a special *Hauptabteilung* concerned with the use of concentration camp labour (*Hauptabteilung* I/5) under *SS-Hauptsturmführer* Burböck. The section probably owes its creation to the increased use after 1938/9 of prisoners in the SS enterprises† directed by Pohl (in his simultaneous capacity as Chief of the *SS-Hauptamt Verwaltung und Wirtschaft*). From 1940 onwards prisoners were also, at first on a small scale, sent to enterprises of military importance.

In his capacity as director of the allocation of camp labour, Burböck was entitled to give direct orders to *Arbeitseinsatzführer* [supervisors of camp labour] appointed in the camps after the start of war. For the purpose of coordination with the Inspectorate of Concentration Camps the former *Hauptabteilung* I/5 of the *Hauptamt Haushalt und Bauten* was dissolved with effect from 30 September 1941 and became part of the Inspectorate of Concentration Camps. There Burböck was given the position of *Beauftragter für den Häftlingseinsatz* [Administrator of Camp labour].

---

*For example, *SS-Obersturmbannführer* Hermann Pister, who replaced *SS-Standartenführer* Karl Koch as Commandant of Buchenwald at the end of 1941, reported that he was told by Glücks on 18 December 1942: 'The *Reichsführer-SS* has appointed you as Commandant of Buchenwald concentration camp. . . .' He (Pister) therefore, as ordered, reported for duty on 20 December in Oranienburg and then together with Glücks presented himself on 21 December to the Chief of the *SS-Führungsamtes*, *SS-Obergruppenführer* Jüttner, 'the then Chief of . . . Glücks' where he was 'officially notified' of his appointment by Himmler as camp Commandant.

†In addition to the DEST enterprises, the SS enterprise, the *Deutsche Ausrüstungswerke* (DAW) [German equipment works], was founded in the spring of 1939.

On the other hand the supervision of all camp buildings (centralized in the *Hauptabteilung* II/C: concentration camp and police buildings, under *SS-Hauptsturmführer* List) remained part of the *Hauptamt Haushalt und Bauten*. In the autumn of 1941 Himmler entrusted Dr-Ing. Kammler, who had come from the Luftwaffe to the SS, with the overall direction of SS building. In this capacity Kammler became head of the *Amtsgruppe* C (Buildings) of the *SS-Wirtschaftsverwaltungshauptamt* (WVHA), set up in February 1942. Under his direction the building activities of the SS increased enormously. In his investigation of 'the economic enterprises of the SS' Enno Georg describes the further development of building activities under Kammler's direction.[1] He says:

The *Amtsgruppe* C of the WVHA controlled several SS building departments (offices for the inspection of buildings, central and regional building offices) entrusted with the execution of individual projects. Planning as a whole, costing and supervision were the responsibility of *Amtsgruppe* C with its six offices.

The labour force on the SS building sites consisted primarily of concentration camp prisoners, prisoners of war, Jews and foreign workers. The use of prison labour in SS building activities continued to grow from 1942 onwards. Towards the end of the war *Amtsgruppe* C employed about 50,000 concentration camp inmates as labourers on its building sites.

From 1943 onwards, *Obergruppenführer* Dr Kammler was increasingly entrusted with special tasks for the armaments industry so that his sphere of activity went far beyond the framework of the SS. The most important of these tasks were:

1 Participation in the so-called fighter programme (production and use of the Me 262 and He 162 jet fighters).
2 Construction of subterranean installations for the armament industry (particularly the manufacture of V-weapons and aircraft) underground (because of the constant risk of air attacks).
3 Manufacture and use of V-weapons (V-1 and V-2).

These duties were the responsibility of the *Sonderstab* Kammler which apart from members of *Amtsgruppe* C consisted of experts from all branches of the armed forces. Kammler was responsible not to the WVHA but to the *Reichsführer-SS* personally and directly. The *Sonderstab* Kammler had its own organization, independent of the WVHA, of so-called *S-Inspektionen* (*Sonder-Inspektionen*) [special inspectorates] and *Führungsstäbe* [control staffs] distributed over the whole of the Reich. It received its orders from the Ministry of Armaments and – for V-weapons – from the *Oberkommando der Wehrmacht*.

The building projects of the *Sonderstab* Kammler consisted of:

1 A-projects (subterranean installations: the preparation of tunnels, the installation of subterranean halls for the manufacture of V-weapons and aircraft); one of the bigger of these ventures was 'Dora' (central building) near Nordhausen, where V-weapons were manufactured.

2 B-projects (installations above ground also intended for the transfer of important armaments concerns).

3 S-projects (special building projects, for example S III, the big subterranean Führer headquarters, set up at the training camp Ohrdruf in Thuringia). Tens of thousands of concentration camp prisoners were used as labour for these immense undertakings which in the last years of the war were developed with great rapidity under the energetic direction of Dr Kammler.

Because of his new tasks Dr Kammler and his *Amtsgruppe* C became increasingly detached from the WVHA. If the war had continued the *Amtsgruppe* C would probably have become an independent *Hauptamt* for 'Buildings' under Dr Kammler.

2 New wave of arrests and first executions in the concentration camps after the start of the War

It seems that as early as the end of August 1939 preparations had been made to take into protective custody a large number of presumed opponents of the régime when war broke out. The legal authorities, that is the Public Prosecutor's Offices, had been informed accordingly. Proof of this is provided by a circular of the Public Prosecutor General at the *Oberlandsgericht* [Supreme Land Court] of Stuttgart, dated 28 August 1939, to the heads of prisons: 'The present tense situation is likely to cause the Secret State Police to take many people into protective custody. I request that you meet applications temporarily to accommodate as many of these detainees as your prison is capable of holding. . . .'

In the days and weeks following the outbreak of war the criminal law was tightened up very considerably (for example, many more offences became liable to the death penalty); this was true both of substantive law (because of a series of new military criminal laws: the decree on special broadcasting measures of 1 September, the war economy decree of 4 September, the decree on subversion of 5 September, the decree on acts of violence of 5 December 1939) and of procedural law (the decree of 1 September simplifying procedure under which the jurisdiction of the special courts was extended to criminal offences, the introduction of shortened proceedings and curtailment of the defence; the law of 16 September 1939 changing the criminal procedure which gave the legal authorities the means of 'extraordinary intervention' against verdicts regarded as too mild: for example, the threat of the death penalty was used much more frequently).

However, this tightening up of the criminal law was apparently not enough for Hitler. At the beginning of the war Himmler was given instructions to use police means against all subversive elements and to use them for the purpose not only of protective custody but in serious cases to liquidate the persons concerned without having recourse to the machinery of the law.

On the basis of the instructions given by Hitler and Himmler, the Chief of the Security Police on 3 September 1939 – the day Britain and France entered the war – issued a circular addressed to senior SS and police leaders, inspectors of the Security Police and Gestapo officers on the 'principles of the internal protection of the State during the war'. The circular said:

Any attempt to destroy the determination and fighting spirit of the German people must be ruthlessly suppressed. In particular any person who voices doubt about the victory of the German people or the just cause of the war must be arrested immediately . . .. Special attention must be paid to all attempts . . . to influence other persons subversively. . . . If there is likely to be any publicity or if there is the possibility that a group might be set up the individuals must in every case be arrested. After the arrest of a suspect the investigations necessary to solve the case as completely as possible must be carried out immediately. . . . Thereafter the Chief of the Security Police will be informed at once and asked for a decision on the further handling of the case, *as, if need be, such elements will be brutally liquidated upon instructions from above*. . . .

A directive which Heydrich sent to the *Stapo(leit)stellen* on 20 September 1939 explained in detail that persons whose actions were particularly reprehensible or dangerous or particularly far-reaching in their 'propaganda effect' must be 'liquidated absolutely ruthlessly (by execution) without regard to person'. Such actions were, for example: 'Attempted sabotage, incitement or demoralization [*Zersetzung*] of members of the army [*sic*] or of a substantial group of persons, hoarding in large quantities, active Communist or Marxist work, etc.' In every case in which in the opinion of the *Stapo(leit)stellen* 'special treatment' (execution) was indicated, 'protective custody [will] be imposed immediately' and the Chief of the Security Police should be informed through an 'urgent telegram'. Furthermore the *Stapoleitstellen* were directed to ensure that in these particularly serious instances the police authorities of the *Kreis* and the *Ort* should immediately inform the Gestapo so that it could issue a protective custody warrant and thus prevent the arrested person from being brought before an investigating judge; the intervention of the judiciary was thus 'avoided'[2] until the Chief of the Security Police had made his final decision. The special directives on the implementation of this order, issued on 26 September to the Gestapa sections concerned,[3] show that cases in which execution was proposed were submitted to Himmler personally.

On the basis of this order, and in some cases also on Hitler's personal instructions, as early as September a number of people in the Reich suspected or guilty of war sabotage or particularly serious crimes were shot without trial. Among those whom the Security Police seized were persons serving sentences in the prisons of the judicial authorities. In such cases, execution by the Security Police represented a particularly drastic disavowal of the law and an extreme instance of interference with its authority.

The Security Police used the concentration camps in which to carry out executions. As early as the first days of September the camps were thus given a new function: they now served also as places of physical destruction, 'sentencing' being preceded either by no trial at all or by a rapid trial in which the judicial authorities played no part. Höss reports that as Adjutant of Sachsenhausen shortly after the start of the war he was in charge of the first execution of this kind. He writes:

The same evening the first execution of the war took place in Sachsenhausen. A communist in the Junker works in Dachau who had refused to do air raid protection work was arrested by the local *Stapo* after being reported by the works police, and brought to the Gestapo in Berlin; the report of his interrogation was submitted to the RFSS who ordered that he be shot at once. According to a secret mobilization instruction all executions ordered by the RFSS or the Gestapa were carried out at the nearest concentration camp.

At 10 pm Müller telephoned from the Gestapa to say that a courier with an order was on his way. This order should be carried out immediately. Shortly afterwards a car arrived with two *Stapo* officials and a handcuffed civilian. The Commandant opened the order which merely said: 'The orders of the RFSS are that the N.N.* will be shot. He will be informed of this under arrest and the order will be carried out one hour later.'

The Commandant informed the prisoner of the orders. The latter was calm although he had not expected to be shot. . . . As adjutant I was in charge of the staff of the Commandant's headquarters. In this capacity I was responsible for carrying out executions – according to the secret mobilization order.[4]

Höss' description clearly shows the successive stages of the first wartime executions in the concentration camps, carried out on the instruction of the Security Police, a procedure which was later followed regularly, particularly at Auschwitz. There is no other evidence of the secret mobilization order referred to by Höss in this connexion. It may be supposed, however, that there was an order, probably issued with the agreement of the Inspector of Concentration Camps, on the procedure for executions in the concentration camps.

Characteristic of the future constitutional development of the Hitler State was the sequel to these first executions in so far as they affected the judicature. In the past it had become a rule that when local Public Prosecutor's Offices heard of high-handed action by the SS or of criminal issues in general which involved Party officials and which were therefore politically delicate, they merely informed their superiors and did not investigate, let alone prosecute, except on express instruction from above. As a result none of the routine investigations was made by the Public Prosecutor's Offices, unless the Ministry of Justice itself decided otherwise. As regards the executions carried out on the instruction of the Security Police in the first weeks after the start of the war, there is fairly exact documentary evidence for the reaction of the Reich Minister of Justice.

*German bureaucratic jargon for someone whose name is not known; from the Latin *nomen nescio*. This use of the letters N.N. is not to be confused with the later so-called NN (Nacht and Nebel) prisoners described on pp. 215 *et seq.* (*translator's footnote*).

Reich Minister of Justice Dr Gürtner had learned in the second half of September, partly from press reports, about three cases in which named prisoners had been shot on the instruction of the Security Police. In addition he had been told by *SS-Brigadeführer* Dr Best, who acted as the representative of the *Reichsführer-SS und Chef der Deutschen Polizei* at the Reich Ministry of the Interior, that the Führer had 'ordered or approved of these executions' and 'further given instruction' that the *Reichsführer-SS* should safeguard the State 'by every means', including 'immediate execution'. To the request of the Ministry of Justice 'to be informed in greater detail about the Führer's order' Heydrich had replied 'that the Ministry of Justice should address himself directly to the Führer about the shootings'.

As a result Gürtner penned a note on 28 September 1939 in which he pointed out, with reference to the three cases and to information received, that there existed in the Reich 'a conflict of authority between the People's Court, the military courts and the special courts on the one hand and the police on the other'. The question was 'according to which criteria [shall] this conflict be resolved in individual cases'. As war legislation provided for a procedure 'which was practically the same as that of the courts martial' there was no need for independent police prosecution in cases of contravention of war legislation. It was merely that the special courts had not been 'described' as courts martial. Gürtner concluded his note with the sentence: 'A general clarification of the question whether crimes in non-occupied territory (Reich territory) are punishable according to the war legislation or shall be dealt with by the police without proceedings or verdict is in my opinion urgently necessary.'[5] Gürtner sent his note to the Chief of the *Reichskanzlei*, Heinrich Lammers, asking him to bring it to Hitler's attention. Lammers spoke to Hitler on 13 October and on the following day 'in the name of the Führer' called personally upon the Reich Minister of Justice to inform him of the result of the interview, the gist of which Gürtner recorded in the following hand-written note, dated 14 October 1939:

He [Hitler] had given no general instruction [with reference to shootings by the Security Police].

The three shootings [which Gürtner had cited] had been ordered by him. He could not renounce this prerogative in individual cases because the courts (military and civil) were proving unequal to the special conditions of the war. – [Just now] he had ordered the shooting of the Teltow bank robbers. Himmler would be approaching me about this today.[6]

This was a clear manifestation of the Führer's will. Gürtner accepted it and the affront to the judiciary which it reflected without resigning. The Reich Ministry of Justice continued to record for some time cases of shootings by the Security Police or the SS in the concentration camps when they came to their notice.[7] But no investigations were made of these incidents which clearly had Hitler's approval, although even under the existing law they constituted murder. As a result of the special SS and police jurisdiction established on 27 October 1939, the ordinary prosecuting authorities were finally deprived of their authority in this sphere.

At first, the main effect of the increased police activity for the so-called 'protection of the State' during the war was that in the weeks following the start of the war many politically suspect former communists and Social Democrats, some of whom had been in a concentration camp before 1939, were once more taken into protective custody. They were joined by other groups, for example between 1,000 and 2,000 German nationals of Polish origin who were regarded as suspect officials of the Polish minority and also by Polish nationals, some of whom had been resident in the Reich for many years (so-called Old Poles). Furthermore a Gestapa order of 9 September 1939 directed the *Stapo(leit)stellen* henceforth to take ruthless action on Security Police grounds against any Polish nationals in the Reich 'who behave at all improperly and to take them into protective custody. They will be accommodated in Dachau camp in a separate section'.

During the same period the Criminal Police ordered the following categories to be taken into protective police custody (to be served in concentration camps): Jews who had been arrested during the 1938 operation and released in order to emigrate but who had not so far seriously tried to do so, and so-called psychopaths 'who because of mental disorder may be suspected of causing unrest among the population'. In October 1939 Himmler further ordered that henceforth all persons picked up during police raids for trying to avoid work should 'be transferred to a concentration camp if they have a previous conviction'. Also from the same period date Himmler's first orders to prepare for the transport of gypsy families from the Reich to the *Generalgouvernement,* an operation which actually began in May 1940.

All these measures were motivated only partially by considerations for the so-called protection of the State. As with Hitler's so-called euthanasia order, some of the new coercive measures were clearly inspired by the thought that the state of emergency provided cover for taking certain violent steps for the 'cleansing of the nation', which appeared fundamentally necessary according to National Socialist ideology but which could not be taken in peace-time in deference to public opinion at home and abroad.

The war was used to embark on a new stage of the National Socialist revolution and the totalitarian transformation of society, which would complete the extermination of political opponents by so-called national political and biological cleansing operations. It was also significant that immediately after the start of the war police activity against the Churches and their representatives increased considerably. Heydrich and above all the *Stabsleiter* of the Führer's deputy, *Reichsleiter* Martin Bormann (from 1941 Chief of the *Parteikanzlei* [Party Chancellery]), thought that the opportunity had come to reopen the fight against the Churches in a more radical form. In a memorandum to Hitler 'on the present political attitude of the Churches and Sects', which Heydrich sent to the Chief of the *Reichskanzlei* on 20 October 1939, he said that the Catholic clergy in particular were the 'sworn enemy of the State' and he recommended ruthless intervention by the Gestapo in all cases where intention of sabotage, incitement of the people, etc., was suspected, regardless of the position and clerical rank of the person concerned. In 1940/1 the number of arrests of Catholic and Protestant clergy and bishops in Germany reached a new peak.

Numerically, however, the largest part of the prisoners taken into protective custody in the first years of the war was composed of nationals of the occupied territories, primarily of Poles but to a lesser degree also of Czechs, Norwegians, Frenchmen, Belgians, Dutchmen and Serbs who as real or potential opponents of the German occupying power were arrested and transferred to concentration camps unless they were accommodated in special police camps and police prisons.

After the start of the war against the Soviet Union, the police proceeded to make even more preventive arrests in the occupied countries. In a circular to the *Stapo(leit)stellen* and commanders of the Security Police (in the occupied territories) the Chief of the Security Police and the SD announced on 27 August 1941:

In view of the increase in subversive activity and comment after the start of the campaign against the Soviet Union, the *Reichsführer-SS* and Chief of the German Police has come to the fundamental decision that all mischief-making clerics, anti-German Czechs and Poles as well as communists and similar riff-raff shall in principle be transferred to concentration camps for a prolonged period.

In the Reich itself, too, the Gestapo considerably intensified its arrests. Their extent is brought home by a table based on the daily reports of the *Stapo(leit)stellen* of all arrests reported in October 1941. It shows that during this month the Gestapo arrested a total of 15,160 persons in the whole of the Reich as it then was (4,384 coming from the Protectorate and the annexed Eastern territories). This was more than ten times the average number of persons taken into protective custody during the years 1935/6. The reasons for the arrests were listed as follows:

Number of arrests made by the State Police in October 1941

	Old Reich and Ostmark	Protectorate and Eastern Territories	Total
Communism and Marxism	544	530	1,074
Opposition	1,518	2,278	3,796
Catholic Church Movement	80	336	416
Protestant Church Movement	12	—	12
Jews	162	314	476
Economic reasons	200	34	234
Ceasing work	7,729	827	8,556
Prohibited association with Poles or prisoners of war	531	65	596
Total	10,776	4,384	15,160

This was also the period when the notorious *Nacht-und-Nebel* [Night and Fog] decree was issued after several attempts on the lives of members of the German armed forces in occupied France during the summer and autumn of 1941, incidents which were attributed to communist partisans. So as not to create martyrs by multiplying the number of military court proceedings in the occupied territories (particularly in France, Belgium and the Netherlands) Hitler, at the end of September 1941, ordered that those suspected of resistance activity should be arrested but that most of them should not be tried and sentenced locally but brought 'in night and fog' across the frontier to Germany where they should be kept in complete isolation without news of their whereabouts being allowed to reach the outside world, a procedure designed to intimidate the population of the occupied territories. On 7 December 1941 Hitler's *Nacht-und-Nebel* instruction went out as an OKW order, signed by Keitel.[8] Directives issued on 12 December 1941 and 16 April 1942 dealt with details and arrangements for secrecy.[9] Only in certain cases, where military matters were concerned, did the order provide for trial by military courts in the Reich and for the transfer of those concerned into military detention (as prisoners of the Wehrmacht); all other arrested persons were to be tried by the special courts or the People's Court [*Volksgerichtshof.*] A further OKW order of 26 June 1942 laid down that those prisoners whose cases were not tried by the military courts because of lack of evidence or who were acquitted should be handed over to the Gestapo.[10] A similar instruction went out on 28 October 1942 about *Nacht-und-Nebel* prisoners released from remand prison pending trial [*Untersuchungshaft*] by the special courts or the People's Court.[11] Thus after 1942 there developed in the concentration camps the special category of *Nacht-und-Nebel* [N.N.] prisoners, most of whom were accommodated in the camps of Gross-Rosen and Natzweiler. Finally in 1944 all N.N. prisoners detained in military prisons or prisons of the Ministry of Justice and not under sentence of death were transferred to concentration camps. In all, approximately 7,000 N.N. prisoners were sent to Germany, 5,000 of whom came from the area of the military commander for France.*

*On 24 September 1943 the *Rasse- und Siedlungshauptamt* ordered 'the transfer of all N.N. prisoners of Germanic descent to Natzweiler concentration camp'. The order was repeated on 20 May 1944 by the *Amtsgruppenchef* D of the WVHA who pointed out 'that in no circumstances are replies to be given to inquiries about the whereabouts of N.N. prisoners. ... Such inquiries shall on principle be forwarded to this office without the inquirer being informed. ...'

After the autumn of 1941 there were also special sections for Soviet prisoners of war in most of the concentration camps. These were camps which were separated from the concentration camps by their own wire enclosure and which were under the control of their own *Schutzhaftlagerführer*. The Soviet prisoners of war transferred by the Wehrmacht to the concentration camps in order to provide forced labour were not regarded as regular concentration camp prisoners. A circular of the Inspector of Concentration Camps to camp Commandants dated 23 October 1941 refers explicitly to 'SS prisoner of war labour camps' being set up. If Soviet prisoners of war died the *Lagerführer* were ordered to inform the *Wehrmachtsauskunftsstelle* (WAST) [Armed Forces Information Office] of the OKW.*

Many of the Soviet prisoners transferred to concentration camps in 1941 or the winter of 1942 were in extremely poor physical condition. Convincing evidence of this, particularly as regards Auschwitz, is provided by Höss and other sources. Of the camp for Soviet prisoners of war set up in Flossenbürg concentration camp, the camp doctor reported on 15 February 1942 that the state of health of the 1,666 prisoners continued to be poor. As causes of sickness he mentioned notably: colds, infectious wounds, general weakness of the body and the heart.

3 New camps; concept of the concentration camps; new protective custody regulations

During the two and a half years between the start of the war and March 1942, when the concentration camps were taken over by the WVHA, the number of camp inmates rose from roughly 25,000 to just under 100,000. Individual camps, for example Buchenwald and Sachsenhausen, were crowded even in the winter of 1939/40 and this lead to the first marked increase in the mortality rate. In Buchenwald, where the number of prisoners had risen to almost 13,000 in November 1939, 2,119 prisoners, i.e. almost 20 per cent, died in the following five months.

*A circular of the RFSS of 19 October 1941 made a characteristic reservation. It said that if the death of Soviet prisoners of war was not due to natural causes, but to 'being shot while trying to escape, suicide, etc.', the SS legal officer in the camp should make a short report to the Inspectorate of Concentration Camps. 'For the time being this will not be sent to WAST. The responsible SS and police courts will . . . also be informed.'

In the winter of 1939/40 Himmler asked the Inspector of Concentration Camps to examine the possibility of setting up new camps and to report whether existing camps or provisional police prisons could be expanded. On the basis of the information received a number of new concentration camps were set up in the spring and summer of 1940: in June 1940 Auschwitz camp (later to become *Stammlager* Auschwitz), composed of old barracks dating from the time of the Empire when Auschwitz was part of Austrian Galicia. The reason for setting up the camp and choosing the locality of Auschwitz – situated in the outlying part of the new Eastern territories incorporated into the *Regierungsbezirk* Kattowitz (about 20 miles east of Kattowitz) at the intersection of eastern Upper Silesia, the *Generalgouvernement* and the *Warthegau* – was apparently primarily, if not exclusively, that a large number of Polish prisoners had been arrested by the Security Police in these areas; they were causing overcrowding in the local police prisons but the police did not want to transfer them to the judicial authorities.

A report from the Inspector of Concentration Camps of 21 February 1940 to Hitler reads: 'Auschwitz, a former Polish artillery barracks (stone and wood structures) is suitable for use as a quarantine camp after some sanitary and structural defects have been dealt with.'

The report shows that on first inspection the buildings and the locality were not regarded as obviously suitable for a big concentration camp. The suggestion contained in the report that Auschwitz should be used as a quarantine camp agrees with statements by Höss who said that when he was appointed Commandant of Auschwitz (4 May 1940) he was ordered to create 'in the shortest possible time out of the existing complex, which is structurally in good condition but completely neglected and crawling with vermin, a transit camp for 10,000 prisoners'. Indeed in the early days of its existence when almost nobody but Polish prisoners were sent to Auschwitz it did partly have the function of a transit camp. Many of the Polish prisoners who in 1940/1 were sent to camps situated in the Old Reich (Sachsenhausen, Gross-Rosen, Dachau, Flossenbürg, etc.) came via Auschwitz. Höss also said that he had hardly taken over the camp which still needed putting in order when the first transports arrived.

It was partly because the *Reichsführer-SS* was completely his own master in the eastern territories incorporated into the Reich and of which Auschwitz formed a part, that at the end of 1940 and then particularly during his first visit to Auschwitz in March 1941, he ordered the extension of the camp area (the so-called 'sphere of interest of Auschwitz concentration camp') into a vast complex covering 15 square miles capable of accommodating more than 100,000 prisoners, and also ordered the installation of special SS experimental agricultural stations and production centres. What he could not do in the Old Reich he could in Auschwitz in his capacity as *Reichskommissar für die Festigung deutschen Volkstums,* namely to order more or less as he wished the confiscation of land for the camp through the Kattowitz Land Office which he controlled; to do so was particularly simple as it was 'only' a question of Polish villages and inhabitants requiring evacuation in order to extend the camp. A determining factor for the extension of Auschwitz was the proximity of the industry of Eastern Upper Silesia where many of the prisoners were employed, particularly as as many works as possible were later transferred to the East where they were less exposed to attack from the air. Another contributory factor was the person of the first Commandant, Rudolf Höss, who proved a very conscientious and energetic executive organ for the ambitious plans of the *Reichsführer-SS*. But it was the decision to make Auschwitz the main centre for the extermination of the Jews that was finally responsible for the extension of the camp and the gathering there of vast numbers of prisoners with the resulting catastrophic side-effects. This decision alone led to the permanent extension of the camp which far exceeded the dimensions of all the other concentration camps.

Instructions given by Himmler during his inspection of Auschwitz on 1 March 1941 led in October 1941 to the establishment of camp Birkenau near the locality of Birkenau (Brzezinka) approximately two miles from the parent camp, and Birkenau was to become the largest of all the concentration camps set up by the National Socialists. The original capacity of 100,000 prisoners suggested by Himmler was doubled in the plans for the camp drawn up in the autumn of 1941 by *Amtsgruppe* C (Buildings) of the WVHA, according to which Birkenau would have a capacity of 200,000 prisoners in roughly 600 huts. This plan, however, was only partly realized. What was completed by the end of the war was Section B I (later the women's concentration camp Auschwitz), designed for 20,000 prisoners, Section B II (the later men's camp) for 60,000 prisoners and part of Section B III, also intended for 60,000 prisoners. Section B IV remained on paper. But even without being completed the camp complex of Birkenau (divided into a women's camp, a men's camp, a family camp, a gypsy camp, etc.) with more than 250 primitive stone and wood huts (so-called stable huts), intended for 300–400 prisoners each, but often occupied by twice that number, formed a vast concentration camp city which covered an area of 440 acres. Two rows of electrified fences 10 miles in length and so-called circular trenches [*Ringgraben*] eight miles in length separated the individual sections and sub-sections of Camp Birkenau. Whereas the parent camp of Auschwitz, which had also been enlarged in 1941, accommodated on average 18,000 prisoners, Birkenau at its peak period, in 1943, contained roughly 100,000 prisoners. It was in the immediate vicinity of Birkenau that the gas chambers and crematoria were set up.

Even before the establishment at Auschwitz of the subsidiary camp of Birkenau, Auschwitz prisoners were, from the spring of 1941 onwards, used for the construction of a Buna (synthetic rubber) factory of IG-Farben AG, situated five miles from Auschwitz parent camp. The consideration that cheap building labour was obtainable from the concentration camp was a decisive factor for those in charge of IG-Farben AG in choosing the vicinity of Auschwitz for this factory. In order to simplify the use of concentration camp labour IG-Farben AG in 1942 set up for the workers in the immediate vicinity of the Buna factory the labour camp of Monowitz, the biggest of the 39 outside detachments [*Aussenkommandos*] of Auschwitz concentration camp which were set up mainly in the industrial area of Upper Silesia, but also further away (e.g. in Brünn [Brno]).

In June 1940, parallel with the establishment of Auschwitz, the concentration camp of Neuengamme near Hamburg was set up where an outside detachment of Sachsenhausen camp had been producing bricks for the SS firm DEST since 1938. The decisive factor in the transformation of camp Neuengamme into an independent concentration camp seems to have been the need, after the campaigns in Norway and against Holland,

Belgium and France, to establish in the west of the Reich a new large centre where political prisoners from these countries could be accommodated. Indeed henceforth French, Belgian, Dutch and Norwegian prisoners constituted a very high proportion of the inmates of Neuengamme.

In August 1940 another camp was established in the east – Gross-Rosen in Lower Silesia. The main motive for this camp was probably the possibility, to which reference has already been made, of using labour in the granite quarries and the need to find accommodation for more Polish prisoners, particularly from the region of the neighbouring Warthegau.

For the northern parts of the annexed eastern territories a similar function was fulfilled by camp Stutthof near Danzig, set up as early as September 1939. In the winter of 1939/40 the huts of Stutthof contained already approximately 4,500 prisoners. The Inspector of Concentration Camps, the Chief of the *Hauptamt Haushalt und Bauten,* Pohl, and the Chief of the Security Police advocated as early as January/February 1940 the transformation of this camp, which was under the control of the *Höhere SS-und Polizeiführer* in Danzig, into a State concentration camp. In fact it was not until February 1942 that the camp came under the control of the Inspector of Concentration Camps. Meanwhile, in 1940, another new concentration camp had been set up, this time in the West, near Natzweiler in Alsace.

The example of Stutthof shows that the concept of concentration camps in the narrower sense no longer applied to all the camps set up after the start of the war in the Reich, and particularly in the newly annexed and occupied territories, controlled by the SS and the police. The evacuation of the Poles from the East and later also that of the Slovenes from Lower Steiermark, or of the Alsatians from the West, led to the establishment of a number of resettlement and transit camps; for instance, for Poles the camps of Soldau in south-east Prussia, Lodz and Potulice, near Bromberg and for Slovenes the camps in Steiermark, some of which had a short life while others survived for the whole war. In 1941, moreover, Himmler ordered the establishment of special *Arbeitserziehungslager* [labour re-education camps] to which the *Stapo* and *Kripo* authorities sent French, Czech, Belgian and other foreign civilian workers employed in the Reich for refusing to work or for similar reasons.*

In some of the occupied territories camps were set up at the initiative of the local SS and police chiefs or Security Police Commanders to which persons suspected of resistance activity were sent or which served as labour camps and which functionally often hardly differed from concentration camps; the main difference was that not being State institutions no provision was made for them in the Reich budget and they did not come under the Inspector of Concentration Camps.

At the beginning of May 1940 the CSSD pointed out in a circular to the Inspectors of the Security Police that:

> The existence of the various camps, such as prisoner of war, internment, transit and labour camps, etc., has sometimes created the impression among the public that they are concentration camps. The *Reichsführer-SS* emphasizes that this description may be used only for the camps under the control of the Inspector of Concentration Camps, such as Dachau, Sachsenhausen, Buchenwald, Flossenbürg, Mauthausen and the women's concentration camp at Ravensbrück.
>
> In order to clarify who is responsible for existing and for possible future camps, I ask you to ensure that no other camp except those mentioned above and those at present being set up by the Inspector of Concentration Camps is described as 'concentration camp'. The appellation *Anhaltelager* [detention camp] is equally not permissible.

Until the end of 1942 the only camps which were recognized as State concentration camps within the meaning of this directive were situated on the territory of the Reich as it then was. In deciding whether certain prisoner or labour camps, as, for example, Stutthof, should be recognized as concentration camps, Himmler seems to have been particularly concerned about the availability of important war work near the camps or of work sites which could be run as SS-owned enterprises. This, for example, was why the relatively small labour camp of Niederhagen (near Paderborn), which had been set up in the vicinity of the Wewelsburg, was made into an independent concentration camp in

*Under Himmler's basic order of 28 May 1941 on the establishment of *Arbeitserziehungslager* only the Inspectors or Commanders of the Security Police and the SD were to be responsible for the establishment of such camps. The camps were to be set up (at the expense of the Reich) as State institutions and to have the 'character of police detention'; they were to be controlled by Gestapo officials or employees and guarded by hired personnel. Detention was to last for a maximum of 56 days which included 'hard labour' for up to 12 hours daily.

1941:* because the SS-controlled building scheme for the Wewelsburg – its proposed transformation into an SS school and a place for SS worship – formed one of Himmler's favourite projects for which he believed that prison labour would be needed for a long time.

This motivation was again reflected in 1943 in the suggestion that the Salaspils camp near Riga should be recognized as a concentration camp. Himmler wrote on 11 May 1943:

One of our *Arbeitserziehungslager* is in Salaspils in the Ostland. This camp is practically a concentration camp but it is under the command of the Security Police. Those who serve their sentence in this camp are Latvian, Estonian and Lithuanian constabulary and volunteers enrolled within the framework of the SS and the police. The inmates are occupied in digging turf, mining, quarrying, manufacturing cement, etc. In no circumstances do I wish this to become a concentration camp of any *Oberabschnitt* and I shall approve of concentration camp Salaspils only under two conditions:
1 if it becomes a concentration camp under the control of the Chief of the *Hauptamt Verwaltung und Wirtschaft*,
2 if this camp includes a genuine and really important armaments enterprise. To have prisoners employed in cement works and digging turf, etc., is well and good but the work is only done to keep them busy. We cannot afford such things during the war.

In 1943/4 the factor of using prison labour for SS projects and SS economic enterprises was decisive in placing the Jewish labour camps of Lublin and Plaszow (near Cracow) which were situated outside Reich territory, under the Inspectorate of Concentration Camps. The inmates of these camps consisted of Jews who, as irreplaceable labour, had been exempted from extermination and from late 1942 onwards had been transferred as working prisoners to the *SS und Polizeiführer* concerned. Both these camps in the *Generalgouvernement* became concentration camps in 1943/4 although their inmates were neither prisoners in protective custody nor detained by the police as a preventive measure. Behind this move was the desire to make available to the joint SS enterprises [*Deutsche Wirtschaftsbetriebe*] and to their central administration through the WVHA such means of production as remained in what was left of the ghettos, and also the productivity of the Jewish camps at Lublin and Plaszow which was at the disposal of local *SS und Polizeiführer*. The same

*It was dissolved in 1943.

applies to the Jews who from 1942 onwards came to Auschwitz in RSHA transports and were selected not for extermination but as potential labour in the camp. All the Jews who came from the erstwhile ghettos and Jewish labour camps in the East or who had reached Auschwitz with an RSHA transport (as part of the 'final solution' programme) and who had in part been transferred to other concentration camps formed a special category of prisoners. Temporarily exempt as 'working Jews' from the 'final solution' programme and taken for this purpose to the concentration camps, they were neither protective custody prisoners nor prisoners arrested by the police as a preventive measure and were registered separately in the camps.

The only camp to the west of the Reich frontier to be placed in January 1943 under the authority of the Inspectorate of Concentration Camps was the former police detention camp s'Hertogenbosch in Holland.

From the preceding observations it becomes clear that even outwardly the sphere of the concentration camps and the various groups of prisoners gathered in them expanded constantly during the war years and that the conceptual distinction between concentration camps, ghettos, police detention camps and labour camps became blurred. Added to this was their multiplicity of functions and to some extent the almost conflicting purposes allotted to, or connected with, them.

In most of the concentration camps – particularly in the second half of the war – Himmler made SS doctors carry out medical, nutritional and other experiments with prisoners. The sacrifice of thousands of prisoners who died or suffered permanent physical damage in the succession of experiments seemed a cheap price to the *Reichsführer-SS* for medical and biological progress. In the same camps from the end of 1941/3 under the secret symbol 14f13 special SS medical commissions selected mental cases, invalids and other undesirable prisoners (Jews) who were either killed by injections in the camps or were taken for extermination to certain institutions previously used for killing incurable mental cases from asylums (Bernburg a.d. Saale, Hartheim near Linz and others).[12] This operation was begun in the camps only when the so-called euthanasia activities outside the camps were stopped because of numerous public protests, particularly from the churches; and the camps also served as a protected place for acts of violence intended to 'purify' the nation biologically, acts which the public could not be expected to tolerate. More or less the same is true of the mass shootings of Soviet Commissars and communists selected in 1941/2 from among the prisoner-of-war camps by special detachments of the Security Police (with the consent of OKW which was responsible for prisoners of war) and sent for execution to the nearest concentration camps. In almost all the then existing concentration camps (Dachau, Buchenwald, Sachsenhausen, Auschwitz and more), thousands of Soviet prisoners of war regarded as communists were murdered in 1941/2. Here the sole purpose of the concentration camps was to serve as places of execution. Those chosen to die were not registered as prisoners and their deaths were not entered in the camp records.

While these extermination operations took place, ever closer links were established between the concentration camps and the growing number of SS-owned concerns and other industries essential to the war effort which, willy-nilly, necessarily regarded the prisoners as a positive labour potential. But even in the use of prison labour extreme differences of result, intention and side-effects emerged.

The fact that from 1941/2 onwards concentration camp inmates were increasingly used for important work had the effect on the whole of relaxing the former rules of internal camp management, designed to terrorize, repress and discriminate. The agonizing roll-calls which often went on for hours, the drill, the senseless bullying and the hard labour were restricted or disappeared completely. In a circular addressed to camp Commandants on 2 December 1942 Himmler ordered that corporal punishment should be used 'in future only as a last resort' when all other forms of punishment (close arrest, withholding of food, hard labour) remained without effect or if a special deterrent was needed (in the case of escape, etc.):

The RFSS has pointed out that corporal punishment is no instrument for . . . commanders and supervisors who are too lazy and incompetent to educate . . . the penal regulations submitted to us hitherto for approval have shown clearly that the purpose and aim of the severest of the camp punishments [corporal punishment] has not in most cases been appreciated.

The Commissioner for the Use of Camp Labour as well as the

firms who employed prisoners were interested in preserving the prisoners' capacity for work and from 1942/3 onwards prizes were introduced for good work and coupons were distributed as rewards enabling prisoners to acquire tobacco and additional food. On 15 May 1943, the Chief of the WVHA, *SS-Obergruppenführer* Pohl, issued a special 'system of rewards' for prisoners. Accordingly:

Prisoners who distinguish themselves by industry, vigilance, good conduct and special achievements at work will henceforth receive privileges. These consist in granting: (1) relaxation of confinement conditions, (2) additional food, (3) money awards, (4) tobacco, (5) permission to visit brothels.*

As the system of rewards shows camp brothels were set up, serviced by prostitutes from women's camps arrested earlier on account of their occupation. In order to use their labour force as productively as possible the SS enterprises even formulated a programme for training and educating skilled workers from among the prisoners whom they employed (particularly for the building industry), a plan which Himmler expected to be of great value also for the post-war period. The training of a labour force for SS enterprises became such an overwhelming consideration compared with the original purpose of detention that provision was even made for the release of prisoners who had become skilled workers on condition that they promised to continue to work in SS enterprises. There were many ways in which labour was used in the camps and some detachments did relatively easy work, as for example in the herb garden of Dachau or the plant propagation establishments of Auschwitz.†

Looked at as a whole, however, the longer the practice continued the more the large-scale use of forced labour from the concentration camps amounted to a ruthless waste of prisoners,

*Nuremberg Document NO-400. Supplementary regulations to this system of rewards were issued by the Chief of the WVHA on 14 February 1944. Under these prisoners were promised as 'further privileges' visits to camp cinema shows, additional money rewards for suggestions for increased productivity by prisoners, etc.

†A letter from the RSHA dated 30 December 1941 to the Inspector of Concentration Camps shows that certain benefits were available even then in particular cases. The letter says: 'Among these benefits are above all transfer to lighter work, particularly office work, permission to smoke, to read, to receive more visitors, to be exempt from having cropped hair, etc., so that protective custody becomes an honourable custody.'

because the depressing psychological and physical working conditions of these prisoners generally obstructed any real increase in productivity. There were also certain instances in which the use of concentration camp labour was combined with the objective of more or less intentional destruction, for example, in the case of those who worked in the quarries of the camps of Mauthausen-Grusen.

In order to differentiate between the conditions of imprisonment and work, Himmler at the beginning of 1941 had ordered the existing concentration camps to be divided into various grades. Grade I *a* was intended for prisoners who stood particularly in need of consideration, older persons or persons almost unable to work for whom the authorities wished to show consideration (in particular prominent political prisoners, members of the clergy, etc.). They were all to be employed in the medicinal herb garden in Dachau. The camps of Dachau, Sachsenhausen and the parent camp of Auschwitz were intended 'for protective custody prisoners with good records who are definitely capable of improvement and also for special cases and solitary confinement'; Buchenwald, Flossenbürg, Neuengamme and the hut camp Auschwitz II (Birkenau), then under construction, were for 'protective custody prisoners with less good records but who are likely to benefit from education and reform' (Grade II). All protective custody prisoners with bad records, particularly those with criminal records and anti-social elements, i.e. those who could not be 're-educated' (Grade III), were to be transferred to Mauthausen.

The order laid down that when a person was taken into protective custody a note should in future be made of his grade and he should be sent to a corresponding camp. In fact, however, this did not always happen. The growth of the concentration camps and of the increasing use of the prison labour left little room for such individual arrangements.

The Development in the second half of the War

1 The WVHA and the use of concentration camp labour

The tendency to transform the concentration camps into an SS-owned arsenal of compulsory labour revealed itself in the winter of 1941/2, and paradoxically it conflicted with simultaneous efforts, also intensified since the start of the war, to exterminate certain undesirable groups. This applied above all to the Jews. Hitler's and Himmler's fundamental decisions on the 'final solution' of the Jewish question had been made by the summer of 1941; henceforth German Jews or European Jews under German sovereignty were systematically moved to the East and killed in selected camps and extermination centres (particularly in Auschwitz, Chelmno, Treblinka, Belzec, Majdanek and Sobibor). But as Himmler also wanted to make greater use of concentration camp labour in the war industry, a number of deported Jews were fitted into the forced labour programme of the concentration camps and were at least temporarily exempt from extermination. In a telegram of 26 January 1942, Himmler informed the Inspector of Concentration Camps:

As no Russian prisoners of war can be expected in the near future, I am sending to the camps a large number of Jews who have emigrated [*sic*!] from Germany. Will you therefore make preparations to receive within the next four weeks 100,000 Jews and up to 50,000 Jewesses in the concentration camps. The concentration camps will be faced with great economic tasks in the coming weeks. *SS-Gruppenführer* Pohl will inform you in detail.

Events in 1942/4, particularly in Auschwitz, were characterized by two conflicting aims with two different authorities in charge; on the one hand the transport and extermination of the Jews, for which responsibility lay with the RSHA, on the other the exploitation of camp labour, for which the Inspectorate of Concentration Camps of the WVHA was responsible. All the other extermination camps in the East (with the single exception of Lublin-Majdanek) had been set up specially and exclusively for factory-like liquidation. In Treblinka, Belzec, Sobibor and Chelmno the Jews who arrived by train or lorry were regularly exterminated almost without exception shortly after arrival. These were not camps in the true sense as there was no intention ever of accommodating prisoners for any length of time. But Auschwitz, with its three big camp complexes (parent camp, Birkenau and Monowitz), was not only the largest of all the concentration camps and as such became a vast arsenal of labour for the armaments industry but, with the big gas-chambers and crematoria set up outside the camp enclosure of Birkenau, developed into one of the largest installations for the extermination of Jews.

This meant that only in Auschwitz, where the two objectives (extermination and use of Jewish labour) competed on the spot did the so-called selection process develop to which almost every arriving transport of Jews was subjected. At the so-called 'ramp' of Birkenau SS doctors and SS officers separated from the mass of deported Jewish men, women and children – probably depending on requirements and the state of health of the transports – a large or small number of persons capable of working (preferably youths, middle-aged men and able-bodied women without children) who were made exempt from extermination, registered as prisoners and sent to the neighbouring camp where they had a chance to survive provided they remained working fit. Selection meant transfer to another authority for a different function, with the objective not of extermination but – at least in theory – of using and to a certain degree preserving the working capacity of the prisoners.

A change in the function of the concentration camps had occurred as early as 1938 when they ceased to serve exclusively for the elimination and compulsory education of so-called enemies of State and people. To the political police motive of combating undesirable elements were added the economic involvements of the SS enterprises connected with the camps. But it was only after the winter of 1941/2 that availability of labour became the dominant factor, determining the future numerical and internal development of the camps. Although the concentration camps did not cease to be places for political persecution they increasingly became institutions for a form of forced labour which was particularly discriminating and draconic. Himmler's decision to put at the disposal of the German war industry the concentration camps and increasingly large contingents of newly received prisoners was very closely connected with increased efforts to mobilize new labour, particularly with the compulsory enrolment of foreign civilian workers which started at the beginning of 1942 and was to compensate for the call-up of Germans and keep up with the increased demand for armaments.

Visible expression of the change in the function of the camps was provided when, on 16 March 1942 on Himmler's instructions, the office of the Inspector of Concentration Camps was transferred from the *SS-Führungshauptamt* to the WVHA under *SS-Obergruppenführer* Oswald Pohl. The WVHA had been set up a short while previously by amalgamating the two *Hauptämter*, *Haushalt und Bauten* and *Verwaltung und Wirtschaft*, and it now formed the central authority of the SS in all economic and administrative matters.

On 21 March 1942, a few days after this reorganization of the concentration camp leadership, Hitler appointed Sauckel, the *Gauleiter* of Thuringia, in the 'civilian sector' as plenipotentiary for labour recruitment [*Generalbevollmächtigte für den Arbeitseinsatz*] with full powers to employ more foreign civilian labour in the war economy of the Reich. Both organizational innovations (as also the simultaneous establishment of a central Armaments Ministry under Albert Speer) were closely connected. Himmler was apparently convinced that by using his powers of coercion he could make his own very significant contribution towards the compulsory mobilization of labour. He obviously regarded the instrument of the concentration camps as more suitable for the mobilization of labour of large groups of the subject populations, particularly in the East, than the 'troublesome' conscription of foreign workers through the labour exchanges. In fact it became police practice during the last years of the war to send larger and larger groups of foreign workers (particularly Poles and 'Eastern workers') to the concentration camps. On the scale, determined by national and ideological considerations, ranging from relative freedom to total coercion in the treatment and position of the recruited so-called foreign workers the concentration camps figured at the extreme end. They represented the form of forced labour which seemed appropriate to groups of peoples regarded as inferior, undesirable or politically dangerous.

Within the WVHA the Inspectorate of Concentration Camps under *SS-Gruppenführer* Glücks as *Amtsgruppe* D formed one of the five big sectors (in addition to *Amtsgruppe* A: *Truppenverwaltung* [military administration], *Amtsgruppe* B: *Truppenwirtschaft* [military economy], *Amtsgruppe* C: *Bauten* [works and buildings] and *Amtsgruppe* W: *SS Wirtschaftsbetriebe* [SS economic enterprises]. Oranienburg continued to be the headquarters of the Inspectorate of Concentration Camps. But its official title now became: *Wirtschafts-Verwaltungshauptamt* –

Amtsgruppenchef D – concentration camps. The new *Amtsgruppe* D of the WVHA had four *Ämter* whose responsibilities were divided as follows (as of March 1942):

Amtsgruppe D: concentration camps
  (Chief: *Brigadeführer* Glücks)
Amt D I: Central Office
  (*Obersturmbannführer* Liebehenschel)
  D I/1: prisoners
  D I/2: communications, camp protection and guard dogs
  D I/3: motorized transport
  D I/4: arms and equipment
  D I/5: military training
Amt D II: Allocation of prison manpower
  (*Standartenführer* Maurer)
  D II/1: allocation
  D II/2: training
  D II/3: statistics and auditing
Amt D III: Medical administration
  (*SS-Standartenführer* Dr Lolling)
  D III/1: medical and dental care of the SS
  D III/2: medical and dental care of the prisoners
  D III/3: camp hygiene and sanitation
Amt D IV: General administration
  (*Sturmbannführer* Burger)
  D IV/1: finance
  D IV/2: welfare
  D IV/3: clothing
  D IV/4: accommodation and billets
  D IV/5: legal, tax and contractual questions

Within each camp there were independent spheres of responsibility corresponding with the spheres of responsibility of *Ämter* I–IV of *Amtsgruppe* D: *Kommandantur, Arbeitseinsatzführer*, garrison or camp doctor and *Verwaltungsführer*. With the exception of *Amtschef* D I, who as representative of the *Amtsgruppenchef* was responsible for the fundamental questions relating to the treatment of prisoners and for the concentration camps (in consultation with the RSHA) and who could not give orders direct to camp Commandants but only via the chief of the *Amtsgruppe*, the other *Amtschefs* were able to give direct instructtions in their own sphere. This meant that the *Arbeitseinsatzführer* of the camp was in constant and direct contact with *Amt* D II and received instructions from it, that the camp doctor was given his orders from the Doctor-in-charge of

Concentration Camps (Chief of *Amt* D III) and that the *Verwaltungsführer* of a concentration camp took his instructions from the *Amtschef* D IV. Camp Commandants were, however, to be kept informed on all important questions.

Responsibility for the supplies and the structural equipment of the concentration camps did not lie with *Amtsgruppe* D. As mentioned already, *Amtsgruppe* C (under *SS-Obergruppenführer* Dr Kammler) was responsible for all matters related to buildings. *Amt* B II was responsible for supplying guards and prisoners with clothing, whereas food supplies for the prisoners were provided by the local civilian food offices, with *Amt* D IV playing merely a co-ordinating role.

Of the three specialist offices (*Amt* II–IV) of *Amtsgruppe* D, by far the most important was *Amt* II (allocation of prison manpower) under *SS-Standartenführer* Maurer. Höss who, after leaving Auschwitz in November 1943, became Chief of *Amt* D I, in his memoirs described *SS-Standartenführer* Maurer as 'the real Inspector' of the concentration camps.

The WVHA retained in particular the right to send prisoners to enterprises of importance for the war effort, to negotiate special conditions for doing so or to refuse to do so. The former Commandant of Buchenwald, *SS-Oberführer* Pister, made the following statement about the process by which prisoners were provided for the armaments industry:

Firms in the armaments industry asked for prisoners from the Inspector of Armaments in Berlin who handed on the demand to *Amtsgruppe* D of the WVHA (Oranienburg). The latter authorized me to inform firms of the conditions for providing prisoners.

On the understanding that the prisoner was regarded by the firm as a worker, the following requirements were laid down:

Good sanitary quarters for the prisoners, beds with mattresses, woollen blankets, good washing and bathing facilities, provision of separate kitchens for prisoners and guards. If at all possible, separate places of work from the civilian workers. The firms frequently emphasized that the standard of accommodation demanded was higher than for the foreign workers.

We for our part agreed to provide free of charge a *Kommandoführer*, guards, a *Verwaltungsführer*, a cook and clerks, tailors and shoemakers. Separate medical staff for SS and prisoners.

Charges for prisoners: skilled workers for an eleven-hour day, whether worked during the daytime or nighttime, per day: RM 6.00
Unskilled workers: RM 4.00

No charge was made for SS personnel but free accommodation had to be provided. . . .

The cost of food was paid for by the free accommodation in concentration camp Bu[chenwald].

In order to avoid a long trek to work, prisoners needed to be housed near their place of work as most of them wore clogs. In every *Aussenkommando* stores for spare clothing were set up. The camp had to be surrounded by barbed wire. Watch towers were required. It was obligatory for the SS guards to be housed outside the enclosure.

Only when all these conditions were complied with was word sent to *Amtsgruppe* D, Oranienburg which then ordered prisoners and guards to be made available. . . .

In the case of outside camps for female labour, for example, munitions and cartridge factories, the enterprise which received the female prisoners was required to provide female employees or workers from its staff as supervisors. After taking a training course lasting several weeks at the women's concentration camp of Ravensbrück, they were taken over by the State, which paid and clothed them. These supervisors were used in the women's camps as block leaders as no member of the SS was allowed to enter a women's camp. They also guarded prisoners at their place of work while it was the task of the SS guards to protect the enterprise and the billets from outside.[1]

In his posthumous notes the Commandant of Auschwitz, Rudolf Höss, also commented on the procedure of providing prisoners for armaments firms and on the practice of using prison labour as it developed during the war in Auschwitz. In particular he described the failure of the guards to observe guard duty regulations and the powerful influence of the prisoner *Capos* on the labour detachments.

The entire prison labour force of a concentration camp was under the command of an *Arbeitseinsatzführer*. He in turn was responsible to *Amt* D II of the WVHA for the correct employment of all prisoners having regard to their professional skills and productivity. The *Arbeitseinsatzführer* kept a card index of the occupations of all the prisoners of a camp. D II required a monthly report on the numerical distribution of individual occupations. Prisoners with important but specialized occupations were listed by name, such as diamond–cutters, optical instrument cutters, precision tool makers, watchmakers, instrument makers, etc. These prisoners were classed as 'ancient monuments' and D II alone was responsible for their use. Any project, and therefore the use of any camp labour, required the written approval of D II. Outside enterprises such as armaments firms, mines or other concerns of military importance which approached the concentration camp for prison labour, were referred to D II via the armaments detachment concerned. D II consulted the Armaments Ministry to establish the urgency of the proposed work. Meanwhile the camp Commandant and the *Arbeitseinsatzführer* investigated what use would be made of the camp labour, how it would be housed and fed, what kind of guards would be required, and they then reported to D II. In the case of major projects the Chief of *Amt* D II investigated the matter personally. On the report by D II, *Hauptamtschef* Pohl granted or rejected the request, depending on the urgency of the work, the availability of prisoners and the result of the investigation carried out by the camp Commandant and the *Arbeitseinsatzführer* or by D II at the enterprise which had made the application. However, on numerous occasions the RFSS ordered the use of prisoners because the work was important for the war effort or made a vital contribution to victory, although the camp Commandant, the *Arbeitseinsatzführer* and D II rejected the application because neither accommodation nor food came up to required standards. . . .

The *Arbeitseinsatzführer* had at his disposal several non-commissioned officers [*Unterführer*] to help him with his duties. Most of the work, however, was done by the prisoners and it took the N.C.O.'s all their time to supervise these to some degree. It was the daily duty of the *Arbeitseinsatzführer* to enlarge or adjust the existing labour detachments. As it was impossible for him to know who, among the thousands of prisoners, was the most suitable for the detachment in question, he was forced to rely on the prisoners of the labour detachment who suggested suitable persons and usually replenished or changed the detachments on their own initiative. The same procedure was followed when a new labour detachment was set up. It was all too natural that this resulted in the worst kind of rackets. It happened countless times that prisoners who were detailed to distant outside detachments were given a chance to escape. Equally, prisoners with friends in the right quarters found it easy to change their occupation and to be sent to the labour detachment of their choice. The *Capos* used the *Arbeitsdienst* [labour service] to protect prisoners whom they liked and to send prisoners whom they found difficult to suitable labour detachments so that the 'sentence' passed on them could be carried out unobtrusively. . . .

The original intention had been that every labour detachment should be supervised by an SS man – a *Kommandoführer* – who remained on the spot until the job was completed. Long before the war, however, the growth of the camps and the increase in the number of projects led to a state of affairs where gradually almost all labour detachments were left completely in the charge of the *Capos* and foremen. Whereas in the case of labour detachments with their own guards some kind of supervision of the *Capos* and prisoners by the sentries-in-charge was possible, depending on the size of the job, labour detachments inside the sentry chain were left completely to the *Capo* and his foremen. Only a few SS men, most of whom were totally unsuited to this kind of work, were available to supervise these detachments. The supervisory staff provided by the firms or building managements could not really be relied upon. These people were all too glad to leave their work to the ever-willing *Capos* and foremen. As a result they soon came to depend completely on the more cunning *Capos* who were, moreover, usually their intellectual superiors. This state of affairs resulted in a reciprocal covering up of all derelictions and transgressions at the expense of the prisoners in their charge and to the detriment of the camp, the enterprise or the firm. The *Capos* and foremen were continually told by the *Schutzhaftlagerführer* that they must not ill-treat prisoners. After their return to camp they were supposed to report any case of misconduct. But this was done by very few *Capos*, most of whom meted out punishment themselves, as they saw fit . . . I also recall that a few SS men of the unit were given severe sentences by the SS court for ill-treating prisoners. Although it was the duty of the SS men who supervised or guarded the prisoners to see that their charges worked properly, they certainly had no right to punish them for any form of misdemeanour. If a prisoner had done wrong, by being obviously idle, negligent or even malevolent at work, he was reported upon return to camp to the *Schutzhaftlagerführer* or the *Arbeitsdienstführer*. Equally the entire supervisory staff of the armaments works, firms, enterprises, etc., were instructed orally by the *Arbeitseinsatz-führer* and by the distribution of leaflets on how to deal with the prisoners; in particular their attention was drawn to the fact that nobody had the right to punish, let alone to ill-treat a prisoner.

Even before the Inspectorate of Concentration Camps was placed under the WVHA, the use of labour became the chief motivation of the orders relating to the camps. One reason for this, in addition to those already mentioned, was Himmler's attempt to create for the SS its own strong economic potential for the period after the war and to acquire an indirect influence on the war economy by mobilizing prisoners for the armaments industry. A circular by Himmler, dated 5 December 1941, addressed to the Chief of the RSHA, the Inspector of Concentration Camps, all camp Commandants and the *SS-Verwaltungschef*, Pohl, states:

The projects of the *Schutzstaffel*, particularly for the post-war period, require that far-reaching preparatory steps are taken now. Among these, the preparation of the necessary building labour takes first place. The SS is in the peculiarly fortunate situation of finding and training this labour force from among concentration camp prisoners. . . .

Every camp Commandant must therefore pay particular attention to the following:

1 To raise the productivity of the prisoners selected for training by sensible, and if need be additional, food and clothing.

2 To stimulate prisoners' interest in their work and therefore to take only such corrective measures as the planned training requires. Willing prisoners must be singled out from the mass of indifferent ones so that they serve as examples.

3 Changes in the prisoners undergoing training must as far as possible be avoided.

4 . . . camp Commandants therefore share in the responsibility for the success of an undertaking which may still seem to many of them impossible. Years ago leading SS experts prophesied that prisoners could not be made into skilled workers and these gentlemen have meanwhile been persuaded to the contrary. It must therefore be possible to achieve the ultimate goal stated above. [2]

During the second half of the war the working hours of most prisoners were raised considerably. Even in the first years of the war they amounted on average to nine or ten hours a day. In 1943 the eleven-hour working day became the rule. In a circular to camp Commandants Pohl wrote on 22 November 1943: [3]

I draw your attention to the fact that the eleven-hour working day laid down for prisoners must be maintained even during the winter months. Outside detachments (for example, building workers) which, in view of the shortness of the day and the consequent onset of darkness, must return to camp in good time are exempt. But prisoners employed in factories or workshops must do eleven hours of work from Monday to Saturday inclusive. In cases of extreme urgency prisoners may also be used on Sundays, but only in the mornings. Because so much work vital to the war effort and to victory is today done by prisoners, it is not in any circumstances permissible for the *real* working day to be less than eleven hours.

At the same time the Inspector of Concentration Camps impressed on Commandants and their assistants in the camps that they should make prisoners work harder than before. On 8 December *SS-Gruppenführer* Glücks wrote:[4]

I have noticed that little or no work is done particularly by the small prisoner detachments.

The *Unterführer* and the sentries stand around the work site hardly paying any attention to the prisoners. One *Unterführer* who was taken to task for this maintained that it was forbidden to make prisoners work.

That, of course, is nonsense. Every *Unterführer* and guard must see that prisoners who stand about are made to work. It is self-evident that in doing so the prisoner must not be hit, pushed or even touched. Words only must be used in making him work. Whether the guard does so in German or in a foreign language is immaterial. The prisoner knows what he is supposed to do. Will you see that every Monday the *Kommandoführer* are instructed on this self-evident duty of guards.

The increase in working hours, the employment of prisoners in physically tiring building work to which many of them were not used led to a progressive sapping of their strength. This was aggravated by the physical and psychological conditions of imprisonment which could not be made up for by rewards and relaxations; the march from camp to work; the waiting and queuing for food; inadequate rations, clothing and rest periods. Debility and prisoner mortality therefore increased rapidly after 1942 and the productivity of the prisoners remained considerably below Himmler's and Pohl's high expectations.

One consequence of the low average productivity of the prisoners was that enterprises which worked with prisoners were forced to employ far more labour to achieve the same output as comparable enterprises employing free labour.[5] As in 1942/3 the daily rate which firms paid for prisoners had been raised to 5 or 6 *Reichsmark* for skilled workers and 3 or 4 *Reichsmark* for unskilled labour (on top of which there were prizes to be paid), the use of prison labour was no longer a financial incentive.*

*Survey of rates for prisoners in Nuremberg Documents NO-516, NO-576 and NO-653. Occasionally industrial firms rejected as unjustified the claims

The majority of the judges at the trials of the American military court, which in 1947/8 in Nuremberg considered the degree to which important German industrial concerns had been responsible for the enslavement and exploitation of concentration camp prisoners, came to the conclusion that these firms did not prefer the employment of concentration camp labour.[6] Most of them, however, had found themselves in some predicament as it would have been difficult for them to reject the prisoners provided through the labour exchanges and armaments detachments as replacements for German labour, particularly as without them they would have been unable to fulfil their production quotas. But the American judges found proof of guilt in the cases where there was evidence that works directors, or members of boards, had got in touch with the SS on their own initiative in order to obtain camp labour – for example in the case of certain directors of IG-Farben AG. It was largely by this criterion that they convicted or acquitted in individual cases. However questionable this yardstick, the participation of many industrial enterprises in the system of using camp labour or foreign workers as slave labour, as happened in the last years of the war, remains a particularly depressing chapter in the history of world-famous German industrial firms.

2 'Simplification' of the protective custody procedure and special regulations for individual groups of prisoners

The instructions issued at the beginning of the war that severe measures should be taken against all politically suspect persons or so-called anti-social elements, and the subsequent mass admission of 'alien nationals' to the concentration camps, led to the modification of some of the regulations governing protective custody procedure.

As early as 24 October 1939 the Chief of the Security Police and the SD announced in a circular:

for charges for prisoners submitted by the concentration camps. For example, the Balingen works (Württemberg) of the Deutsche Bergwerks- und Hüttenbaugesellschaft stated in a letter to Natzweiler concentration camp, dated 12 October 1944, that it could 'in principle pay only for what is really used for us, and, at the most, for those connected with the construction of the camp. You can certainly not charge us for prisoners . . . reported sick'.

In general prisoners will not be released from protective custody during the war. In particular there will be no release of officials and other conspicuously active prisoners or of enemies of the State with criminal records or of markedly anti-social elements. If in a particular case release appears essential for special reasons, a detailed report must be made on the determining factors.

The same order also laid down a simplified procedure for the revision of protective custody orders. Unless there was a special reason to apply for release, protective custody was now automatically extended for three months when cases came up for quarterly revision by the *Stapo* authorities and the State Secret Police Office (RSHA, *Amt* IV). The conduct reports which the camps used to make when detention orders came up for review as well as the applications for release or for extension made regularly at the same time were now dispensed with. It was only on special instruction from the Gestapa that the concentration camps were required to submit reports on the conduct of prisoners. The main difference of the new regulation was the following: whereas hitherto justification had been necessary for the extension of custody, prolongation now became automatic and it was the exception for detention orders to be revised and prisoners to be released.

Indeed the practice of issuing protective custody orders was 'simplified' soon after the start of the war. A circular from the Chief of the Security Police and the SD, dated 16 May 1940, informed the Security Police authorities that in urgent cases protective custody applications could be made by telegraph to the protective custody section of the Gestapa (Section IV C2) and that in such cases the Gestapa would telegraph authority to make a protective custody order and send a written confirmation later. The practice of sending telegraphic instructions meant that the issuing of protective custody orders by the RSHA became a quick, routine procedure. An objective investigation of the justification of protective custody applications was hardly possible in such circumstances. In practice the decision came to rest even more than before with the local *Stapo* authorities. The order, moreover, authorized the Commanders of the Security Police in the *Generalgouvernement* to set aside protective custody orders on their own authority. The RSHA (or the Gestapo) thus ceased to be responsible for the regular revision of protective custody orders of Polish prisoners from this region. A further very significant special regulation concerning Polish protective custody prisoners was contained in the circular of the Chief of the Security Police and the SD on 4 May 1943. The *Stapo(leit)-stellen* and the Commanders of the Security Police were authorized 'to issue protective custody orders for all Polish prisoners and to arrange for their transfer to concentration camps . . . on their own authority'. The only exceptions to this rule were members of the Polish aristocracy, political and intellectual leaders, former senior officers and senior clergy ('from bishops upwards').

'In order to prevent . . . any misuse by the prisoners', the RSHA ordered on 22 August 1941 that henceforth all concentration camp prisoners of foreign nationality and also German Jews and German nationals of Polish or Czech origin should not be left in possession of their protective custody orders; these should merely briefly be 'handed to them and then taken away on the same day and put on the files'.

Completely outside normal protective custody procedure were the transfers to concentration camps of Soviet civilian workers (so-called 'eastern workers') of which there were an increasingly large number of cases after 1941/2. Orders regarding the announcement of deaths among these prisoners show that they were sent to concentration camps by special arrangement between the *Stapo* authorities and the labour exchanges. On the basis of an instruction of the RSHA of 18 June 1942 the Inspector of Concentration Camps informed camp Commandants on 1 August 1942 that 'the relevant departments of the RSHA would keep a numerical check only on . . . the transfer of Soviet Russian civilian workers' to concentration camps. 'In order to save paper and time' it was unnecessary in future to give details 'either of the arrival of such a prisoner or of his transfer to another camp'. The preparation of camp registers for the RSHA, otherwise required by the authorities, could be omitted, nor was there any need for reports to the Inspectorate of Concentration Camps (*Amtsgruppe* D of the WVHA). As Soviet civilian workers were sent to concentration camps only by the *Stapo(leit)stellen* 'all correspondence about these prisoners [will] take place exclusively with the state police authorities concerned'. Announcements of deaths should be made to these authorities only and reports to the RSHA and the Inspectorate of Concentration Camps on cases of death 'of Soviet Russian civilian workers [are] unnecessary'. Nor was there any need for action by the records department of the political sections of the camps 'because the transfer of Soviet civilian workers did not occur within the normal framework of protective custody arrangements'.

At first these so-called 'eastern workers' were sent to the concentration camps only temporarily for the compulsory re-education of work-shy persons or similar cases. But on 26 February 1943 the Chief of the *Amtsgruppe* D informed camp Commandants:

In response to a request from this office, the RSHA has ordered that Soviet Russian civilian workers (eastern workers) shall not, except in very special cases, be released from concentration camps.

The old arrangement, originally made because of its educational effect, by which eastern workers were released from the concentration camps after a certain period of time and sent back to their old places of work, is abandoned so as to safeguard the current armaments programmes of the concentration camps. The *Stapo(leit)stellen* have been informed accordingly by the RSHA.

In the spring of 1944, during the withdrawal of German troops from the east, it became customary forcibly to evacuate Russian civilian workers and to send them *en masse* as workers to the concentration camps. In the case of these large-scale transfers, registration was further simplified. On 26 April 1944 the Chief of the Security Police and the SD ordered that:

1 Eastern nationals arriving in concentration camps in collective transports from the East will not for formal purposes be treated in accordance with the guide-lines issued for the Reich territory;
2 in particular none of the otherwise customary notifications of change in the case for individual prisoners is necessary and
3 these prisoners will be registered *only* in the concentration camp itself. Reports about transfer, death or other changes concerning these prisoners are therefore superfluous.

Referring to this order the Inspector of Concentration Camps on 9 May 1944 instructed camp Commandants to act accordingly. Only in the case of eastern workers sent by the State police authorities to the Reich was there any need for 'the hitherto customary reports of any change'.

3 Numerical developments of the camp population and mortality up to the end of the War

The RSHA continued to be responsible for issuing protective custody orders as well as for authorizing releases, reduced to a minimum since the outbreak of the war. It also went on exercising a strong influence on the concentration camps through the *Stapoleitstellen* and the political sections of the camps. During the second half of the war the camps were regarded not only as a means of eliminating opponents of the régime but primarily as a source of labour, and the indirect effect of the WVHA, therefore, as the new authority concerned with the camps, was to send more and more people there. Shortly after taking over the camps, on 30 April 1942, the Chief of the WVHA wrote to Himmler:

The mobilization of all camp labour at first for military tasks (to raise armaments production) and later for peace-time building programmes is becoming increasingly important. This realization demands action which will permit a gradual transformation of the concentration camps from their old one-sided political form into an organization suited to economic requirements.

Himmler himself made it clear involuntarily that a coercive system of this kind, which primarily served economic aims, meant a complete shift of the bases of the concentration camps. In replying to Pohl on 29 May 1942 he said that he was in agreement with all innovations but that in his view the concentration camps should continue to have an educational function and to offer the opportunity of release. 'Otherwise the suspicion might gain ground that we arrest people, or if they have been arrested keep them locked up, in order to have workers.'[7]

Pohl in his letter had emphasized that many Commandants and *Schutzhaftlager- Rapport-* and *Blockführer* employed in the camps continued to treat their charges as enemies of the State who required terrorizing, that they showed little interest in a rational use of labour and thereby defeated his efforts. He was particularly concerned to reduce the prisoner mortality which, because of inadequate accommodation, lack of camp hygiene, etc., had reached a new high in 1942.

Subsequent statistics of *Amt* D III (medical administration) show that in the second half of 1942 alone, of an average total of approximately 95,000 prisoners not less than 57,503 died, i.e. roughly 60 per cent in 6 months.[8]

When Pohl in December 1942 (through Himmler) urged the RSHA to order the transfer of more prisoners to the camps in order to increase the labour contingents, the Chief of the Security Police announced on 31 December 1942 that measures had meanwhile been taken to increase the number of prisoners in the concentration camps:

1 Anti-social prisoners handed over by the judicial authorities will immediately be sent to concentration camps.* So far approximately 12,000 prisoners have been named by the Reich Minister of Justice, some of whom have been or are being transferred to concentration camps.
2 The subordinate authorities are – as already announced – instructed to transfer immediately to the concentration camps approximately 35,000 prisoners arrested under the simplified proceedings.
3 Arrangements are made to transfer immediately to concentration camps all Poles held in custody in prisons of the *Generalgouvernement* who need to be detained for a prolonged period.

As soon as these operations are completed I shall make further announcements. But meanwhile I wish to point out in this connexion that as a result of the high mortality rate in the concentration camps it has not been possible, in spite of sending more people there, to increase the total number of the prisoners, and that if the mortality rate continues to remain as high or to rise any improvement is unlikely even if there is a bigger intake.[9]

The Inspector of Concentration Camps, *SS-Gruppenführer* Glücks, for his part instructed Commandants on 20 January 1943 'to make every effort to reduce the mortality figure in the camp': 'I hold the camp Commandant and the head of camp administration personally responsible for examining every possibility of preserving the prisoners' capacity for work'.[10]

In the eight months between January and August 1943 a further 60,000 prisoners died in the concentration camps.[11] Relative mortality, however, dropped visibly, though the mortality rate continued to be very high, for example among the prisoners in preventive detention who in the winter of 1942/3 had been transferred from prisons administered by the judicial authorities to the concentration camps. The draft of a letter from

*The *Reichsführer-SS* and the Reich Ministry of Justice had agreed in the autumn of 1942 to transfer from the prisons administered by the judicial authorities to the concentration camps 'prisoners serving sentences of preventive detention in penitentiaries who upon completion of their sentence will be kept in preventive detention [*Sicherungsverwahrung*] and prisoners with several previous convictions'.

the Chief of the WVHA to the Reich Minister of Justice, dated April 1943, states that of a total of 12,658 prisoners in preventive detention taken over by the concentration camps not less than 5,935 had died by 1 April 1943. Most of these deaths occurred in Mauthausen-Gusen, the camp to which most of the preventive detainees [*Sicherungsverwahrten*] had been sent. In order to disguise the deaths the *Reichsführer-SS* on 26 May 1943 instructed the Inspector of Concentration Camps that henceforth camp register offices should cease to number deaths and death certificates consecutively and should hide by a code system the total annual number of deaths in the camps:

Future cases of death shall be given consecutive Roman numbers with consecutive subsidiary Arabic numbers, so that the first case of death is numbered I/1, the second I/2, etc., up to I/185. Thereafter further cases of death shall be numbered II, from II/1 to 185. When number II/185 has been reached further cases during the year shall be numbered III/1 to 185, IV/1 to 185, etc. Each new year will be started again with number I/1.

The increase in mortality in the concentration camps since the beginning of the war also led to various changes in the regulations concerning the announcement of deaths and the notification of relatives. By 1941/2 at the latest, cases of death in the concentration camps were not recorded any longer by the local register offices but by the camp register office. From then on all camps had their own crematoria for the incineration of the bodies of dead prisoners.

Referring to the fact that the customary telegraphic notification of relatives of dead prisoners had led to hardship and disquiet which should be avoided in the interest of the community and the 'standing of the Security Police', the *Reichsführer-SS* ordered on 21 May 1942 that camps should no longer notify relatives but only the *Stapo* authority responsible for the deceased prisoner; this authority would then make a suitable announcement to the relatives. As after the outbreak of war, relatives were as a general rule not allowed to receive the bodies of prisoners,[12] relatives should be told that the body would be cremated. 'The desire of relatives to see the deceased for the last time shall be granted except in the case of Poles and all Jews' unless there were medical reservations. At the same time, however, Himmler made a significant special regulation for Grade III prisoners (Mauthausen):

> As regards Grade III prisoners of concentration camp Mauthausen ... relatives shall be notified of the death of the prisoner *after* the body has been cremated.

As regards Soviet civilian workers the *Reichsführer-SS* on 8 May 1943 issued a special instruction to the effect that notification of death should be made exclusively by the labour exchanges, which should be informed of the date of death, cause, etc., by the authority (Gestapo) responsible for sending the prisoner to the camp. The order said explicitly: 'Information to the effect that the person concerned has died in a concentration camp will be avoided in all circumstances'.

Reports to the authorities of the RSHA or the Inspector of Concentration Camps were also 'simplified' a number of times for cases of death among certain groups of prisoners in the camps. A circular from the Inspector of Concentration Camps, dated 21 November 1942, to camp Commandants laid down the following new guide-lines:

1 Deaths of Jews will be recorded only on a collective list (one copy) containing the following information:
   number,
   name, Christian name, for women also the maiden name,
   date and place of birth,
   nationality,
   last place of residence,
   date of death,
   cause of death,
   authority responsible for admission of prisoner to concentration camp.

   In the case of Jews taken into protective custody or preventive detention upon the order of *Amt* IV C2 or *Amt* V of the RSHA, the names of the person concerned will be underlined in red on these lists and the number given to the prisoner by *Amt* IV or V will be mentioned. The lists will be arranged by date of death and submitted at the end of the month up to the third day of the following month.

   Express letters and final reports on deaths of Jewish prisoners are therefore superfluous.

2 Notification of deaths of all other prisoners will be sent in one copy only on the form used hitherto (express letter) to the RSHA – *Amt* IV C2 or *Amt* V – and the SS-WVHA – *Amtsgruppe* D. These forms will be sent regularly by the normal postal services to the RSHA or to this office.

Paragraphs 1 and 2 apply whether the death is due to natural causes or not. The authorities responsible for the prisoner's admission to the camp will, as hitherto, be informed at once by telegraph in order to notify the relatives, to the extent laid down in the regulations.

While Himmler, Pohl and Glücks told camp Commandants to reduce the death rate in their camps, the SS camp doctors were given more or less clear instructions to kill sick inmates or prisoners too weak to work again as unobtrusively as possible by phenol injections or by other means. Hygiene and killings were used as interchangeable means to make the camps 'fit for action' and to free them from all ballast.

In his posthumous Cracow notes, Höss said of the SS doctors in Auschwitz that it had been their regular duty to select 'for extermination . . . in Auschwitz and Birkenau and in the labour camps, Jews no longer able to work and who were unlikely to be fit again within four weeks'.

Jews suspected of epidemic diseases were also exterminated; the bed-ridden by injections, the others in the crematoria or in the bunkers by gas. To my knowledge phenol, Evipan and hydrocyanic acid were used for the injections.

Höss added that as well as Jews other prisoners in the sick bay were 'also killed inconspicuously by injections'. In those cases the doctor responsible would enter 'an illness quickly causing death' on the death certificate.

It seems that this practice was silently tolerated and approved of, but being, unlike the extermination of the Jews, not formally sanctioned by order of the Führer a cover-up was therefore needed for bureaucratic purposes. Typical is a note on the files of *SS-Untersturmführer* Heinrich Kinna of 16 December 1942, who was responsible in Kreis Zamosc (district Lublin) for sending transports of Poles to Auschwitz and who recorded that the leader of the Auschwitz *Schutzhaftlager*, Aumeier, had stated after accepting a transport:

Only able-bodied Poles should be sent in order to avoid as far as possible any useless burden on the camp and the transport system. Mentally deficient persons, idiots, cripples and the sick must be removed as quickly as possible by liquidation so as to lighten the load on the camp. Appropriate action is, however, complicated by the instruction of the RSHA that, unlike Jews, Poles must die a natural death.

Verbal expression is here given to the thoughtless cynicism which accompanied the bureaucratic concealment of liquidations.

The investigations of SS Judge *Hauptsturmführer* Dr Morgen show[13] that in 1943/4 sick prisoners and prisoners unfit for work were killed by camp doctors in other camps also, for example in Buchenwald. Morgen confirms explicitly that these killings were not regarded as criminal acts within the meaning of SS jurisdiction.

But it was probably only in Auschwitz that the extermination of inmates incapable of doing further work assumed very large dimensions. The main reason obviously was that the technical requirements for liquidation were readily available here and were therefore used on a large scale also for non-Jewish inmates who were in the sick quarters or who could do no more work. Höss reports that the process of giving lethal injections was used in Auschwitz as a form of 'disguised execution' for those Polish prisoners 'whose execution was ordered by the RSHA or the Commander of the Security Police and the SD of the *Generalgouvernement*' but 'for political or security reasons [should] not become known', so that 'the cause of death [was] given as one of the usual ones in the camp'.

From 1943 onwards the numerical development of the concentration camps took the form of a steeply rising curve because of new waves of arrests and the admission of Poles, compulsorily evacuated Russian civilian workers,* Jews and other groups.

By August 1943 the total of concentration camp inmates had risen to 224,000 as compared with 88,000 in December 1942. Approximately a third of this total, 74,000, fell to the share of the three Auschwitz camp units (parent camp, Birkenau and Monowitz), by far the biggest of all the camps; the next biggest at that time were: Sachsenhausen with 26,000 and Dachau and Buchenwald with 17,000 inmates each. Mortality was also highest in Auschwitz where there were still 2,370 cases of death in August 1943.[14]

On 5 April 1944 the head of the WVHA proudly announced to Himmler the existence of a total of twenty concentration camps with an additional 165 subsidiary labour camps.[15]

---

*According to the *Schutzhaftlager* report of 11 December 1943 there were in Sachsenhausen 12,626 Russian civilian workers out of a total of 35,671 inmates (the second largest groups being 11,407 political *Schutzhäftlinge* and 7,262 Poles); Nuremberg Document NO-1538.

In the weeks that followed still more camp labour was mobilized, in particular for the big building projects in connexion with the transfer underground of certain branches of the armaments industry. It seems that Hitler and Himmler regarded the coercive instrument of the concentration camps as specially suited to this particularly heavy work under very primitive conditions. In May 1944 Hitler gave instructions to use for this purpose many of the Jews expected to become available as a result of the deportation of Hungarian Jews. At the same time it was agreed to strengthen the guard units by making available a substantial number of soldiers unfit for further service in the field. Himmler announced to the chiefs of the RSHA and the WVHA on 11 May 1944:

The Führer has ordered that for the purpose of guarding the 200,000 Jews whom the *Reichsführer-SS* has sent to concentration camps in the Reich for use in the big building programme of the OT [Organization Todt] and for other nationally important tasks, 10,000 men with officers and N.C.O.s will be transferred to the *Waffen-SS*. They will be taken from the reserves. . . .

These quotas do not seem to have been 'fulfilled', but it may be assumed that of the deported Jews destined for extermination, approximately 100,000 were 'shunted' in the summer of 1944 into concentration camps and used as labour.

According to a WVHA report of 15 August 1944 the total number of concentration camp inmates was 524,286 persons, 379,167 of whom were men and 145,119 women.[16] But even then the highest level had not been reached. Particularly in the last months of the war during the withdrawal of troops from the East further tens of thousands of Jews and other forced labour from the occupied countries were transferred to concentration camps in the Reich and pressed into labour detachments. Camp Dora (Mittelbau), raised to the status of an independent concentration camp in 1944, with its labour detachments for the subterranean production of aircraft in Thuringia and the Harz mountains alone received a further 60,000 prisoner workers in the last months of the war. According to a survey of 15 January 1945 there were at that time in the Reich 714,211 concentration camp inmates (511,537 men and 202,674 women). At the same time the SS guards numbered approximately 40,000 men.

Hitler's fateful order to evacuate the camps at the approach of the enemy and to transfer their inmates into existing camps further back led to a chaotic finale for the concentration camp prisoners in the spring of 1945 when Soviet troops penetrated into the Reich from the East and Anglo-American troops from the West. Probably at least a third of the more than 700,000 inmates recorded in January 1945 lost their lives on the exhausting evacuation marches, in the transport trains which took weeks to reach their destination, and (particularly) in the hopelessly overcrowded reception camps in the months and weeks immediately before the end of the war. According to existing incomplete figures the total number of prisoners who died in the concentration camps during the war from weakness and disease must be put at not less than half a million.

Notes

The Persecution of the Jews

Social Darwinism
1 Address to the officers of the *Leibstandarte Adolf Hitler* on 7 September 1940 (Nuremberg Document PS 1918); Speech to the *Gauleiters* in Poznan on 3 August 1944 (*Vierteljahrshefte für Zeitgeschichte*, vol. 1, 1953).

2. *Lehrplan des SS-Hauptamptes von 1943/4.*

Hitler's Jewish Policy and the Nazi Party before 1933
1. *Mein Kampf* (Munich edition 1940).

The First Years of Persecution
1. Report of the American consul in Leipzig, April 1933, Nuremberg Document PS 2709.

2. The Greater Berlin Medical Gazette.

The Nuremberg Laws and their Consequences
1. Handwritten notes by Hitler's former senior officer and later adjutant, Consul General Fritz Wiedeman (retired). [Photocopy in the Institut für Zeitgeschichte, Munich.]

2. Speech at the unveiling of the Belsen memorial on 30 November 1952.

3. Nuremberg Document NG 327.

The Pogrom of 9–10 November and the Destruction of the Economic Existence of the Jews
1. Nuremberg Document PS 3063; *IMT*, vol. XXXII, pp. 20 *et seq.*

2. Nuremberg Document PS 3058; *IMT*, vol. XXXII, pp. 1 *et seq.*

3. See *IMT*, vol.XXV, pp. 337 *et seq.*; XXX, pp. 516 *et seq.*

4. *Documents on British Foreign Policy 1919–37*, Third Series, vol. III, London, 1950, p. 227.

5. See the typed deposition in: *IMT*, vol. XXVIII, pp. 449 *et seq.*; and also Göring's statement at Nuremberg, vol. IX, p. 314.

The Road to the 'Final Solution'

1. *IMT*, vol. XVIII, pp. 538 *et seq.*

2. *IMT*, vol. XXVIII, pp. 532 *et seq.*

3. Hannah Arendt, *Eichmann in Jerusalem, A Report on the Banality of Evil* (New York, 1963), pp. 38 *et seq.*

4. Nuremberg Document NG 2586 (copy).

5. During the Polish campaign they were known as *Einsatzgruppen der Sicherheitspolizei.*

6. Document WB [Manstein Trial]. Microfilm in the Institut für Zeitgeschichte, Munich.

7. Nuremberg Document NOKW 129; Document MAR 1514, 1518, 1525, 1539, 1543 [Manstein Trial]. The deportations went on until the winter and were discontinued at the insistence of the Soviet Union.

8. The situation report of the SD *Einsatzkommando,* Bromberg.

9. Minutes of the meeting of heads of departments and field sections [*Amtschef- und Einsatzgruppenleiterbesprechung*], 21 September 1939.

10. Nuremberg Document EC 307 (also PS 3363). R. Hilberg, *The Destruction of the European Jews* (Chicago/London, 1961).

11. 'Instructions given verbally by Major Radke': Reports of the Special Duties Division [*Abteilung z. b. V*] at General Staff Headquarters. Microfilm in the Institut für Zeitgeschichte, Munich.

12. Secret teletype from OKH (Quartermaster General) to the armies, 1 October 1939. Document WB 2752.

13. *IMT*, vol. XXXVI, p. 306 (Himmler, 12 February 1940).

14. Nuremberg Document(s) NG 2586.

15. Nuremberg Document(s) NG 5764.

The Final Solution

1. *The Kersten Memoirs, 1940–1948* (London, 1956).

2. Nuremberg Document L-180; *IMT*, vol. XXXVII, pp. 670–717.

3. Warlimont, *Inside Hitler's Headquarters* (Weidenfeld and Nicolson, 1964).

4. Nuremberg Document PS 447. My italics.

5. Nuremberg Documents NOKW 256 and 2080.

6. *IMT*, vol. XXXII, p. 472.

7. *IMT*, vol. IV, p. 350 and vol. XXXI, p. 39 (Ohlendorf, 5 November 1945 and 3 January 1946). Also Nuremberg Document NO 4145 (Dr Walter Blume, 29 June 1947).

8. Nuremberg Document NO 2890 (24 April 1947).

9. Nuremberg Document PS 078. Also PS 502; and *IMT*, vol. XXVI, pp. 111 *et seq.*

10. *IMT*, vol. XXXVII, pp. 672 and 687. The commander of *Einsatz-kommando* 3, *Standartenfuhrer* Jager, said: ' The executions carried out by the Lithuanian partisans on my instructions and by my orders . . .' That this was not one of the local pogroms referred to by Heyrich is obvious from the final statemeet in Jager's general report: 'Before the security police tasks were undertaken by *Einsatzkommando* 3, the partisans had liquidated 4,000 Jews by pogroms and executions.'

11. Undated report from *Einsatzgruppe* A, presumably February 1942. *IMT*, vol. XXX, p. 72.

12. A report sent to General Thomas (Head of the Economics and Armaments Office in the OKW) on 2 December 1941. *IMT*, vol. XXXII, p. 72.

13. *IMT*, vol. XXXVIII, pp. 87 and 92.

14. Nuremberg Document PS 1997 (also NG 1866). See *IMT*, vol. XXIX, p. 234.

15. Nuremberg Document NO 2405 (photocopy in the Institut für Zeitgeschichte, Munich). My italics.

16. Nuremberg Document NG 3104. My italics.

17. Nuremberg Document NG 2586/PS 710.

18. Eichmann Trial. Document of evidence No. 1209. Italics in the original.

19. Nuremberg Document NO 626; see also NG 5035 and 4848 (Photocopy in the Institut für Zeitgeschichte, Munich).

20. Himmler Files. (Microfilm in the Institut für Zeitgeschichte, Munich.) My italics.

21. *IMT*, vol. XXVII, pp. 19 *et seq.* Italics in the original.

22. Field detachment C's report of 19 November 1941, Nuremberg Document NO 2832. (Photocopy in the Institut für Zeitgeschichte, Munich.) See also NO 3146.

23. *IMT*, vol. XXXV, p. 85 (italics in the original). Also Nuremberg Documents NOKW 309 and PS 4064. (Photocopy in the Institut für Zeitgeschichte, Munich.)

24. Document WB 1642. Manstein Trial. (Photocopy in the Institut für Zeitgeschichte, Munich.)

25. Nuremberg Document NO 5655. (Photocopy in the Institut für Zeitgeschichte, Munich.)

26. *IMT*, vol. XXXIII, p. 435.

27. *IMT,* vol. XXXVI, p. 137; Nuremberg Document NO 3146. (Photocopy in the Institut für Zeitgeschichte, Munich.)

28. Order issued to the *Höhere SS und Polizeiführer,* Ukraine, Nuremberg Document NO 2027. (Photocopy in the Institut für Zeitgeschichte, Munich.)

29. Nuremberg Document NO 2403. (Photocopy in the Institut für Zeitgeschichte, Munich.)

30. Nuremberg Document NG 2499. (Photocopy in the Institut für Zeitgeschichte, Munich.)

31. Repeated in a 'confidential' decree issued by the Reich Ministry of the Interior on 2nd June 1942. Nuremberg Document NG 2620. (Photocopy in the Institut für Zeitgeschichte, Munich.)

32. Nuremberg Document NG 299 (8 and 22 April 1941).

33. *IMT,* vol. XXXIII, p. 536.

34. Nuremberg Document NG 1123; 8 May and 7 June 1941. (Photocopy in the Institut für Zeitgeschichte, Munich.)

35. Text of paragraph 5 of an order of the Reich Minister of the Interior concerning the handling of war damage suffered by Jews. 20 July 1941.

36. *IMT,* vol. XXVI, p. 200 (Document PS 654).

37. *IMT,* vol. XXXVIII, p. 9.

38. Nuremberg Document PS 709. (Photocopy in the Institut für Zeitgeschichte, Munich.)

39. Nuremberg Document(s) NG 2586. (Photocopies in the Institut für Zeitgeschichte, Munich.)

40. Hilberg, *op. cit.* p. 374.

41. *IMT,* vol. XXIX, pp. 498 *et seq.*

42. Nuremberg Document NO 907. (Photocopy in the Institut für Zeitgeschichte, Munich.)

43. Nuremberg Document NG 205. (Photocopy in the Institut für Zeitgeschichte, Munich.)

44. Globocnik to von Herff, 29 October 1943. (Original in the Document Centre, Berlin.)

45. *IMT,* vol. XLII, p. 564 (19 July 1946).

46. Nuremberg Document NO 365. (Photocopy in the Institut für Zeitgeschichte, Munich.)

47. Reitlinger, *op. cit.* p. 156.

48. *Commandant at Auschwitz, Autobiographical Notes of Rudolf Höss,* edited by M. Broszat (Stuttgart, 1958), p. 153.

49. Nuremberg Document No 205. (Photocopy in the Institut für Zeitgeschichte, Munich.)

50. Globocnik's letter to *SS-Gruppenführer* von Herff on 13 April 1943. (Original in the Document Centre, Berlin.)

51. Goebbels' Diary. Photocopy in the Institut für Zeitgeschichte, Munich.

52. *IMT,* vol. XXIX, p. 572. And Nuremberg Document NO 2207. (Photocopy in the Institut für Zeitgeschichte, Munich.)

53. According to the testimony of the SS and Police Commander in the Warsaw district, *SS-Brigadeführer* Stroop (in his ill-famed report of 16 May on the rising in the Warsaw ghetto), 'in the first large-scale deportations ... during the period 22 July to 3 October 1942'. *IMT,* vol. XXVI, pp. 634 *et seq.*

54. Katzmann Report (Nuremberg Document L-018). *IMT,* vol. XXXVII, pp. 394–7.

55. *Ibid.* p. 398.

56. Nuremberg Document NO 5574. (Photocopy in the Institut für Zeitgeschichte, Munich.)

57. As Himmler put it. Hilberg, *op. cit.* pp. 334 *et seq.*

58. Himmler's files, folder 126. (Microfilm in the Institut für Zeitgeschichte, Munich.)

59. Nuremberg Document NO 1611. (Photocopy in the Institut für Zeitgeschichte, Munich.)

60. Nuremberg Document(s) NOKW 134. (Photocopy in the Institut für Zeitgeschichte, Munich.)

61. Katzmann Report. *IMT,* vol. XXXVII, p. 398.

62. In the Government General, the eastern territories annexed by the Reich and the Bialystok district. Report of the Head of the Statistics Branch in the Office of the *Reichsführer-SS,* Dr R. Korherr, of 19 April 1943. Nuremberg Document NO 5193. (Photocopy in the Institut für Zeitgeschichte, Munich.) Also Hilberg, *op. cit.* p. 337.

63. Letter from Krüger, 11 January 1943. Nuremberg Document NO 1882. (Photocopy in the Institut für Zeitgeschichte, Munich.)

64. *IMT,* vol. XXVI, p. 693.

65. Nuremberg Document NO 1903. (Photocopy in the Institut für Zeitgeschichte, Munich.)

66. Nuremberg Document NO 2496. (Photocopy in the Institut für Zeitgeschichte, Munich.)

67. *IMT*, vol. XXXVII, p. 495.

68. Katzmann's report. *IMT*, vol. XXXVII, pp. 401, 405 *et seq.* Reitlinger, *op. cit.* pp. 309, 317 *et seq.*

69. Nuremberg Document NO 5179. (Photocopy in the Institut für Zeitgeschichte, Munich.)

70. Hilberg, *op. cit.* p. 334.

71. Minutes of the conference at Cracow on 31 May 1943. *IMT*, vol. XXXIX, p. 670.

72. Reitlinger, *op. cit.* pp. 317 *et seq.*

73. Nuremberg Document NO 599. (Photocopy in the Institut für Zeitgeschichte, Munich.)

74. Minute written by Globocnik (who had by this time been appointed *Höhere SS und Polizeiführer,* Adriatic Coastal District) to Himmler, 4 November 1943. Nuremberg Document NO 056. (Photocopy in the Institut für Zeitgeschichte, Munich.)

75. Nuremberg Document NO 5193. (Photocopy in the Institut für Zeitgeschichte, Munich.)

76. *SS-Oberführer* Bierkamp's order of 20 July 1944. *IMT,* vol. XXXVII, p. 487. (Nuremberg Document L 053.)

77. *IMT*, vol. XXVII, p. 49. (Nuremberg Document(s) PS 1166.) My italics.

The Concentration Camps 1933–45

The Phase of Revolutionary Takeover 1933–4

1. Rudolf Diels, *Lucifer ante Portas* (Stuttgart, 1950), pp. 222 *et seq.*, and cf. Hans Bernd Gisevius, *To the Bitter End* (London, 1948).

2. Rudolf Diels, *op. cit.* pp. 394 *et seq.*

3. Nuremberg Documents PS-775 (undated).

The Structure of the SS Concentration Camp System 1934–7

1. Nuremberg Document PS-783.

2. Nuremberg Document PS-784.

3. Nuremberg Documents PS-786–788.

4. Cf. Nuremberg Document PS-1216.

5. *IMT,* XXVI, PA-645.

6. *IMT,* XXVI, PS-778.

7. Nuremberg Document PS-1216.

8. Called thus in Eicke's service regulations of 1 October 1933; Nuremberg Document PS-1216.

The Concentration Camps during the first years of the War 1939–41/2
1. Enno Georg, 'Die wirtschaftlichen Unternehmungen der SS', *Schriftenreihe der Vierteljahreshefte für Zeitgeschichte* No. 7 (Stuttgart, 1963), p. 37.

2. Nuremberg Document NO-2263.

3. Nuremberg Documents NO-905.

4. Rudolf Höss, *op. cit*. pp. 69 *et seq.*

5. Nuremberg Documents NG-190.

6. *Ibid.*

7. *Ibid.* a list with 18 such cases for the period 6 September to 20 January 1940.

8. Nuremberg Document PS-1733.

9. Nuremberg Documents PS-699 and PS-836.

10. Quoted in Nuremberg Document NOKW-2579.

11. Nuremberg Document NG-226.

12. Cf. Nuremberg Documents NO-860, NO-907, NO-1007, NO-2366, NO-2799, PS-1151.

The Development in the second half of the War
1. Nuremberg Document NO-254.

2. Nuremberg Document NO-385.

3. Nuremberg Document NO-1290.

4. Nuremberg Document NO-1544.

5. Nuremberg Document NO-1914.

6. Cf. for example the Judgement of the United States Military Tribunal, VI, p. 150.

7. Nuremberg Document NO-717.

8. Nuremberg Document NO-1010.

9. Nuremberg Document NO-1523.

10. *Ibid.*

11. Nuremberg Document NO-1010.

12. Circular of the Reich Criminal Police Office of 3 October 1939.

13. Nuremberg Document NO-2366.

14. Nuremberg Document NO-1010.

15. Nuremberg Document NO-020.

16. Nuremberg Document NO-399.

3   Appendix

The Glossary has been compiled by Brian Melland.

Glossary

All ranks, unless otherwise stated, are SS

AA	(see Auswärtiges Amt)
Abs.	(see Abschnitt)
Abschnitt	A regional subdivision of the territorial organization of the SS, subordinate to an Oberabschnitt. Also a regional HQ of the SD
Abt.	(see Abteilung)
Abt. L	(see Abt. Landesverteidigung)
Abt. Landesverteidigung	
	The National Defence Branch in OKW
Abteilung	i A branch, section or subdivision of a main department or office (Amt, Hauptamt, or Amtsgruppe)
	ii A military unit or detachment up to battalion strength or equivalent level of command
Abw.	(see Abwehr)
Abwehr	lit. defence. Specifically the Espionage, Counter-espionage and Sabotage Service of the German High Command – Amt Ausland/Abwehr
Abwehrpolizei	Counter-espionage police. A function of the Grenzpolizei controlled by the Gestapo
Abzeichen	Badge of rank, appointment or distinction (see also Hoheitsabzeichen)
a. D	(see ausser Dienst)
Adjutantur	i A staff department dealing with routine personnel and administrative matters
	ii The earlier title of the Persönlicher Stab RfSS
Ahnenerbe Forschungs- und Lehrgemeinschaft	
	Society for Research into and Teaching of Ancestral Heritage. Administered by the Pers. Stab. RfSS it promoted the study of family and national hereditary history and the dissemination of racial theories
Allg. SS	(see Allgemeine SS)

Allgemeine SS	The general body of the SS composed of part-time, full-time and inactive, or honorary, members, distinct from the Waffen-SS
Allgemeines Wehrmachtsamt	
	The General Armed Forces Office in OKW concerned principally with personnel, training and equipment
Amt	A main office, branch or directorate of a ministry; or an independent ministry, e.g. Ausw. Amt
Amtsgericht	Law court of the first instance with functions ranging over the whole field of legal affairs
Amtsgruppe	A branch of a Hauptamt. Amtsgruppe D of WVHA was responsible for the administration of the concentration camps
Anhaltelager	A temporary detention camp
Anordnung	An order, instruction or regulation
Anwärter	A cadet, candidate
AO	(see Auslands-Organisation)
AOK	(see Armee-Oberkommando)
Arbeitsdienstführer	
	In control of the labour performance in a concentration camp and responsible to the Arbeitseinsatzführer
Arbeitseinsatzführer	
	A wartime supervisor of labour in a concentration camp, senior to the existing Arbeitsdienstführer
Arbeitserziehungslager	
	Workers educational camps for released prisoners requiring special training to refit them for industry
Armee-Oberkommando	
	An Army HQ
Aufklärung	lit. enlightenment. Reconnaissance (mil.)
Ausb.	(see Ausbildung)
Ausbildung	Training
Ausl/Abw.	(see Ausland/Abwehr)
Ausland/Abwehr	
	An Amt (previously Amtsgruppe) in OKW. The Armed Forces Espionage, Counter-espionage, Sabotage and Foreign Information Office under Admiral Canaris. Disbanded in 1944 and absorbed into the RSHA

Auslandsnachrichtendienst
> The intelligence service covering foreign countries; one of the functions of the SD as Amt VI of the RSHA

Auslands-Organization
> The NSDAP agency concerned with the care and supervision of Germans abroad. Ranked as a Gau

Aussendienststelle
> Outstation or outpost of the Sipo and SD (alternative form of Aussenstelle)

Aussenkommando
> A working detachment of prisoners billeted outside a concentration camp

Aussenstelle   (see Aussendienstelle)
ausser Dienst   Retired, on the inactive list
Aust   (see Aussenstelle)
Auswärtiges Amt
> The Ministry of Foreign Affairs

AWA   (see Allgemeine Wehrmachtsamt)

Bahnschutzpolizei
> Railway protection police with the status of auxiliary police (Hilfspolizei). Transferred to the SS in 1942

Bann   A subdivision of the Hitler Youth Region (Gebiet) approximately equal to a Kreis
Barbarossa   The code-word for the German attack on Russia, 22 June 1941 (= B-Tag)
Bauinspektion   Building Inspectorate, part of Amtsgruppe C of the WVHA
Bauwesen   A branch of Amtsgruppe C of the WVHA which controlled works and buildings undertaken by concentration camp prisoners
BdO   (see Befehlshaber der Ordnungspolizei)
BdS   (see Befehlshaber der Sicherheitspolizei)
Beamter   An official or functionary
Beauftragter   A representative, commissioner or administrator
Bef.   (see Befehl and Befehlshaber)
Befehl   An order or command

Befehlshaber	A senior military commander, e.g. of a Wehrkreis
Befehlshaber der Ordnungspolizei	
	Commander of the Uniformed Police at regional and Wehrkreis level and in occupied territories, subordinate to the HSSPF (previously entitled Inspekteur der Ordnungspolizei)
Befehlshaber der Sicherheitspolizei und des Sicherheitsdienstes	
	Commander of the Security Police and Security Service in occupied territories, subordinate to the HSSPF for particular tasks but under direct RHSA control. Latterly the title of the IdS in certain areas of the Reich
Behörde	An authority; an administrative body
Bekanntmachung	
	A proclamation
Bereitschaft	An emergency or alarm detachment of the Party or police (see also Politische)
Bereitschaftspolizei	
	Mobile barrack police units of the Landespolizei administered by the various Länder before the centralization of the police in 1935–36
Bevollmächtigter	
	Plenipotentiary
Bewachungsmannschaft	
	A guard detachment of the SS in a concentration camp
Bezirk	A district, an administrative unit
Blockführer	i An SS n.c.o. i/c of a block or company of prisoners in a concentration camp, responsible to the Rapportführer
	ii The lowest official of the NSDAP, responsible for the political supervision of forty to sixty households and responsible to the Zellenleiter
Brif. or Brigf.	(see Brigadeführer)
Brigadeführer	The SS equivalent of a Major-General in the British Army
Bürgerwehr	Citizens defence force (in the early post-1918 period)
Bürgermeister	The mayor (burgomaster) of a medium-size town or a smaller community

Capo (or Kapo)
: lit. chief, head (Italian). A works boss in a concentration camp who assisted the Arbeitsdienstführer. Capos were mostly selected from the common criminals in the camps

CdZ
: (see Chef der Zivilverwaltung)

Chef des Generalstabes des Heeres
: Chief of the General Staff, Army

Chef der Sicherheitspolizei und des SD
: Chief of the Security Police and Security Service (i.e. Heydrich to 1942 then Kaltenbrunner)

Chef der Zivilverwaltung
: Head of the Civilian Administration of an occupied territory (e.g. Alsace, Luxembourg)

Chefsache
: A top secret document

CSSD
: (see Chef der Sicherheitspolizei)

DAF
: (see Deutsche Arbeitsfront)

DAG
: (see Deutsche Ansiedlungsgesellschaft)

DAW
: (see Deutsche Ausrüstungswerke)

DEST
: (see Deutsche Erd- und Steinwerke)

Deutsche Ansiedlungsgesellschaft
: The German Settlement Company, affiliated to the RKF in 1940

Deutsche Arbeitsfront
: The German Labour Front, the largest of the NSDAP's 'Affiliated Organizations' (angeschlossene Verbaende). It comprised all the guilds, corporations and professional associations. Its leader was Robert Ley

Deutsche Ausrüstungswerke
: The German Equipment Works, an SS enterprise established in 1939

Deutsche Erd- und Steinwerke GmbH
: lit. German Clay and Brickworks Co. An SS enterprise formed in 1938 primarily to set up brick works and exploit quarries, using concentration camp labour

Deutsches Rotes Kreuz
: The German Red Cross. Its president was SA Gruppenführer the Duke of Saxe-Coburg, its vice-president Ogruf. Dr Grawitz

Deutsche Umsiedlungs-Treuhand GmbH
:   The German Resettlement Trust Ltd affiliated to the RKF

Deutsche Wirtschaftsbetriebe GmbH
:   German Economic Enterprises Ltd. Created by the SS and controlled by the WVHA

Dienstgrad
:   A rank or grade

Dienststelle
:   A headquarters, administrative office, station or depot

Dienstvorschrift
:   A service manual or regulations

DRK
:   (see Deutsches Rotes Kreuz)

Dulag
:   (see Durchgangslager)

Durchgangslager
:   A transit camp

DUT
:   (see Deutsche Umsiedlungs-Treuhand GmbH)

DVL
:   (see Volksliste)

DWB
:   (see Deutsche Wirtschaftsbetriebe)

Ehrenführer
:   Honorary SS generals. A distinction accorded by Himmler to leading Party and State figures, e.g. Bormann, Ribbentrop, Weizsäcker, who were nominally attached to his staff

Einsatzbefehl
:   An operation order

Einheit
:   A unit

Einsatz
:   Employment, operation, action

Einsatzgruppe
:   An operational group or task force of the Sipo and SD for special missions in occupied territory, composed of up to six Einsatzkommandos

Einsatzkommando
:   A detachment of the Sipo and SD forming part of an Einsatzgruppe

Einsatzstab
:   i An operational staff of the Sipo/SD employed in occupied territory
    ii An operational staff of the RuSHA concerned with the appropriation of real estate in the eastern territories

Einsatztrupp
:   The smallest unit of an Einsatzgruppe

Einwandererzentralstelle	
	Central Immigration Office controlled by the RSHA and also part of the RKF
Einwohnerwehr	
	Citizens defence force (of the early post-1918 period)
Endlösung, die	The final solution, i.e. the extermination of the Jews
Erlass	Edict, decree or order
Ernste Bibelforscher	
	(see IVB)
Ersatzheer	The Replacement Army
e. V	Eingetragener Verein. A registered society
EWZ	(see Einwandererzentralstelle)

Fachreferat	A specialist subsection or 'desk' in an office or headquarters
Felddägerkorps	A shock formation of the SA dissolved in 1935 and incorporated in the police
Feuerschutzpolizei	
	The Fire Fighting Police, a branch of the Orpo under the Generalinspekteur des Feuerschutzpolizei und Feuerwehren
Feuerwehren	The Fire Brigades controlled by the Orpo (see also Feuerschutzpolizei)
FHA	(see Führungshauptamt)
FHQ	(see Führerhauptquartier)
Fla.	(see Flugabwehr)
Flüchtlingslager	
	A refugee camp
Flugabwehr	Anti-aircraft defence (hence Flak = Flugabwehr Kanone)
Fördernde Mitglied der SS	
	Patron member of the SS paying a monthly contribution, under WVHA administration
Freiwilliger	A volunteer
Führer	A leader, commanding officer, chief. Never used as a sole title except in relation to Adolf Hitler (der Führer)
Führerhauptquartier	
	Hiter's Field HQ
Führungshauptamt	
	The Operations Department of the whole SS,

Führungshauptamt *cont.*

responsible for the organization and employment of its formations, but not for the tactical employment of Waffen-SS formations in the field which were controlled by OKW and OKH. Its chief was Ogruf. Hans Jüttner

Führungsstab   An operations staff

Funk   Wireless, radio

Gau   The main territorial unit of the Nazi Party which divided Germany into 42 Gaue: the Auslands-Organization was the 43rd. The Gau was also the Civil Defence Region (see also Reichsgau)

Gauleiter   The highest ranking NSDAP official below the Reichsleitung. Responsible in each Gau for all political and economic activity, also for mobilization of labour and civil defence

Geheim   Secret

Geheime Feldpolizei

The Secret Field Police, the executive arm of the Abwehr for security tasks in the Armed Forces. Largely taken over by the Sipo and SD in 1942

Geheime Kommandosache

A secret military document (its civilian equivalent was 'geheime Reichssache')

Geheime Staatspolizei

The Secret State Police, i.e. Amt IV of the RSHA. Its chief was Ogruf. Heinrich Müller

Geheimes Staatspolizeiamt

The national HQ of the Secret State Police absorbed into the RSHA in 1939

Geh. Kdos. (or g. Kdos.)

(see Geheime Kommandosache)

Gemeinde   A municipality, community

Gemeindepolizei

The municipal police
(also Gemeindeschutzpolizei)

Gendarmerie   The rural police, including motorized units for traffic control

Generalbevollmächtigter

A Commissioner General or Plenipotentiary

266

Generalgouvernement
> The Government General, i.e. German-
> occupied Poland administered by a German
> civilian Governor with HQ in Cracow.
> Classed as a Nebenland (appended territory)
> of the Reich

Generalkommando
> An Army Corps HQ

Generaloberst   Literally Col. General. No equivalent in either
> British or U.S. armies

GenQudH   (see Generalquartiermeister)

Generalquartiermeister des Heeres
> The Quartermaster-general of the Army

GenStdH   (see Generalstab)

Generalstab des Heeres
> The General Staff, Army

Gericht   A court of law, tribunal

Germanische Leitstelle
> The Germanic Liaison Office in the SS
> Hauptamt responsible for the supervision of
> the Germanic SS and for special HQs, e.g.
> the Germanic House in Hanover

Germanische SS
> The Germanic formations in the Waffen-SS,
> the various native Germanic organizations in
> the occupied territories, eg. Norway,
> Belgium, controlled by the Germanische
> Leitstelle

Gesamt SS   lit. the total SS, a term used to cover all its
> branches

Geschäftsführer
> The executive chief or manager of an office or
> business

Gestapa   (see Geheime Staatspolizeiamt)

Gestapo   (see Geheime Staatspolizei)

Gewerbepolizei   Administrative officials of the uniformed police
> concerned with trade establishments and the
> application of price controls in conjunction
> with the regional Price Control Bureaux

GFP   (see Geheime Feldpolizei)

Gliederung   lit. an organization. A para-military formation
> of the NSDAP, e.g. the SA, SS, HJ

GmbH   Geschäft mit beschränkter Haftung.
> Limited Liability Company

Grenzpolizei	The Frontier or Border Control Police, controlled by the SD. Personnel wore SS uniform
Grenzpolizei Kommissariat	
	A regional frontier HQ of the Grenzpolizei. Controlled Grenzposten (outposts)
Grenzüberwachung	
	Border control. Carried out by SSG units to reinforce the Grenzpolizei. Dissolved in 1937 and absorbed into the Grepo
Grepo	(see Grenzpolizei)
Gruf.	(see Gruppenführer)
Gruppe	lit. a group. An elastic term applied, e.g. to a territorial command HQ of the SA, or an *ad hoc* military formation, or a section in a ministry
Gruppenführer	The SS equivalent of a Lieutenant-General in the British Army
Gruppenkommando	
	An Army Group HQ
Gruppenstab	The HQ staff of an SA Gruppe, the highest regional command (cf. the SS Oberabschnitt)

HA	(see Hauptamt)
Häftling	A prisoner
Hakenkreuz	The swastika (the hooked cross). The emblem of the Nazi Party and, from 1935, of the Third Reich
Hauptamt SS	The Central Office of the SS responsible for the recruitment, training, education, welfare, etc., of the whole SS including the Germanic SS. Its chief was Ogruf. Gottlob Berger
Hauptamtchef	Head of a Hauptamt
Hauptamt SS Gericht	
	The SS Legal Department responsible for applying the special disciplinary and penal code governing all SS and Police personnel. Its chief was Ogruf. Franz Breithaupt
Hauptamt Haushalt-und Bauten	
	Main Office for Budget and Buildings which controlled the allocation of concentration camp labour and construction work; part of the later WVHA. Its chief was Ogruf. Oswald Pohl, later chief of WVHA

Hauptamt Sicherheitspolizei

> The HQ of the Security Police (Gestapo and Kripo) integrated with the SDHA to form the RSHA in September 1939

Hauptamt Verwaltung – und Wirtschaft

> (see Wirtschafts- und Verwaltungshauptamt)

Hauptaussenstelle

> A main outstation of the SD

Hauptmannschaft

> A 'captaincy'. A gendarmerie unit of about 150 men

Hauptscharführer

> The SS equivalent of a Sergeant-Major in the British Army.

Hauptsturmführer

> The SS equivalent of a Captain in the British Army.

Haupttreuhandstelle Ost

> Main Trust Office East. A public corporation created by Göring for the seizure and administration of Polish and Jewish property

HDv. (see Heeresdruckvorschrift)

Heer The Army

Heeresdruckvorschrift

> An army manual

Heeresgruppe An Army Group

Heeresverordnungsblatt

> Army Orders and Gazette

Hegru. (see Heeresgruppe)

Heimatbund, Steirischer

> The Styrian Home Defence League, founded in 1941. Operated on the Slovenian frontier in the SA Gruppe Südmark, organized in Wehrmannschaften

HIAG Hilfsgemeinschaft auf Gegenseitigkeit. Mutual Help Association. The present welfare organization of former Waffen-SS personnel. HQ in Lüdenscheid, Westphalia

HIGA (see Hilfsgrenzangestellte)

Hilfsgrenzangestellte

> Pre-war Auxiliary Frontier Personnel employed to reinforce the Customs Service, recruited from the Allgemeine SS

Hilfspolizei	Auxiliary Police, recruited largely from Nazi Party Formations, which assisted the regular police in various functions (e.g. the Bahnschutzpolizei) but were not an intergral part of the Orpo
Hipo	(see Hilfspolizei)
Hitler Jugend	The Hitler Youth, one of the principal Gliederungen of the Nazi Party formed in 1935. Originally the junior branch of the SA
HJ	(see Hitler Jugend)
Hochverrat	High Treason. An attempt to overthrow the government or change the constitution by force, defined in articles 80–87 of the Reich Penal Code (cf. Landesverrat)
Höherer SS- und Polizeiführer, Senior SS and Police Commander	
	Himmler's personal representative in each Wehrkreis and liaison officer with the military district commander and other senior regional authorities. Also established in occupied territories, e.g. the HSSPF Frankreich. Nominally the commander of all SS and police units in his area
Hoheitsabzeichen	
	National badge, emblem or marking: in particular the Nazi eagle worn on the right breast by the Wehrmacht and on the upper left arm by the Waffen-SS and police
Hoheitsträger	lit. bearer or representative of sovereignty. A Party official
HSSPF	(see Höherer SS- und Polizeiführer)
Hstuf.	(see Hauptsturmführer)
HTO	(see Haupttreuhandstelle Ost)
HVBl	(see Heeresverordnungsblatt)

Ia	The operations officer in a military HQ or formation
IA-Abteilung	The section of the former Berlin Police Presidency responsible for the collection of political-police intelligence. Its functions were taken over by the new Gestapa in 1933–34

Ic-Dienst	Intelligence Service. The title of the SS organization set up under Heydrich, precursor of the SD.
	(the 'Eins C.' is the intelligence officer in a military HQ or formation)
IdO	(see Inspekteur der Ordnungspolizei)
IdS	(see Inspekteur der Sicherheitspolizei)
IMT	The International Military Tribunal, Nuremberg

Inspekteur der Ordnungspolizei
      The original title of the BdO

Inspekteur der Sicherheitspolizei und des Sicherheitsdienstes
      Inspector of the Security Police and Security Service at regional Wehrkreis level, subordinate to the HSSPF for particular tasks but under direct RSHA control (see also BdS)

Internationale Vereinigung Ernster Bibelforscher
      The International Association of Serious Bible Researchers or 'Jehovah's Witnesses' founded by Charles Russell. The German branch was established in 1927

| IVB | (see Internationale Vereinigung Ernster Bibelforscher) |

| Jagdverbände | SS sabotage and subversive units employed in occupied and ex-occupied territories, controlled by Ostubaf. Otto Skorzeny, chief of RSHA Amt VI S |
| Junkerschule | An officer cadet training school of the SS |

Kanzleiobersekretär
      A senior clerical officer in a government office or headquarters

| Kapo | (see Capo) |

Kasernierte Hundertschaften
      Early SS para-police units formed from SS Sonderkommandos and later named Politische Bereitschaften

Kasernierte Polizei
      The militarized barrack police organized in motorized units, employed extensively in the Eastern occupied territories

KdO	(see Kommandeur der Ordnungspolizei)
Kdo.	(see Kommando)
Kdr.	(see Kommandeur)
KdS	(see Kommandeur der Sicherheitspolizei)
Kgf.	(see Kriegsgefangener)
KL	(see Konzentrationslager)
Kom. Gen.	(see Kommandierender General)
Kommandant	i Commandant of an Army L. of C. District
	ii Commandant of a concentration camp

Kommandantur

        i a Garrison HQ

        ii a concentration camp HQ

Kommandeur   The officer commanding a unit

Kommandeur der Ordnungspolizei

        The Commander of the regular police in a
General Kommissariat subordinate to the
BdO (cf. KdSipo).

Kommandeur der Sicherheitspolizei und des
Sicherheitsdienstes

        The Commander of the Security Police and
Security Service in a sub-district (General
Kommissariat) of a Reichskommissariat in
occupied territory. Also the commander of a
Sipo/SD Einsatzkommando

Kommandierender General

        A Corps Commander

Kommandoamt (or Kommando) der Waffen-SS

        The department within the
Führungshauptamt responsible for the general
operational control of the W-SS

Kommandoamt der Orpo

        The Operations Branch of the HQ of the
Ordnungspolizei

Kommandoführer

        The n.c.o. in charge of a party of prisoners
working outside a concentration camp

Kommissarischer Polizeipräsident

        A provisional police president

Kommissariat   A regional HQ of the Grenzpolizei situated on
the Reich frontier. (See also
Reichkommissariat)

Konzentrationslager

        A concentration camp

KPD	Kommunistische Partei Deutschlands. The German Communist Party
Kreis	An administrative district; also the principal subdivision of a Gau
Kreishauptmann	The principal district official in Saxony, also in the Government General
Kreisleiter	The lowest salaried official of the Nazi Party. Responsible for a Kreis within a Gau
Kriegsgefangener	A prisoner of war
Kriegsgerichtbarkeit	The sphere within which military law is exercised
Kriegstagebuch	A war diary
Kriminalkommissar	The lowest rank in the upper officer class (Gehobener Dienst) of the Criminal Police (=Obersturmführer). Promotion to Kriminalrat, thence to Kriminaldirektor (=Hauptsturmführer, Sturmbannführer)
Kriminalpolizei	The Criminal Police, which, together with the Gestapo, formed the Security Police (Sipo). Became Amt V of the RSHA in 1939. Its chief was Gruf. Arthur Nebe
Kriminalrat	(see Kriminalkommissar)
Kriminalsekretär	The lowest rank in the intermediate officer class (mittlerer Dienst) of the Criminal Police (=Untersturmführer). Promotion to Ober-sekretär, thence to Inspektor (=Untersturmführer, Obersturmführer)
Kripo	(see Kriminalpolizei)
KTB	(see Kriegstagebuch)
KZ	(see Konzentrationslager)
Laenderreferat	A 'desk' within a department responsible for all matters concerning a specific country or countries
Lagebericht	A situation report
Lager	A camp
Lagerführer	An assistant commandant in a concentration camp in charge of the Häftlinge and responsible for their discipline to the Lagerkommandant

Lagerkommandant
The chief officer in a concentration camp responsible for the external security and internal order of the whole camp

Land
One of fifteen territorial divisions of Republican Germany each with its independent government. From 1933 control of the Länder by the central Reich Government was exercised by Reichsstatthalters

Landesbauernschaft
The farmers' organization in a Land

Landeskriminalpolizeiamt
The Prussian Criminal Police HQ transformed into the RKPA in July 1937

Landespolizeibehörden
The police authorities in each state of Germany, renamed under the Nazi Höhere Polizeibehörden

Landespolizeibezirk
A Land police district

Landesverrat
Treasonable activity against state security in its relation to other countries, e.g. divulging state secrets (cf. Hochverrat)

Landgericht
A County or District Court of the first instance dealing with more important civil and criminal cases than an Amtsgericht

Landkreis
A rural administrative district

Landrat
The chief authority in the administration of a Landkreis corresponding to the Oberbürgermeister of a Stadtkreis. Was frequently the Party Kreisleiter

Landtag
The chamber of deputies or diet in a Land, abolished by the Nazis

Landwacht
The auxiliary rural police established in 1942 to assist the regular police, recruited principally from the SA and ex-servicemen of W.W.I.

Lebensborn e.V. The Fountain of Life. An SS society founded in 1936. Attached to the Pers. Stab RfSS and affiliated with the RuSHA. Its main functions were to adopt suitable children for childless SS families, to succour racially sound pregnant women and their offspring, and in general to promote the racial policy of the SS

Legationsrat	Legation or embassy counsellor in the Foreign Service
Leibstandarte SS Adolf Hitler	
	The Bodyguard Regiment A.H. Oldest of the SS militarized formations (later W-SS). Formed in 1933 from the Stabswache Berlin. Reached divisional status in 1941. Fought in Russia and the West. Commanded by Obstgruf. Sepp Dietrich 1933–43
Leibwache	Bodyguard. Specifically Hitler's first assault squad, the Stosstrupp Hitler, precursor of the SS detachments of 1925
Leitabschnitt	A regional HQ of the SD coinciding approximately with a Wehrkreis
Leiter	The leader, chief or commander of an office, station or authority
Leitstelle	A regional HQ of the Gestapo or Kripo established at Wehrkreis HQ or in the administrative capital of a Land or Reichsgau
LKPA	(see Landeskriminalpolizeiamt)
LSSAH	(see Leibstandarte)
Luftschutzpolizei	
	The ARP police formed in 1942 from personnel of the SHD and Teno as part of the Schutzpolizei. Recruited mainly from police reservists

Machtergreifung, die	
	The 'seizure of power', the Nazi term for 30 January 1933
Mann, SS	A Private.
Mannschaft	Troops; a ship's company
Marktpolizei	Market police, supervision of regulations governing markets and fairs. A function of the local police authorities (Gemeindepolizei-behörden)
MBLiV	Ministerial Blatt für die innere Verwaltung. The official gazette of the Ministry of the Interior dealing with administrative matters
Meldewesen	Police registration
Militärbefehlshaber	
	The military governor of an occupied territory
Militärgericht	A military court or tribunal

Ministerialdirektor
Head of a department in a ministry. A senior official in the higher Civil Service approximately equivalent to an Assistant Secretary

Ministerialrat A senior counsellor, usually head of a section (Referent) in a Ministry. Approximately equivalent to a Principal

Ministerpräsident
The Prime Minister of a Land government

Mitglied Member

Nachrichten Information, intelligence or signals

Nachrichtendienst
Information, intelligence or signals service

Nachrichtenführer
A chief signals officer

Nacht-und Nebel
Lit. Night and Fog, the title given to the OKW decree of 12 December 1941 which directed that persons in occupied countries guilty of activity against the Reich or the armed forces were to be deported to Germany for trial by special courts and held in the concentration camps

Napola (see Nationalpolitische Erziehungsanstalten)

Nationalsozialistische Deutsche Arbeiter Partei
The National Socialist German Workers' Party, the full title of the Nazi Party

Nationalpolitische Erziehungsanstalten
National Political Educational Institutes. Secondary Schools organized on Hitler Youth lines and controlled by an SS Inspector General (Ogruf. August Heissmeyer)

Nationsozialistische Kraftfahr-Korps
The National Socialist Motor Corps, one of the para-military formations of the Nazi Party. Its tasks included the pre-military training of recruits for the Army's motorized and armoured formations. Its chief was Erwin Kraus

Nationalsozialistische Volkswohlfahrt
The NS People's Welfare Organization responsible largely for the care of mothers and juveniles. Its chief was Erich Hilgenfeldt

Nebenstelle	A sub-station of the Grenzpolizei
NN	(see Nacht-und-Nebel)
Notdienstverordnung	
	An emergency regulation
NPEA	(see Nationalpolitische Erziehungsanstalten)
NSDAP	(see Nationalsozialistische Deutsche Arbeiter Partei)
NSKK	(see Nationalsozialistisches Kraftfahr-Korps)
NSV	(see Nationalsozialistische Volkswohlfahrt)

Oa.	(see Oberabschnitt)
ObdH	(see Oberbefehlshaber das Heeres)
Oberabschnitt	The main territorial division of the SS in greater Germany approximately equal to a Wehrkreis
Oberbefehlshaber das Heeres	
	The Commander-in-Chief of the Army (von Brauchitsch 1938–41, vice von Fritsch, Hitler 1941–45)
Oberbürgermeister	
	The lord mayor of a large town
Oberdienstleiter	
	A rank in the Nazi Party approximately equal to a Colonel
Oberf.	(see Oberführer)
Oberführer	The SS equivalent of a Brigadier in the British Army
Obergruppenführer	
	The SS equivalent of a General in the British Army
Oberkommando das Heeres	
	The High Command of the Army
Oberkommando der Wehrmacht	
	The High Command of the Armed Forces (the supreme commander was Hitler, with Keitel as ChefdOkdosdWM)
Oberkriegsverwaltungsrat	
	A senior administrative councillor in occupied territory
Oberlandesgericht	
	A Court of Appeal; usually at least one in each Land and Prussian province

Oberpräsident   The senior administrative official in a Prussian province

Oberregierungsrat

A senior government councillor in the Higher Civil Service

Oberscharführer

The SS equivalent of a Quartermaster-Sergeant in the British Army

Oberste SA Führer

The Supreme Commander of the SA, i.e. Hitler from 1930, replacing Pfeffer von Salomon

Oberste SA Führung

The High Command of the SA

Oberstes Parteigericht

The Supreme Court of the Nazi Party under Reichsleiter Walter Buch. It dealt with all ranks higher than Kreisleiter

Oberstgruppenführer

An SS rank for which there is no equivalent in the British or U.S. armies. Literally Col. General

Obersturmbannführer

The SS equivalent of a Lieutenant-Colonel in the British Army

Obersturmführer

The SS equivalent of a Lieutenant in the British Army

Oberverwaltungsgericht

The chief administrative tribunal in Prussia

Oberverwaltungsrat

A senior administrative councillor

Obstgruf.   (see Oberstgruppenführer)

Ogruf.   (see Obergruppenführer)

OKH   (see Oberkommando das Heeres)

OKW   (see Oberkommando der Wehrmacht)

OLG   (see Oberlandesgericht)

Ordnungspolizei

lit. 'order police'. The regular, uniformed police comprising the Schutzpolizei, Gendarmerie, Feuerschutzpolizei and certain technical and auxiliary services

Organisation Todt
A semi-military government agency (Reichs-
behörde) established in 1933. Its main
function was the construction of strategic
highways and military installations. After
Todt's death in 1942 Speer, Minister of
Armaments and War Production, became its
chief

Orpo (see Ordnungspolizei)

Ortsgruppenleiter
The Nazi Party official in charge of one or
several communes of a part of a town and
subordinate to Kreisleiter

Ortspolizei The local police
OSAF (see Oberste SA Führer)
Oschaf. (see Oberscharführer)
Osti (see Ostindustrie)

Ostindustrie GmbH
Eastern Territories Industries Ltd. An SS
company founded in March 1943 under
Ogruf. Pohl of the WVHA and directed by
Brigf. Globocnik. It ran factories in the
Lublin area, employing Jewish prisoners

Ostministerium (see Reichsministerium für die besetzten
Ostgebiete)

Ostubaf. (see Obersturmbannführer)
Ostuf. (see Obersturmführer)
OT (see Organization Todt)
OVG (see Oberverwaltungsgericht)

Parteigericht A Nazi Party disciplinary court at Kreis and
Gau level (see also Oberstes Parteigericht)

Parteikanzlei Hitler's chancery as leader of the NSDAP,
directed by Martin Bormann

Persönlicher Stab RfSS
Himmler's Personal Staff, ranking as a
Hauptamt of the SS. Its chief was
Ogruf. Karl Wolff

Personalhauptamt
The SS Personnel Department responsible for
records of all SS officers. Its chief was Gruf.
Maximilian von Herff

Personalkanzlei	
	The pre-war precursor of the SS Personal Hauptamt
Pioniere	Engineers, sappers, also pioneers (US)
Politische Bereitschaften	
	Political alarm squads previously named Kasernierte Hundertschaften. Precursors of the SS Verfügungstruppe (e.g. the Politische Bereitschaft Hamburg)
Politische Leiter	
	lit. political leaders. The hierarchy of NSDAP officials
Politische Polizei	
	The Political Police of the Weimar period, absorbed by and expanded as the Gestapo in and after 1933
Polizeiabschnitt	
	A municipal police (Schupo) section controlling five or more Polizeireviere
Polizeibehörden	
	Ex officio Police Authorities at Land, Kreis and Ort level, e.g. the Regierungspräsident or Reichsstatthalter, the Bürgomeister, the Landrat
Polizeidirektion	
	The HQ of the municipal police in a medium-size town, headed by a Polizeidirektor
Polizeidivision	A fully militarized formation of the Waffen-SS raised in 1939 from regular police personnel
Polizeigruppe	A municipal police group controlling three to five Polizeiabschnitte
Polizeipräsidium	
	The HQ of the regular police in a large city, headed by a Polizeipräsident
Polizeirevier	A municipal police ward, precinct or station
Präsidialkanzlei	Hitler's chancery as President, directed by Meissner
Quartiermeister	
	A senior General Staff Officer responsible for supply and administration (G 4)
RAD	(see Reichsarbeitsdienst)

Rapportführer   An SS n.c.o. in a concentration camp
                responsible for taking roll-calls and general
                administrative duties
Rasse-und Siedlungshauptamt
                The SS Central Office for Race and
                Settlement. Controlled the racial purity of the
                SS and was responsible for organizing the
                settlement and welfare of SS colonists in the
                conquered eastern territories. Its last chief was
                Ogruf. Richard Hildebrandt
Rechtswahrerbund
                The Lawyers' League, one of the Affiliated
                Organisations (angeschlossene Verbaende) of
                the Nazi Party, previously called Juristenbund
Referat   A subsection or 'desk' within a Gruppe
Referent   The official in charge of a Referat, an expert
                (cf. Sachbearbeiter)
Regierungsbezirk
                The subdivision of a Prussian province, also a
                Bavarian administrative district
Regierungspräsident
                The senior government official in a
                Regierungsbezirk
Regierungsrat   A government councillor, the lowest rank in
                the Higher Civil Service
Reichsarbeitsdienst
                The National Labour Service, compulsory for
                the youth of both sexes. Its chief was
                Konstantin Hierl
Reichsbevollmächtigter
                The German Plenipotentiary controlling civil
                affairs in certain occupied countries, e.g.
                Denmark
Reichsführer-SS and Chef der Deutschen Polizei
                Reich Chief of the SS and Head of the German
                Police. Himmler's full title from June 1936
Reichsführung-SS
                The Supreme Command of the SS,
                comprising the Persönlicher Stab RfSS and
                the Hauptämter (incl. the RSHA)
Reichsgau   One of eleven regions formed of territories
                annexed from 1939 and administered by a
                Reichsstaathalter

Reichsgesetzblatt
>The official legal gazette issued in two Parts by the Ministry of the Interior: Pt I current legislation, Pt II international treaties, etc.

Reichskanzlei
>The chancery of the Chancellor (Kanzler) directed by Lammers. One of Hitler's four chanceries

Reichskanzler
>The Chancellor of the Reich, i.e. Adolf Hitler

Reichskommissar für die Festigung des deutschen Volkstums
>Reich Commissioner for the Consolidation of German Nationhood. An office created by Hitler in 1939 under Himmler for the repatriation of Volksdeutsche and settlement of German colonies in eastern occupied territory

Reichskommissariat für das Ostland
>The German Civil Administration in occupied Soviet territories, excepting the Ukraine for which a separate RK was formed. It was divided into General Kommissariate with subordinate Gebiets (district) and Stadt (city) Kommissariate

Reichskriminalpolizeiamt
>The Criminal Police HQ included in the RSHA as Amt V. Its chief was Gruf. Arthur Nebe

Reichsleiter
>The highest ranking Party official, most of whom also held ministerial and administrative posts

Reichsministerium des Innern
>The Ministry of the Interior under Himmler from 1943 (replaced Frick). Also called Reichsinnenministerium

Reichsministerium für die besetzte Ostgebiete
>Reich Ministry for the Occupied Eastern (Soviet) Territories, created in 1941 under Rosenberg (also called Ostministerium)

Reichsministerium für Ernährung und Landwirtschaft
>Reich Ministry of Food and Agriculture under Ogruf. Herbert Backe from 1943 (replaced Darré)

Reichsregierung
>The Reich Cabinet

Reichsschatzmeister
The Treasurer of the Nazi Party and head of its administration (Reichsleiter Schwarz)

Reichssicherheitsdienst
A special Security Service responsible for guarding Hitler and other leading Nazis, drawn from the criminal police and commanded by Brigf. Rattenhuber

Reichssicherheitshauptamt
The Central Security Department of the Reich, formed in 1939 and combining the existing Police (Gestapo and Kripo) and the Security Service (SD). It was both a central office (Hauptamt) of the Reichsführung-SS and of the Reich Ministry of the Interior

Reichsstatthalter
The Reich Governor of a Land or a Reichsgau. Frequently identical with the Party Gauleiter

Reichstag
Parliament. During the Third Reich it was shorn of its legislative function, which was assumed by the Reich Government (i.e. Hitler and his ministers) under the Enabling Act of 24 March 1933

Reichsverteidigungsbezirk
A Reich Defence District. Created in 1942 and equivalent to a Gau with the Gauleiter as Commissioner for (Civil) Defence

Reichswehr
The 100,000 man Army to which Germany was limited by the Treaty of Versailles. Under Defence Law (Wehrgesetz) of 21 May 1935 the term Reichswehr was replaced by Wehrmacht (the Armed Forces)

Ressort
An administrative department or sphere of activity

Revier
(see Polizeirevier)

RfSSuChdDtPol
(see Reichsführer SS)

Richtlinien
Guide lines, directives

RKF
(see Reichskommissar für die Festigung, etc.)

RKPA
(see Reichskriminalpolizeiamt)

RMBliV
(see Ministerial Blatt)

RMEuL
(see Reichsministerium für Ernährung, etc)

RMd.
(see Reichsministerium des Innern)

RMO	(see Reichsministerium für die besetzte Ostgebiete)
Rotte	i A number of men in a file
	ii The smallest unit in the SS equivalent to a half section
Rottenführer	The SS equivalent of a Corporal in the British Army
RSHA	(see Reichssicherheitshauptamt)
Rückwärtiges Armeegebiet	
	An L. of C. area (formerly the Etappe)
Rückwärtiges Heeresgebiet	
	A rear army area
Rüstung	Armament
Runderlass	A circular instruction
RuSHA	(see Rasse- und Siedlungshauptamt)

SA	(see Sturmabteilungen)
Sachbearbeiter	An officer or official responsible for a particular subject
Sanitätsdienst	Medical service
Scharf.	(see Scharführer)
Scharführer	The SS equivalent of a Staff-Sergeant in the British Army
Schuma	(see Schutzmannschaft)
Schupo	(see Schutzpolizei)
Schutzhaft	Protective custody
Schutzhaftlager	
	A camp for prisoners in protective custody, i.e. a concentration camp
Schutzmannschaft	
	Auxiliary police recruited in the eastern occupied territories from the local population, e.g. in the Ukraine where the first Schuma bn was formed in August 1941
Schutzpolizei	lit. Protection Police. The regular uniformed municipal and country constabulary (the 'bobby' or 'cop'), which formed the bulk of the Ordnungspolizei
Schutzstaffel	lit. protection or guard detachment. Formed in 1925 from the earlier Stosstrupp Hitler, the SS became under Himmler, appointed RfSS in 1929, the most powerful Gliederung of the Nazi Party. It was a state within the State

SD	(see Sicherheitsdienst)
SD-Raute	The diamond patch or lozenge worn by SD personnel on the left sleeve
Selbstschutz	i A German nationalist Self-Protection organization active in Silesia in 1920 ii A Self-Help militia recruited by the SS from Volksdeutsche in Poland iii The Self-Protection Service, part of the Luftschutzdienst comprising air raid wardens and other civilian ARP personnel
SHD	(see Sicherheits- und Hilfsdienst)

Sicherheitsdienst des RfSS

The Security Service of the SS formed in 1932 under Heydrich, later also Chief of the Security Police (Sipo), as the sole intelligence organization of the NSDAP. The HQs of the Sipo and SD formed the core of the 1939 RSHA

Sicherheitshauptamt

The Central Security Department of the SS under Heydrich, also known as the SD Hauptamt

Sicherheitspolizei

The Security Police composed of (*a*) the Gestapo, and (*b*) the Kripo, under Heydrich

Sicherheits-und Hilfsdienst

The Security and Assistance Service, an auxiliary police force responsible for all tasks resulting from air raids. Replaced by the Luftschutzpolizei in 1942

Sicherungsverwahrung

Preventive detention

Sigrunen	The runic double S flash of the Schutzstaffel (and the police)
Sipo	(see Sicherheitspolizei)

Sonderbehandlung

lit. special treatment. The Nazi euphemism for killing detainees

Sondergerichtsbarkeit

The special disciplinary jurisdiction of the SS and Police administered by SS and Police Courts

Sonderkommando

        A special detachment of the SS employed for police and political tasks. (See Kasernierte Hundertschaften)

SP   (see Sicherheitspolizei)

SS   (see Schutzstaffel)

SSOS   (see Selbstschutz Oberschlesien)

SSPF   (see SS und Polizeiführer)

SS und Polizeiführer

        District SS and Police Commanders in Eastern occupied territories subordinate to the HSSPF

Staatsanwalt   A public prosecutor attached to district courts, courts of appeal, the Supreme Court and the People's Court

Staatsschutzkorps

        The semi-official term used to describe the combined functions of the Gestapo, Kripo and SD for the protection of the State

Staatskommissar

        Special State Commissioners appointed by the Nazis to Land ministries, e.g. in Bavaria

Staatspolizei   i The former Prussian Political Police
        ii The Nazi Political Police, i.e. the Gestapo

Staatspolizeileitstelle

        The regional HQ of the Gestapo in a Wehrkreis or capital of a Prussian province or a Land or Reichsgau and controlling Stapo-Aussendienstellen

Staatspolizeistelle

        The regional HQ of the Gestapo in a Regierungsbezirk or smaller Land or Reichsgau. Its work was coordinated by the larger Staatspolizeileitstelle, but it was not subordinate to the latter. Also controlled Stapo-Aussendienststellen

Staatssekretär   A State Secretary, the permanent head of a Ministry equivalent to a Permanent Under-Secretary of State

Stab   A staff

Stabschef   The Chief of Staff of the SA and its Commander under the OSAF (Hitler). The last chief was SA Ogruf. Wilhelm Schepmann, former Polizeipräsident, Dortmund

Stabsführer	The Chief of Staff of the Führer of the Allgemeine SS in an Oberabschnitt (the HSPPF) and reponsible for their conduct and control
Stabshauptamt	The Central Office of the RKF. Its chief was Ogruf. Ulrich Greifelt
Stadthauptmann	
	The senior administrative official in a Stadthauptmannschaft, a subdivision of a District in the General Government (Poland)
Stabswache	The original Party HQ guard detachment formed in 1923 from the SA and absorbed into the Stosstrupp Adolf Hitler (see also Leibstandarte)
Stadtkreis	A municipal administrative district
Stadtwacht	The auxiliary urban police created in 1943 and recruited mainly from the SA
Staf.	(see Standartenführer)
Stahlhelm	The Nationalist ex-servicemen's organization founded by Franz Seldte in 1918. Compulsorily absorbed by the SA in 1933
Stalag	(see Stammlager)
Stammlager	A permanent P/W camp (also the original Concentration Camp at Auschwitz)
Standarte	An SS (and SA) formation approximately equivalent to a regiment
Standartenführer	
	The SS equivalent of a Colonel in the British Army
Standgericht	A regimental court martial
Standortführer	A garrison commander
Standrecht	Martial law
Stapo	(see Staatspolizei)
Stapolste	(see Staatspolizeileitstelle)
Stapostelle	(see Staatspolizeistelle)
Stelle	A place, position, appointment, establishment
Stellv.	(see Stellvertreter)
Stellvertreter	A deputy or representative
StHA	(see Stabshauptamt)
Stosstrupp	Assault or shock troop
Strafverfahren	A criminal procedure or suit
Streifendienst	i Patrol service
	ii The Patrol Service of the Hitler Youth trained and officered by the SS

Stubaf.   (see Sturmbannführer)
Sturm   An SS (or SA) unit equivalent to a company
Sturmabteilungen

                  The SA (the 'Brownshirts' or Stormtroopers).
                  The original shock troops of the NSDAP
                  founded in 1921. After the 1934 purge,
                  eclipsed politically by the SS. From 1939
                  responsible for the pre-military training of all
                  able-bodied males (see Wehrmannschaften)
Sturmbann   A unit of the SS (and SA) approximately
                  equivalent to a battalion
Sturmbannführer

                  The SS equivalent of a Major in the
                  British Army
Sturmführer   An SA rank equal to an SS Untersturmführer
Sturmmann   The SS equivalent of a Lance-Corporal in
                  the British Army

Technische Nothilfe

                  The Technical Emergency Corps, an
                  auxiliary police force of the Orpo consisting
                  of engineers, technicians and specialists
                  concerned with construction work, public
                  utilities, communications, salvage, etc. Largely
                  engaged on air raid damage and also employed
                  as field units with the army and air force.
                  First established in 1919
Teilkommando   A sub-unit
Teno   (see Technische Nothilfe)
TN   (see Technische Nothilfe)
Totenkopfverbände

                  Death's Heads units originally composed of
                  volunteers from the Allgemeine SS, organized
                  in four Standarten and employed as concen-
                  tration camp guards. In 1939 formed the
                  nucleus of the SST Division, one of the first
                  SS field formations of the Waffen-SS
Trupp   A squad, detail or party, An SS (and SA)
                  unit equivalent to a platoon
Truppenübungsplatz
                  A training area
TV   (see Totenkopfverbände)

Unabkömmlich	Irreplaceable, indispensable (UK gestellt, in a reserved occupation)
Untersuchung	Investigation, interrogation
Umwandererzentralstelle	
	The Central Transfer Office concerned with the resettlement of Polish deportees from the Wartheland. Part of the RKF organization controlled by the RSHA
Unterführer	A subordinate commander. Generically a non-commissioned officer (cf. Unteroffizier)
Unterscharführer	
	The SS equivalent of a Sergeant in the British Army
Untersturmführer	
	The SS equivalent of a Second-Lieutenant in the British Army
Uschaf.	(see Unterscharführer)
Ustuf.	(see Untersturmführer)
UWZ	(see Umwandererzentralstelle)
VDA	(see Volksbund für das Deutschtum im Ausland)
Verband	A formation
Verbindungsoffizier	
	A liaison officer
Verfügungstruppe	
	The militarized formations of the SS renamed Waffen-SS in the winter of 1939–40
Vernichtungslager	
	An extermination camp
Verordnung	A decree, regulation, order
Versorgungsanwärter	
	A serviceman or official entitled to a pension
Vertrauensmann	
	An intelligence agent or informer
Verwaltung	Administration
Verwaltungsführer	
	The SS officer i/c administration in a concentration camp responsible for its whole economy
Verwaltungspolizei	
	The administrative arm of the Orpo and Sipo

V-Mann	(see Vertrauensmann)

Volksbund für das Deutschtum im Ausland

> The League for Germans Abroad. A pre-Nazi organization concerned with the activities of Volksdeutsche. Taken over by the Party in 1930. Its chief was Ogruf. Werner Lorenz, also chief of Vomi

Volksdeutsche Mittelstelle

> The Racial German Assistance Office. Formed in 1936 as the Büro von Kursell and renamed in 1937. Its chief was Ogruf. Werner Lorenz. It was largely run by the SS

Volksgruppe	A racial minority group
Volkskartei	The National Register kept by the administrative police. Introduced in 1939 to facilitate induction of men and women into the Armed Forces, Labour Service, etc.

Volksliste, Deutsche

> The List of Racial Germans, introduced by decree in Poland in 1941 and later extended to other territories. Divided into four sections of which I and II covered persons eligible for Reich citizenship; III, State membership by naturalization (Germans on approval); IV, provisional State membership (Germans on trial)

Volkstum	Nationality (in the ethnic and cultural sense)
Vollzugspolizei	The excutive arm of the police
Vomi	(see Volksdeutsche Mittelstelle)
VO	(see Verbindungsoffizier, also Verordnung)

Vorbeugungshaft

> Preventive arrest

Vorschrift	Regulation(s), instruction(s), or a manual
VT	(see Verfügungstruppe)

Wachmannschaft

> An early SS concentration camp unit (cf. Wachsturm, Wachtruppe, Wachverband). All these *ad hoc* units developed into the SSTV

Wachsturm	An early SS concentration camp guard company, precursor of the SS Sturmbann and Standarte and SSTV
Wachtmeister	A police, cavalry or artillery sergeant

Wachtruppe	An early SS guard unit in a concentration camp
Wachverbände	SS concentration camp guard formations, later the SS Totenkopfverbände
Waffen SS	The fully militarized combat formations of the SS composed initially of the Verfügung-struppe and Totenkopfverbände. Included non-German SS units after 1940. Put nearly 40 divisions into the field in World War II. The term W-SS became current in 1939–40
WAST	(see Wehrmachtauskunftstelle)
Wehrbauer	SS ex-servicemen settled in the Eastern territories as colonist-peasants
Wehrdienstpflicht	
	The obligation to serve in the Armed Forces
Wehrkreis	A Military District, roman numbered. In peace time it contained the HQ and subordinate formations of an active infantry corps, carrying the same roman numeral, whose commander was also the District commander. Before the war the four motorized corps were served by the Districts in which their HQs were stationed (cf. the current Wehrbereich)
Wehrkreisbefehlshaber	
	The Commander of a Military District
Wehrmacht	The Armed Forces, i.e. Army, Air Force and Navy
Wehrmachtauskunftstelle	
	The Armed Forces Information Office. Responsible for recording casualties, prisoners of war, deserters, etc., of the three Services. A missing persons bureau (still active in Berlin)
Wehrmachtbefehlshaber	
	The C.-in-C. of an occupied territory
Wehrmachtführungsstab	
	The Armed Forces Operations Staff. Its chief was Generaloberst Alfred Jodl
Wehrmannschaft	
	i Defence units of the Styrian Heimatbund ii Military training units of the SA established in 1939, also Home Guard units of the SA
Wehrverband	lit. defence formation. A term applied to the irregular Freikorps troops and later to the SA

Wehrwirtschaft Military or war economy
Wehrwirtschaftsamt
        The War Economics Directorate of OKW
Weisung   A directive
WFST   (see Wehrmachtführungsstab)
Wirtschaftsbetriebe
        Economic enterprises (of the SS)
Wirtschafts- und Verwaltungshauptamt
        The SS Economic and Administrative Office.
        Formed in 1942 from the Verwaltungsamt of
        the SS Hauptamt. It controlled the economic
        enterprises of the SS and administered the
        concentration camps. Its chief was Ogruf.
        Oswald Pohl
WKr.   (see Wehrkreis)
WM   (see Wehrmacht)
W-SS   (see Waffen SS)
WVHA   (see Wirtschafts-und Verwaltungshauptamt)

ZAL   (see Zentralarbeitslager)
z.b.V   zur besonderer Verwendung: for special
        employment
Zellenleiter   lit. cell leader. A Nazi Party official (Hoheits-
        träger) responsible for four to five blocks of
        households and subordinate to an
        Ortsgruppenleiter
Zentralarbeitslager
        A central labour camp for the Jews as organized
        by the SSPF Cracow
Zollgrenzdienst The Border Customs Service
Zollgrenzschutz
        The Border Customs Protection Service.
        Personnel recruited from Customs officials
        controlled by the Sipo
z.V   zur Verfügung

Chronology

16 April 1925	First appearance of Hitler's new 'Head-quarters Guard'. First *Schutzstaffel* (SS) formed in this year.
6 January 1929	Heinrich Himmler becomes *Reichsführer-SS*.
Autumn 1931	SS Security Service set up under Reinhard Heydrich.
31 December	SS 'Race and Resettlement' Office set up under Walter Darré Marriage authorization made obligatory for SS men.
28 February 1933	The day following the Reichstag fire. 'Ordinance for Protection of People and State' lays foundation for National Socialist dictatorship.
9 March	Himmler becomes Police President of Munich and Reinhard Heydrich Head of Political Desk of Munich Criminal Police.
17 March	Formation of the *Leibstandarte Adolf Hitler* (120 strong), a special SS detachment under Sepp Dietrich.
20 March	Dachau Concentration camp set up on Himmler's orders.
1 April	Himmler becomes Commander of the Bavarian Political Police.
26 April	Formation of the Secret State Police Office (Gestapo) Berlin.
30 November	Law on the Prussian Secret State Police.
1 December	Law on 'Guarantees for the Unity of Party and State'.
20 April 1934	Himmler becomes Deputy Head and Inspector of the Prussian Gestapo.
22 April	Heydrich becomes Head of the Gestapo.
9 June	The SD constituted as the sole political information and counter-espionage service of the NSDAP.
30 June	Murder of Röhm and other SA leaders.

30 June *cont.*	
	Elimination of the SA as a political power factor. Formation of armed SS units (*SS Verfügungstruppe*) begins. All concentration camps placed under the SS.
4 July	Theodor Eicke becomes Inspector of Concentration Camps and Commander of the SS Guard formations.
20 July	Hitler declares the SS an independent organization (removing it from the authority of SA Headquarters)
30 January 1935	Formation of the *SS Hauptamt* (including the concentration camp, *Verfügungstruppe* and *Totenkopfverbände* Inspectorates). The Race and Resettlement Office given *Hauptamt* status.
1 June	Oswald Pohl becomes SS Chief Administrator on the personal staff of the *Reichsführer-SS*.
Early March 1936	Formation of the NSDAP *Volksdeutsche Mittelstelle*.
10 February	New Gestapo law.
29 March	SS Guard formations renamed *SS Totenkopfverbände* and increased to 3,500 men.
17 June	Himmler nominated *Reichsführer SS und Chef der Deutschen Polizei*. Formation of *SS-Hauptämter* for the *Ordnungspolizei* under Kurt Daluege and *Sicherheitspolizei* under Heydrich.
20 September	The Gestapa takes over the responsibilities of political police commanders in all the *Länder*
10 May 1937	Commencement of the process of merging the SS and *Ordnungspolizei*.
13 November	Designation of HSSPF in the event of mobilization.
23 June 1938	Decree concerning the acceptance of *Sicherheitspolizei* personnel into the SS.
8 October	First *Sicherheitspolizei Sonderkommandos* formed for move into the Sudetenland.
20 April 1939	Formation of the SS Administrative and Economic *Hauptamt* (from the office of SS Head of Administration) under Oswald Pohl.

1 June	SS Legal Office in the personal staff of the *Reichsführer-SS* raised to the status of SS Legal *Hauptamt*. Formation of the SS Personnel Chancellery in the Personal Staff of the *Reichsführer-SS*.
1 September 1939	On the outbreak of war strength of the *SS Verfügungstruppe* raised from 8,000 to 9,000 and of the *SS Totenkopfverbände* to 6,500. Units of the *Verfügungstruppe* and of the *Totenkopfverbände* take part in the Polish campaign. *Einsatzgruppen* from the *Sicherheitspolizei* and SD commence activity in Poland.
22 September	Formation of the RSHA from the SS *Sicherheitspolizei Hauptamt* and *RFSS Sicherheitsdienst* (under Heydrich).
October	Formation of the SS division *'Das Reich'* and of one *SS Totenkopf* division.
7 October	Himmler becomes 'Reich Commissar for the strengthening of Germanism' (RKF).
17 October	Institution of special SS and police jurisdiction.
2 November	HSSPF in occupied territories given the additional responsibility of RKF representatives.
January 1940	Introduction of the title *Waffen-SS*.
1 June	The *SS Verfügungstruppe* Inspectorate becomes '*Waffen-SS* Headquarters' including the concentration camp Inspectorate. Strength of the *Waffen-SS* 100,000 men, raised to 150,000 men by the end of the year.
15 August	Formation of the SS Operational Head-quarters (from various offices of the previous SS *Hauptamt*) as the Military Headquarters of the *Waffen-SS* under Himmler himself. Gottlob Berger becomes head of the new SS *Hauptamt*.
Mid June 1941	The RKF office becomes an SS *Hauptamt*, as does the *'Vomi'* under Werner Lorenz.
22 June	*Sicherheitspolizei* and SD *Einsatzgruppen* begin work in Russia: *Einsatzgruppe A* under Walther Stahlecker in the Baltic area (Army

22 June *cont.*

Group North).
Einsatzgruppe B under Arthur Nebe in
White Russia (Army Group Centre).
Einsatzgruppe C under Otto Rasch in
North Ukraine (Army Group South).
Einsatzgruppe D under Otto Ohlendorf
in South Ukraine (11th Army)
Overall strength of each *Einsatzgruppe*
500 to 1,000 men.

1 July — Decree on SS and Police rank parity.
Overall strength of SS troops by the end
of the year 230,000 men.

1 February 1942 Formation of the WVHA (SS Economic
and Administrative *Hauptamt*)

16 March — Concentration camps placed under the
WVHA.

6 June — Heydrich dies of wounds from a bomb
attack.

25 August 1943 Himmler becomes Minister of the Interior.

30 June 1944 Overall strength of the *Waffen-SS*
594,443, of the *Allgemeine SS* 200,498
(official SS statistics), of concentration
camp guards 24,000 (approx.).

21 July — Himmler becomes C.-in-C. Replacement
Army.

Autumn — Peak of *Waffen-SS* manpower 910,000.
38 primarily motorized or armoured
divisions including 310,000 racial Germans,
50,000 'germanic volunteers', 150,000
non-Germans.

23 May 1945 Himmler commits suicide.

Select Bibliography

This consists only of books mentioned by the authors in the original edition. To these have been added the English translations, where known.

THE PERSECUTION OF THE JEWS

Adler, H. G. *Theresienstadt 1941–1945, Das Antlitz einer Zwangsgemeinschaft*, Tübingen 1960 (2nd edn.)
  Die verheimlichte Wahreit, Theresienstädter Dokumente, Tübingen, 1958
Arendt, Hannah. *Eichmann in Jerusalem, A Report on the Banality of Evil*, New York 1963
Blau, Bruno. *Das Ausnahmerecht für die Juden in Deutschland 1933–1945*, Düsseldorf 1954 (2nd edn.)
Buchheim, Hans. *Das Dritte Reich, Grundlagen und politische Entwicklung*, Munich 1958
  The Third Reich, its Beginnings, Development and End, London 1961
Burckhardt, C. J. *Meine Danzige Mission 1937–1939*, Munich 1960
Daim, Wilfred. *Der Mann, der Hitler die Ideen gab, Von den religiösen Verirrungen eines Sektierers zum Rassenwahn des Diktators*, Munich 1958
Dietrich, Otto. *Zwölf Jahre mit Hitler*, Munich 1955
Domarus, M. *Hitler, Reden und Proklamationen 1932–1945*, Würzburg 1963
Genoud, F. *Le testament politique de Hitler, Notes receuilles par Martin Bormann*, Paris 1959
Glum, Friedrich. *Der Nationalsozialismus*, Munich 1962
Graml, H. Die *Auswanderung der Juden aus Deutschland zwischen 1933 und 1939, in Gutachten des Institut für Zeitgeschichte*, Munich 1958
Heuss, Theodor. *Hitlers Weg*, Stuttgart, Berlin and Leipzig 1932
Hitler, Adolf. *Mein Kampf*, Munich 1940
Hohlfeld, J. *Dokumente der deutschen Politik und Geschichte*, Vol. 3, Berlin 1953

Kochan, L. *Pogrom, 10 November 1938*, London 1957

Kossey, E. *Handbuch zum Entschädigungsverfahren*, Munich 1958

Lenz, Friedrich. *Die Rasse als Wertprinzip, Zur Erneuerung der Ethik*, Munich

Lorenzen, Sievert. *Die Juden und die Justiz*, Berlin 1943

Martius, Hedwig Conrad-. *Utopien der Menschenzüchtung*, Munich 1955

Poliakov, L. *Brévaire de la Haine*, Paris 1951

Reichmann, Eva. *Die Flucht in den Hass*, Frankfurt a/M 1956

Reitlinger, G. *Die Endlösung*, Berlin 1956
The Final Solution, London 1953

Rauschning, H. *Hitler Speaks*, London 1939
Gespräche mit Hitler, Zürich, Vienna, and New York 1940

Schefler, W. *Judenverfolgung im Dritten Reich 1933–1945*, Frankfurt a/M

Warlimont, W. *Im Hauptquartier der deutschen Wehrmacht 1939–1945*, Frankfurt 1962
Inside Hitler's Headquarters 1939–1945, London 1964

Documents on British Foreign Policy 1919–1937, Third Series, vol. III, London 1950

Documents on German Foreign Policy 1918–1945, Series D (1937–1945).
  Vol. IV *The Aftermath of Munich*
  Vol V *Poland : The Balkans : Latin America : The Smaller Powers*, London 1951 and 1953

THE CONCENTRATION CAMPS 1933–45

Diels, Rudolf. *Lucifer ante Portas*, Stuttgart 1950

Fraenkel, Ernst. *The Dual State*, New York 1941

Geigenmüller, Otto. *Die Polizeiliche Schutzhaft im national-sozialistichen Deutschland*, Leipzig 1937

Gisevius, Hans Bernd. *To the Bitter End*, London 1948
Bis cum bitteren Ende, Hamburg 1960

Höss, Rudolf. *Kommandant in Auschwitz*, ed. M. Broszat, Stuttgart 1958

Jochmann, Werner. *Im Kampf um die Macht. Hitlers Rede vor dem Hamburger Nationalklub (28 February 1926)*, Frankfurt a/M 1960

Kogon, Eugen. *Der SS-Staat*, Frankfurt a/M 1946
The Theory and Practice of Hell, London 1950

Index